The Trend Forecaster's *Handbook*

Martin Raymond

Laurence King Publishing

LAURENCE KING

Published in 2010 by
Laurence King Publishing Ltd
361–373 City Road
London EC1V 1LR
United Kingdom

T: 020 7841 6900
F: 020 7841 6910
e-mail: enquiries@laurenceking.com
www.laurenceking.com

A catalog for this book is available
from the British Library.

ISBN: 978 1 85669 702 6

Design: Gerard Saint & Edward Vince at
Big Active, London
Picture Research: Allison Weldon,
Tom Hopkins

Printed and bound in China

Contents

Related study material is available on the Laurence King website at
www.laurenceking.com

Foreword

THERE IS A SAYING among trend forecasters; those who can't do, and those who can, forecast. Working with clients on a global basis, I am aware of this again and again. Always concerned about the here and now, they forever fail to see the new and next. They "do" without thinking, and what thinking they do is done without imagination. Part of the forecaster's job is to challenge this process, and the job of this book is to provide you with the tools, techniques, and methodologies to become the kind of forecaster that makes these challenges profitable, innovative, and professionally accurate.

Yes accurate! If a company hires you, invests in you, and asks you to identify the next social, cultural, ethical, or environmental trend that is set to impact on consumer behavior, they'll expect you to get it right – especially if they are expected to commit a sizable chunk of their annual budgets to finance the recommendations you have made.

Forecasting can therefore leave little to chance, and the skills used by the forecaster leave little room to be questioned, challenged, or brought into doubt. They must be transparent, measurable, robust, and above all provable. This book has been written to provide you with such collateral. It also provides you with a range of approaches that can be amplified or dampened down depending on the industry you are eventually employed in, or the lifestyle sectors within these industries you are asked to focus your efforts on. All trends can be predicted; all shifts in the culture anticipated and accounted for – as long as you understand what trends are, where to look for them, what to look for when you are looking for them, and how to read or "braille" them when you actually find them!

All of this is explained in the opening chapters alongside the hidden and scientifically-proven laws and principals that govern the spread of trends throughout our culture. In the later chapters you are introduced to the people who create, mitigate, and drive these trends – our Innovators and Early Adopters, as well as the groups that make them popular – "social tribes" that forecasters refer to as the Early and Late Majorities.

Once these groups have been defined and understood, it is at once easier to appreciate the methods used by forecasters to identify, analyze, and determine the impact of trends on a local, national, and global basis. The many disciplines a forecaster calls upon in their day-to-day activities are also identified and explored – strategic intuition, neuro-psychology, memetics, behavioral economics, complexity theory, and even scenario planning, network science, and ethnography.

All are complex areas of study in their own right – but in this book they are all explained in a way that hopefully makes them intelligible to the student who needs to understand the sometimes invisible (and traditionally difficult to explain) talents many forecasters have, or learn to develop, without realizing they are indeed skills that can be quantified, honed, learned, and passed on in the first place! Techniques designed to sharpen your ability to imagine, dream, and envision are also discussed – again these are skills most of us have, but tend to put aside when we work in more corporate and commercial environments.

As we shall see, however, these tools – and they are tools – are every bit as important as the ones traditionally used to measure a person's tastes or to pin down their views – focus groups, quantitative surveys, depth interviews, and so on – all covered in these pages. However, while these activities can be used to determine a percentage shift in people's taste, or their views on a particular product, they are less useful in telling us what these tastes look, feel, sound, or smell like. Or for that matter, if the product itself is likely to go viral – the forecaster's term for a product, idea, or service that is likely to kick-start a trend.

This can only be done by fieldwork, social observation, exercising empathy, or utilizing your imagination, or even a daydream, to envision future scenarios. All these skills are addressed, and the many ways to deploy them unpacked. In the end, however, good trend forecasting comes down to three things: practice, perseverance, and the patience to follow through on a clearly-mapped-out set of methodologies. Forecasting, as you will see, isn't about guesswork or inspirational "flashes," but rather it is about applying quantitative and qualitative skills in a way that allows you to identify new and emerging shifts in the culture as they happen, and then to map and forward project these shifts in a way that makes them visible and transparent to less observant people.

This is what *The Trend Forecaster's Handbook* has been designed to do: to open your eyes, sharpen your senses, hone your cognitive and cultural skills, and also to remind you that there is one command that underpins and drives all forecasters – *sapere aude* (dare to know). It is an old phrase from an ancient language, but one that becomes more relevant and important in a world where there is so much to know, where any decision to reject knowledge must be robustly challenged – and in the final analysis, this is what good forecasting teaches you; to dare, to know, to challenge, and to use what you have learned to dare and challenge others.

Martin Raymond
October 2009

Timeline

This timeline charts the types of products, services, trends, and even ways of living that seem likely to become mainstays of our culture over the next two decades.

2011

"Nano" car revolution

2015

Le Labo multi-use retail

REDUCE REUSE RECYCLE
REFILL

"Medi-beauty"

"Fruitelligent" foods

Green Depot recycling

QR codes

"Homedulgent" delivery

Epson PictureMate printer

Tomy/Zink Camera/Printer

The School of Life

Aivan slide radio

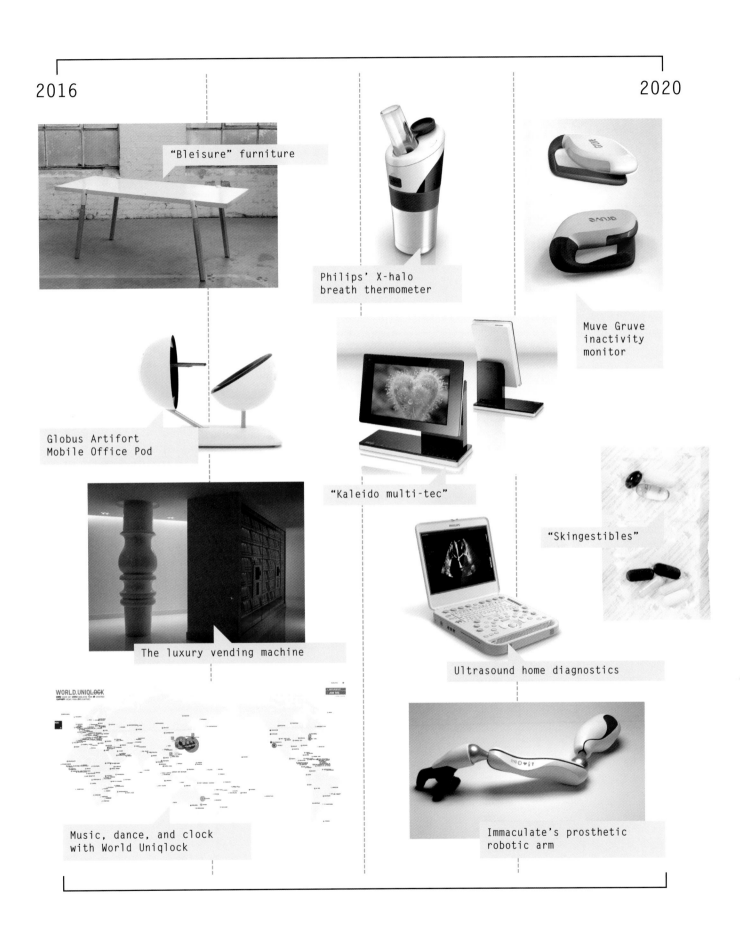

2016

2020

"Bleisure" furniture

Philips' X-halo
breath thermometer

Muve Gruve
inactivity
monitor

Globus Artifort
Mobile Office Pod

"Kaleido multi-tec"

"Skingestibles"

The luxury vending machine

Ultrasound home diagnostics

Music, dance, and clock
with World Uniqlock

Immaculate's prosthetic
robotic arm

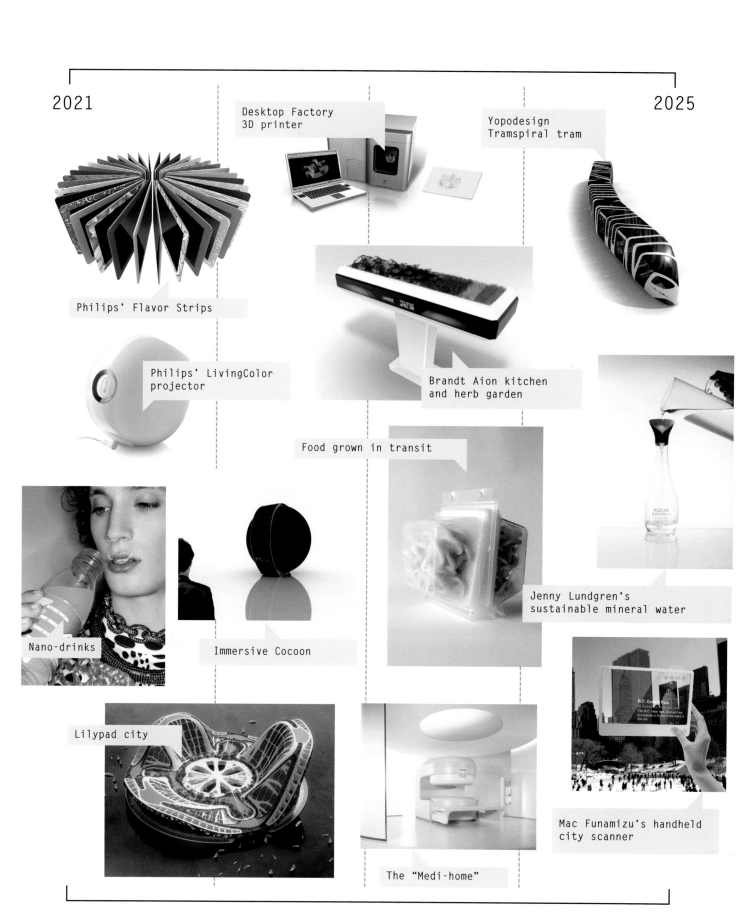

2021   2025

Desktop Factory
3D printer

Yopodesign
Tramspiral tram

Philips' Flavor Strips

Philips' LivingColor
projector

Brandt Aion kitchen
and herb garden

Food grown in transit

Nano-drinks

Immersive Cocoon

Jenny Lundgren's
sustainable mineral water

Lilypad city

Mac Funamizu's handheld
city scanner

The "Medi-home"

2026

2030

Andrea Nimtschke's
Firo cooking tube

Christelle Boule's
biodegradable urns

Susana Soares'
Bee diagnostics

The Moixa Interface Sphere

Podle mist
sprays

Philips' food cubes

Brittany Bell's "Seed Archive"

IDEO Aquaduct bike

GINA car by BMW

Waterpod
floating
homes

"Light-foot" living

The Colim Modular Camper

Hydro-Net city

Chapter One
The Anatomy of a Trend

THE "OCTOPUS"
chandelier by
Autoban is a
fantastical blurring
of a chandelier and
anglepoise lamp.
It is a design that
also echoes a trend
among designers such
as Maarten Baas,
Tobias Rockenfeld,
and Nacho Carbonell
to produce work
that resembles
phantasmagorical
monsters and
mechanical
creations.

"I'm losing my edge to the Internet seekers who can tell me every member of every good group from 1962 to 1978. I'm losing my edge. To all the kids in Tokyo and Berlin. I'm losing my edge to the art-school Brooklynites in little jackets and borrowed nostalgia for the unremem- ered eighties."

James Murphy, LCD Soundsystem[1]

THE WORDS OF THE LCD Soundsystem song "Losing My Edge" sum up the dilemma faced by all trend forecasters today: the fear that sooner or later, as the lyrics of the song suggest, they will lose their edge. For if trend forecasting is about anything, it is about staying plugged into the new and the next: to those areas of the culture where our "art-school Brooklynites," and their future equivalents, live, flourish, and bring into being a set of lifestyle choices contrary to those that have gone before.

> DEFINITION OF A TREND FORECASTER

By definition and activity, trend forecasters are lifestyle detectives: men and women who spend their time detecting patterns or shifts in attitudes, mindsets, or lifestyle options, that run against current thinking or how people normally behave, live, dress, communicate, and trade. To do this, as we shall see in the

A trend can be an "idea" as well as a set of similar shapes or interrelated objects. Here, a range of different products and locations represent portability, dual functionality, and a sense that work and play spaces are no longer segregated, but interchangeable as people no longer make distinctions between where, how, and when they work. This trend has been dubbed "Bleisure"; a blurring of "business" and "leisure."

coming chapters, trend forecasters use a battery of techniques and processes that have been derived from disciplines as diverse as sociology, psychology, and ethnography, and from methods such as military and scenario planning, and even role playing.

A relatively recent discipline, trend forecasting now underpins all aspects of society where it is important to understand the short, medium, and long-term impact of new and emerging changes taking place in the culture around us. These can be large scale changes impacting on the world of science, technology, fashion, interiors, architecture, or the arts, or they can be more subtle and difficult-to-identify shifts in how we will live tomorrow vis-à-vis the food we eat, the way we listen to music, or even the way we consume media.

> DEFINITION OF A TREND

To be a trend forecaster, it is vitally important to know what a "trend" is. It is not, as some people think, a term exclusively associated with the world of fashion. Nor is it a term that simply refers to processes which affect physical or aesthetic changes in our culture. A trend can be emotional, intellectual, and even spiritual. At its most basic, a trend can be defined as the direction in which something (and that something can be anything) tends to move and which has a consequential impact on the culture, society, or business sector through which it moves.

The word "trend" is an old one, and its origins can be traced back to Middle English and High German, where it meant "to turn" or "to spin" or "to revolve." At the beginning of the twentieth century, it was a term more familiar to economists, mathematicians, and statisticians who used it to describe an upward or downward shift on a graph, or a set of plotted figures, which allowed them to predict more long-term changes in a market or economic sector. However, from the 1960s onward, thanks to the work of economists, writers, mystics, and social scientists such as Herman Kahn, Pierre Wack, Michel Godet, and Peter Schwartz, it also became associated with aspects of our culture that are more difficult to quantify – those emotional, textural, psychological, or lifestyle changes that cause people to buy frozen produce over fresh, wear short skirts over long ones, choose one brand of car over another, or become a PC person rather than an Apple Mac one. Within this context, a trend can also be described as an "anomaly" – an oddity, inconsistency, or deviation from the norm, which becomes increasingly prominent over a period of time as more people, products, and ideas become part of that change. The words "style" or "movement" are sometimes used to describe these changes, or shifts, but strictly speaking a style is a distinctive manner, aesthetic, method, or way of expressing something "new" (in design, fashion, architecture, etc.), while a trend is the "direction" in which something new or different moves. A style then is about difference, while a trend is about difference and the direction along which that difference travels.

Trends in the broadest sense of the word are found in all aspects of our culture. In architecture, for instance, the repetitive raw-looking concrete work of architects like Peter and Alison Smithson and Sir Denys Lasdun – known as

A trend can also be a "meme" – a compelling or infectious idea that runs through the culture like a virus, cutting through all opposition, including what would otherwise be considered the dominant trend. For instance, at a time when organic, free-range, and seasonal food trends dominate consumer thinking, late-teen consumers are instead buying vitamin water and synthetically-inspired drinks.

Brutalism – can be categorized as a trend; likewise the block colors and randomly fixed shapes of Milan's Memphis Group (see page 16). In furniture, product design, and fashion, similar shifts can be noted on a yearly, monthly, or weekly basis. In design, thanks to the economic downturn in the middle of the first decade of the twenty-first century, a trend emerged which was called variously the "New Sobriety," the "New Seriousness," or (as the fashion designer Karl Lagerfeld called it) the "New Modesty."[2] This trend used sober palettes, solid shapes, and a restrained design aesthetic to project a mood that was more formal, cool, and controlled – the antithesis of trends and styles such as bling (an ostentatious lifestyle choice and visual aesthetic that encouraged and demanded conspicuous consumption and the love of gaudy material, products, and clothing labels). "Eve-olution"[3] – a play on the name of the biblical Eve and the word "evolution" – is a more niche but hugely important trend that has recently come to the fore and represents an emotional shift in how products need to be designed in a more female-focused and intuitive way, and one that continues to impact on the work of male and female designers today.

But a desire, a mood, or an idea can also be a trend. In the 1980s, the reduction and removal of national barriers to encourage the flow of goods, capital, and people gave birth to a trend we now call "Globalization." In the 1990s, growing concerns about how we sourced our food, coupled with the desire to eat pesticide-free products, kick-started a trend for buying organic products. Similarly, changes in how some of us consume information (via social media rather than newspapers), listen to music (via downloads rather than on CDs), or even describe ourselves ethically (more eco-friendly as opposed to being environmentally indifferent), can be classified as a trend.

Trends are, therefore, a fundamental part of our emotional, physical, and psychological landscape, and by detecting, mapping, and using them to anticipate what is new and next in the world we live in we are contributing in no small way to better understanding the underlying ideas and principles that drive and motivate us as people. Thus, much of a trend forecaster's time is spent telling people "why" trends happen, as well as "how," "where," and "when" they happen. Trends, as we shall see, are compulsive, addictive, and, in some cases, viral – infecting us when we least expect it, and on occasion whether we want them to or not.

To understand how and why this infection happens, it is important to understand some of the hidden qualities of trends themselves. To do this we need to delve into the world of evolutionary biology, and into the work on memes of author, biologist, ethologist, and humanist Richard Dawkins.

> MEMES AND TREND VIRUSES

As Dawkins describes it in his book, *The Selfish Gene,*[4] a "meme" is a cultural version of a gene in that it self-replicates in response to social, ethical, biological, or environmental changes which might impact on its survival. The entomology of the word relates to the Greek word *mimema*, to "mime" or "mimic," but it is also similar to the French word *meme* for "same," also a vital component in the make-up of a meme.

In art, trends are sometimes referred to as "movements," such as the Memphis movement, as represented here in the shelving unit of Ettore Sottsass (opposite), but really trends and movements are the same thing. The Surrealist art movement has also inspired furniture and product designers to create a shift in furniture styles that has been called "Surreality" by forecasters. Feature products (from top) include the "Etagère" by Camille Debons and Grégory Parsy, the "Sculpt Wardrobe" by Maarten Baas, and the "Lathe" chair by Sebastian Brajkovic.

According to Dawkins, memes can be anything – "tunes, ideas, catch-phrases, clothes, fashions, ways of making pots, or building arches."[5] Just as genes propagate themselves in the gene pool by migrating from one body to another via sperm or eggs, Dawkins, and many other evolutionary biologists, believe that memes propagate themselves in the meme pool by passing from brain to brain via a process called "imitation," whereby one person imitates a behavioral characteristic of another because of the advantages in doing so.

We do this, Dawkins believes, because evolution has encoded us with certain traits that make it easier for us to survive socially, intellectually, and culturally if we mirror or mimic the characteristics of others – especially if those characteristics offer us (and them) clear advantages in terms of being more competitive, beautiful, intellectual, or culturally or socially superior.

Being a meme, a trend infects us in much the same manner. We buy a fashion item, a product, or a piece of furniture because we like it, but also because possessing this product has a certain social, cultural, or psychological value attached to it. It makes us feel cool, edgy, conservative, different, or perhaps more fulfilled, because we have seen the product in the possession of people who we associate with these values. Some of us do this consciously, but for many of us it can be an unconscious decision in that we are merely going with the flow. Or are we? Sociologists would say that we are not. Deep down in our subconscious, and around us in society, there are seen and unseen forces and subtle social, environmental, and psychological pressures at work – from friends, family, the media, even total strangers – that cajole us into going with the flow more than we would like to think. These pressures or influences were first noted in 1962 by Everett M. Rogers, an American sociologist, when he started looking at why some farmers in a particular part of America were more innovative than others when it came to adopting new ideas.

> DIFFUSION OF INNOVATIONS

Everett M. Rogers called his theory the "Diffusion of Innovations,"[6] and identified it by studying the findings of previous research projects which had been carried out by fellow sociologists, including Bryce Ryan and Neal Gross. Ryan and Gross studied the activities of farmers in Iowa and were specifically interested in how long it took them to adopt an innovation – in this case a hybrid corn seed designed to improve their annual crop yields.[7] They measured the rate of adoption by noting the speed at which the innovation passed from farmer to farmer, and by identifying and isolating any factors that speeded up or slowed down this process.

Building on the work of Ryan and Gross, and on the findings of similar programs of research throughout the state of Iowa, Rogers was able to determine that, regardless of the innovation, the pattern of diffusion through a particular group, community, or social tribe was the same. It started with an idea or with an "Innovator" who had the idea. He or she in turn passed this idea on to a group called "Early Adopters." Adjusting the idea slightly, Early Adopters in turn passed it on to a group called the "Early Majority," who in turn transmitted the idea to yet another group, referred to in Rogers' studies as the "Late Majority."[8] These, in turn, communicated the idea to members of the community he dubbed "Laggards," because they were the most resistant group of all to new ideas and changes.

Although Rogers focused his early studies on such areas as hybrid corn, as his later research indicated,[9] he could also have been looking at the rise of organic farming, rap, cell phone usage, the Internet, a fashion trend, or any of the design or architectural trends mentioned or visualized in this chapter. All of these are different, but all follow the same pattern as they move through the culture via a number of very distinctive but always overlapping social types which Rogers divided up into five categories. These categories, which you will find in any community, city, or country, remain more or less the same size in percentage terms regardless of which culture, or sector within a culture (as in the retail sector, the technology sector, the organic food sector, etc.), you measure them in. They are called the "Diffusion of Innovation types."

> DIFFUSION OF INNOVATION TYPES

Although Rogers' research was carried out four decades ago, trend forecasters today still use his "types" and the percentage divisions within them to calculate the size of each group in any overall society or sector they are asked to study. His categories include:

__Innovators are those individuals who are responsible for the development of an innovation or the introduction of a new idea. Percentage-wise they make up about 2.5 percent of any overall group. In themselves they may not be the ones who created the original idea, or kick-started the new trend, but they are the ones who can articulate it in a way which makes sense to other members of their tribe or the groups they come into contact with.

In terms of mapping a trend, they are among the first people a trend forecaster needs to track down within any community or sector if he or she is keen to identify a trend in its early stages and chart its progress through society as a whole.

__Early Adopters are usually close friends or colleagues of the Innovator. They are happy to be exposed to new ideas and ways of doing things from an individual or group of people they trust and respect. They represent about 13.5 percent of any overall group and usually have a high degree of interconnectedness or involvement with other groups. Early Adopters are usually more integrated into a social group, style tribe, or community and, because they are more familiar with the community they live in, are more trusted and valued.

If Innovators are global in their tastes and knowledge streams, Early Adopters are local, highly visible, and well connected. Potential adopters of an idea also look to them for advice and information about any new trend or innovation. This can be anything from a fashion or technological innovation to a website or a niche-but-growing consumer group. When isolating, identifying, and measuring the spread and impact of a trend, forecasters focus their efforts

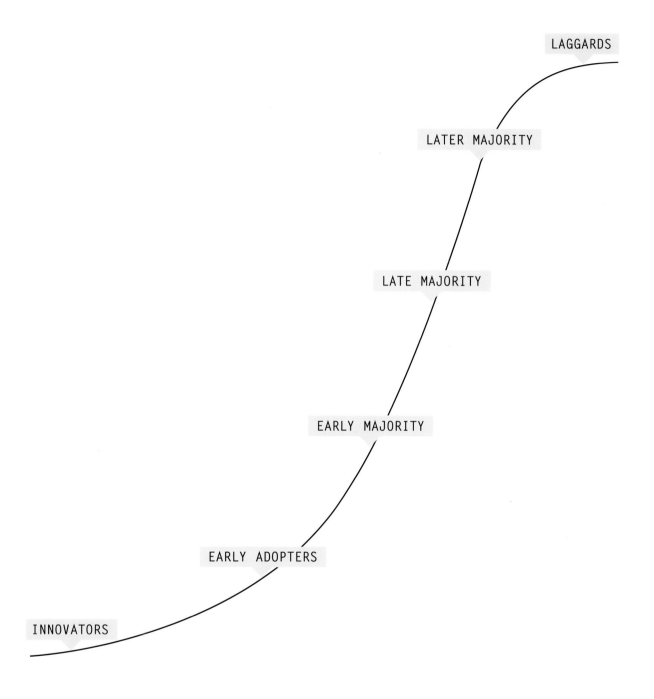

LAGGARDS

LATER MAJORITY

LATE MAJORITY

EARLY MAJORITY

EARLY ADOPTERS

INNOVATORS

The Diffusion of Innovation curve

The Diffusion of Innovation curve seen here is a simplified version of the mapping process used by Bryce Ryan and Neal Gross, to describe how an idea, innovation, or product development passes from the fringes of our culture into the Late Majority mainstream. It does so in the form of an S-shape curve, the lower part of the S being occupied by our Innovators and Early Adopters, the upper parts by our Early Majority, Late Majority, and Laggards. Forecasters refer to the turn in the lower curve as the tipping point (where the trend is about to go "viral" or big), and the top tip of the upper S as the "flat-line" or Laggard's Leap, when the trend is effectively burned out or dead.

An innovation does not have to be a radical departure in future-faced technology. It can simply be about "no frills elegance." Here a television by Westinghouse, a Palm Pre phone, and Hewlett-Packard's HP 2140 Mini notebook use "cheap chip" technology and toughened plastics to create a trend that has been called "Utilitec" (as in utilitarian technology).

on identifying the Early Adopter within any community, along with the Innovator.

These two groups, more than any of the other types, are crucial to spreading a trend because they "help trigger the critical mass when they adopt an innovation."[10] Forecasters use the term "critical mass" to describe the point at which a trend becomes so infectious few people can resist it. This is also known as the "tipping point," or the point at which the trend tips over from being a minority concern to a majority one that is highly visible and influential.

__Early Majority are those who need to see how the Early Adopters relate to, and grapple with, any new idea. They make up a sizable, and thus influential, 34 percent of any overall group. Although they are not opinion leaders in their own right, they nonetheless know many of the opinion leaders within the Early Adopters, and thus act as a bridge of reassurance between them and the Late Majority, who are always more sceptical of new or emerging trends unless they can see direct benefits from buying into them.

Early Majority members are highly sociable, unusually active online, but do not necessarily have thoughts or ideas designed to lead or to direct – they are invariably followers, but followers other people trust as they are seen to be sensible enough not to adopt something if it is too radical or outlandish. While never the first to have an idea, the Early Majority nonetheless stick with it longer than most, and hold on to it as they pass it over to the Late Majority – the next most important group in terms of volume-buying power.

Trend forecasters tend to monitor which ideas or trends the Early Majority are concerned with to determine which ones are set to become more popular than others with the Late Majority. They may even establish test groups or panels among this segment to test an idea, or to establish the validity of a trend if they are still unsure about it. Because the Early Majority is so connected to the Late Majority group, and because both groups make up the largest number of people within the groups overall, many forecasting and marketing agencies concentrate their efforts here because these are the areas where they can determine more precisely if the trend they are focusing on is set to be a profitable and long-lasting one.

__Late Majority are those who are conservative by nature and who require high levels of reassurance and explanation about how a new idea will work and how they can benefit from using or buying into it. They represent about 34 percent of any overall group, so in terms of influence they are a powerful body to deal with. Late Majority members tend to adopt things in watered-down forms and formats, and do so only after they have seen enough examples of it among the Early Majority and among, on, or with people they respect and whose opinions they trust (such as celebrities or their more adventurous friends).

Because of this, the Late Majority are easier to target and their tastes easier to define. They are the greatest imitators of all the types: keen to go for the "look," to kit their house out in the latest style, to buy that "must-have" bag, or to travel to that must-see holiday destination. Many companies, therefore, concentrate their efforts in servicing this group because it is easier to imitate than it is to innovate.

(text continues on page 26)

Case Study:
Henrik Vejlgaard

HENRIK VEJLGAARD (trend-forecasting.com) refers to himself as a "cultural flirt." A trend sociologist, he also writes for fashion and design magazines on a range of topics from shopping and fashion to consumer behavior. But at the heart of his activities is a desire to braille the culture (see page 36) and "flirt" with people that live at the edge of the lifestyle firmament. As he says: "It is here that change happens, and here that newness erupts. Traditional analysis is important, but "non-verbal observation" is the best skill a forecaster can nurture because most groups are better at showing us what is new and next, rather than telling us."

After that, Vejlgaard says, comes "context": "Once you have identified a trend or a new movement, you need to decode and determine the factors that will influence or impede its spread. Something happening in Williamsburg, New York, for instance, may spread to Shoreditch in London, or Shinjuku in Tokyo, quicker than it spreads to other parts of America."

To map this process, and to determine the ebb and flow of a trend, Vejlgaard has developed his "Diamond-Shaped Trend Model" to represent how trends migrate from the extreme edges of the culture to the more mundane mainstream. With a nod toward Everett Rogers' Diffusion of Innovation curve,

When "decoding" a streetscape,it is important to break it down into a number of clear and separate zones. These should include a street's façade (the retail, business, and leisure spaces it contains), its sidewalk traffic (the style, ethnicity, and sartorial characteristics of the people using it), and finally, activities or mixed-use areas that define the street's overall sense of purpose — for recreation, retail, leisure, business.

If a street is located in an "edge," fringe, or Innovator zone, then it is important to note the technology people use, how they use it, where, and when. Are they texting, talking, or using instant messaging? And how do they behave when they are doing this? Do they walk and talk, pause and talk, choose "pause" areas where there is less foot traffic? Or a space perhaps that is suggestive of a private office — a doorway, a free café chair. In each instance, a forecaster is scanning for a potential trend, habit, or insight that will suggest a future opportunity to one of their clients.

Observation, intuition, and interrogation are the three processes many forecasters use when street watching. For the first you should always use a notebook, camera, or digicam; for the second, the ongoing knowledge you have stored in your head about this and the many other streets you have visited; and for the third, a recording device that allows you to stop people you are keen to talk to and to capture verbally details about their dress sense, or their attitudes.

and the cultural types that inhabit it, Vejlgaard's Diamond-Shaped Trend Model (see illustration opposite), is broken down into six different personality profiles: Trendsetters, Trend Followers, Early Mainstreamers, Mainstreamers, Late Mainstreamers, and Conservatives. He developed this model in the early 1990s, he says, when attempting to identify how long it took a fashion trend observed on the fringes of society to migrate into the mainstream: "The more visual and observable a trend was the faster it moved." He noticed, for instance, that cosmetic trends took one to two years to pass from the Trendsetters' stage to the Mainstream, while clothing and accessories both took two to three years, and home design five to seven years (because it was less observable, most costly to change, and highly dependent on a collective decision-making process within the home).

The speed at which a trend spreads through the Diamond-Shaped Trend Model, explains Vejlgaard, is highly dependent on any number of factors, and these should be noted at all times. For instance, if the trend can be easily observed (for example, if it is in the public domain), listened to, copied, photographed, or in any way replicated in a manner that makes it easier to "show" someone as opposed to "tell him or her about it," then the trend will spread faster and be more readily assimilated and adapted. If, on the other hand, it is a trend with an emotional dimension, or one that is highly subjective in terms of how we understand or describe it – the organic food or eco-clothing movement, for instance – then its spread will be slower.

Observing, however, must be accompanied by a process Vejlgaard refers to as "synthesizing." This, he says, is the final bit of the puzzle and must be done if you are to map accurately the process of a trend through the Diamond-Shaped Trend Model. Constant vigilance is the key, he stresses: watching and listening, but also using everything at your disposal – cell phones, digital cameras, the Internet, notepads, sketchbooks, your memory – to observe and then to interpret your observations in a way that is useful. "This is what it comes down to in the end – the insights you apply to observation. But first and foremost comes the observation."

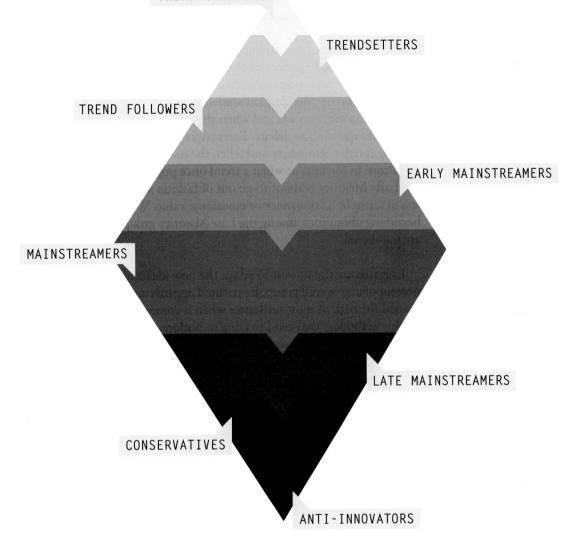

TREND CREATORS

TRENDSETTERS

TREND FOLLOWERS

EARLY MAINSTREAMERS

MAINSTREAMERS

LATE MAINSTREAMERS

CONSERVATIVES

ANTI-INNOVATORS

The Diamond-Shaped Trend Model

Henrik Vejlgaard's Diamond-Shaped Trend Model offers forecasters a clear and easy route to map a particular trend through. Working with Vejlgaard's rough calculations it is possible to plot the speed, or velocity, of a particular trend or product through each of the shaded zones. He calculates, for example, that cosmetics take one to two years to pass along the diamond; clothes and accessories two to three years; home design five to seven years.

The speed of a trend is also influenced by the country, city, or town you measure it in, as well as social groups within which you track it. It is therefore important to factor in all issues that may influence the take-up of a trend in a particular area, including levels of technological usage (from cell phones to laptops, social networking activities to television viewing patterns), to the predominant social, political, and religious views your "test" group may have, etc.

Even the most simple driver can have an impact on the rate and intensity of adoption. City dwellers, for instance, may be keen to buy into all trends organic and rural, but people in the country may want the urban ideal. Therefore a trend toward living the rustic "good life" might not be adopted in the countryside at all – because there it is neither new nor, given the hardships such a life can bring, even desirable.

Above all others, the Late Majority is a group governed by "social norms" (a set of moral, social, and lifestyle rules that the majority of their friends and associates subscribe to) as much as they are by market or economic ones. Because of this, they are among the quickest to drop a trend or to fall out of love with a celebrity, a piece of clothing, a bag, or a food brand, if these brands are shunned by their peers, or are no longer considered to be part of accepted public opinion or taste. Market studies are littered with the damage the Late Majority can exact on a brand when they believe it is likely to bring their sense of self into question or debate. Forecasters monitor the activities of this group because it tells them where and when the market is about to experience a downturn in fortune, or when a trend once popular among Early Adopters and the Early Majority is about to go out of fashion and, therefore, be worth a lot less in terms of its monetary or emotional value. When forecasters see a trend becoming ubiquitous among the Late Majority group, they know that its days are numbered.

___Laggards are the slowest to adopt the new idea and make up about 16 percent of any overall group. By nature Laggards are conservative and err toward the path of most resistance when it comes to trying something new. Highly orthodox, they tend to cling to notions that are traditional, familiar, and long-tested. This is usually the case whether we are talking about fashion, fragrances, interiors, household goods, or laptops. Laggards are reluctant to change, suspicious of the new, and wary of ideas that are likely to challenge the status quo. However, when everybody else has finally settled into a trend and now regard it as the norm (sustainability, gay marriages, genetically-modified food, for example) Laggards at last begin to come around and tacitly subscribe to the idea, albeit to a more watered-down version. Eventually, they become the base-line or foundation against which the next set of radical ideas is judged.

Forecasters observing a trend being adopted by Laggards refer to it as a trend that has "flat-lined," in other words a trend that has reached the end of its usefulness as far as the forecaster is concerned. This however does not mean you should be dismissive of this group or indifferent to its tastes and views. When Laggards embrace an idea it also tips forecasters off to the fact that somewhere back along the Diffusion of Innovation cycle, new ideas are once more emerging. Innovators and Laggards then are the bookends to the same journey – to observe and understand one, it is important to observe and understand the other.

The Diffusion of Innovation types can also be viewed as a series of interlocking circles that have characteristics in common where and when they overlap. It is easy to imagine an idea or a trend starting out among Innovators (cell phone usage, social networking, using "emoticoms" in text messages, etc.) and working its way through to the Early Adopters, Early Majority, Late Majority, and Laggards. But imagine for a moment mapping or plotting the progression of that journey as a flow chart, as a set of figures or activities on an X/Y axis. How would it look? A bit like an "S" that has been tripped up on its face (see page 19). The starting point of the "S" would begin with the Innovator, then curve up to meet the Early Adopters, then on to the Early

Double dressers

In a culture where looking different is prized, a growing number of teenagers are choosing conformity as a way of demonstrating their "individuality" as well as their friendship. In this sense, Innovators Antonya Allen (left) and Amy Harrison (right), are using conformity to define their difference or "otherness." They serve as a reminder to forecasters that Innovators are not always outlandish, but merely people

running against accepted norms – in this case the desire among many teenagers to stand out and look different.

Some forecasters, however, argue that double dressing is merely a more intimate example of "mirroring" – the need to imitate those we respect or admire – a kind of behavior typical within social groups distinguished by a self-defined difference or coolness. It could therefore be argued that double dressing is a meme with limited

evolutionary potential because it sees clear and distinct advantages in being so limited. Trends like this, however, tend to be short lived and remain ultra-niche and localized. Because they control creativity, and curb (albeit in a limited way) the underlying need among people to alter certain aspects of their dress, they become less and less appealing and ultimately die out as the incentives for buying into them become less compelling.

In the age of supersonic and subsonic jets, the "anomaly" forecasters may be identifying is a return to more eco-friendly and stylish modes of travel, such as the airship. Featured (from top) are the "Aeolus" by Christopher Ottersbach, the "Manned Cloud" by Jean-Marie Massaud, and Nau's "Strato Cruiser," all designed to evoke a new spirit of freedom, escape, and spirited adventure – a trend that has been called "Slowtopia."

Majority, and so on as more and more people become infected with an idea, until it hits the Laggards where it would begin to plateau and flat-line. This shape and phenomenon is referred to as the "S-shape curve" or, as it is better known to trend forecasters, the "Diffusion of Innovation curve."

> DIFFUSION OF INNOVATION CURVE

The "Diffusion of Innovation curve" is a pathway or trajectory forecasters look for, and attempt to map, when they are noting a new trend's passage through the culture. The "S" shape describes the curve or line you get when you statistically plot the rate at which something is adopted (the X axis), against the length of time it takes for a particular group to adopt an idea or trend (the Y axis).

The Diffusion of Innovation curve was first noted by Jean-Gabriel de Tarde (Gabriel Tarde), a French nineteenth-century lawyer and judge, who analyzed a wide range of trends he identified through the court cases over which he adjudicated. As Rogers reports it, Tarde observed that "the rate of adoption of a new idea usually followed an S-shaped curve over time."[11] But to accurately plot a trend's progress through a community, or to determine the point at which it is about to "tip" and go viral, you have to consider a number of other issues as well: how a trend is communicated (ideas are disseminated more swiftly online than they are in books or on television), the time it takes to communicate it, and the social or societal norms that might influence the speed or the level of intensity at which a trend is adopted.

Rogers and Tarde also recognized that "the take off in the S-shaped curve of adoption begins to occur when *opinion leaders* in a system use a new idea."[12] This is why when you are identifying or tracking a new trend you will spend a lot of time with opinion leaders among the Early Adopters, or in identifying Innovators within a group who are never far away from the Early Adopters. But there is another, more vital reason why ideas or trends spread they way they do.

Rogers noted, for example, that some Innovators or Early Adopters were more outgoing and gregarious than others, while some had fewer friends and smaller social networks. He likewise observed that Innovators and Early Adopters overall had larger social networks than the Late Majority and Laggards, and that their social networks contained more people within them who were socially diverse and culturally different in one way or another from the majority of people within the overall Innovator or Early Adopter groups. This is not as common as you think. If you look at a group of friends, work colleagues, or people that frequent the same club, you will find that they tend to have the same social backgrounds, ethnic origins, and similar social and cultural references. People, in other words, tend to hang out with people who most resemble themselves. This is known as a group with high levels of "homophily."

___HOMOPHILY

"Homophily" is a term which was coined by sociologists in the 1950s to describe processes and activities that they referred to as "love of the same." It is a word, and an idea, that denotes the bonds, similarities, and social activities that tie groups of people together in a way which makes them similar in terms of how they think, look, act, and engage with other people. According to sociologists, "sameness" – or the desire to be similar to others – makes most people feel comfortable and secure. Because of this, homophily is more common among groups like the Late Majority and Laggards, who by nature are more conservative and less open to newness or change in their day-to-day lives. This means that they are more resistant to change and less likely to be infected by a meme or a trend than the Innovator and Early Adopter groups. It does not mean, however, that they are immune to them, merely that the infection process takes longer, and can become more diluted as their higher resistance levels wear down and dissipate the intensity of the trend. "Homophilous" types are found in all groups, and by detecting and monitoring them trend forecasters can quickly gauge the speed at which an idea or a trend will pass through to the mainstream.

__HETEROPHILY

"Heterophilous" groups are the polar opposite to homophilous ones. If the latter is about having smaller networks, and fewer social, intellectual, and philosophical encounters, the former is about having these in abundance. Heterophilous people and groups tend to be more open, keener on change, and have larger and more ethnically and socially diverse networks. Because of this, they encounter new ideas, attitudes, and outlooks more frequently than their homophilous counterparts. As a consequence, they are more likely to embrace, disseminate, and dispense with the ideas or experiences in a shorter and more concentrated period of time as new ones fight for their attention. Forecasters tend to spend a lot of time studying heterophilous groups and using the observations and insight gleaned from doing this to inform their decisions about what is likely to be new or next in terms of trends among the Early Majority, Late Majority, and Laggards.

The more heterophilous people you find in a group, the more likelihood it is that this group will be an Early Adopter group and one, therefore, as a forecaster you should be interested in studying. This is common on university campuses and in university towns, where student bodies come from diverse social, ethnic, and cultural backgrounds. As a student, this is something you should cherish, and explore. Later in life you will notice that this is not the case at all, that such difference and diversity (unless you live in a truly global city such as London, Paris, New York, São Paulo, Buenos Aires, Rotterdam, Berlin, etc.) is very rare. People for the most part, unless they are Innovators or Early Adopters, tend to live (if they have a choice) among those who are like-minded. This is why homophilous neighborhoods or communities are more common in most of the areas we live in today. They tend to have few heterophilous types among them and, therefore, are more suspicious of anything that threatens their stability or sameness until they are absolutely sure it is a safe, unchallenging route to take. You are unlikely to find any bars, clubs, shops, stores, businesses, or buildings in these places that challenge the norm or which are kick-starting new ideas.

For forecasters then, groups that are highly heterophilous by nature (Innovators and Early Adopters) are of greater interest than those that are

Stelarc is an
Australian-based
performance artist who
explores the body's
relationship with
technology and the
growing influence of
surgery and genetic
modification on how
we look. He is one
of a growing body
of artists that
forecasters look to
for inspirational
leads on how we will
respond to a world
where genetic
modification and the
latest advances in
stem cell research
will make even the
most unusual forms
of body augmentation
possible.

homophilous, because part of a forecaster's job is to focus his or her efforts on areas of the culture, or the people within them, who encourage the exchange of ideas, and especially new ideas.

> SUMMARY

By nature trend forecasters are heterophilous types – enamored with the new, the next, and the innovative. They are always open to ideas, keen to embrace change, and to be with, or part of, groups who are similarly disposed. Trend forecasters are curious and keenly observant of new and emerging patterns or anomalies in the culture that alert them to more profound cultural shifts. These changes can be in any area – fashion, retail, design, interiors, the arts, architecture, even science and technology. A trend can also be an idea, philosophy, or political or social movement.

As we have seen, a trend tends to spread along set lines and via key groups such as Innovators, Early Adopters, and so on. This "Diffusion of Innovation" process is governed by a complex set of social, psychological, cultural, and evolutionary rules and compulsions that impact on the speed, tenacity, and integrity of a trend as it passes from one Diffusion of Innovation type to another. Some of you might argue that there is no such thing as a trend or a meme that can affect you in the way that has been outlined: that we are by our own definition individuals, are we not? But dig into your cupboard, spin through those old playlists, or look at your previous tastes in boyfriends or hairstyles and, again and again, you'll find yourself asking: "Did I really buy that/listen to this/sleep with him or her?"

We did, we do, and will continue to do so, because these compulsions for the most part are unconscious. They are the public ways in which we register our decision to conform or be different, to be an Innovator, an Early Adopter, or a member of the Late Majority. They are the decisions that in retrospect make us part of a tribe, subgroup, fashion or design clan: they hone our tastes, attitudes, and outlooks. But if we are aware of them, and try to assess and study them objectively, they are also traits we can draw on to make us more effective and observant forecasters. For if forecasting is about anything, it is about being able to observe, interrogate, and draw insight and inspiration from the world around us – and from people we may have nothing in common with.

Forecasting, as we shall see in the following chapters, isn't just about focusing on the new and the next, it is also about paying attention to the different and the diverse, the patterns that we recognize, and the anomalies that disrupt and confound them.

Chapter Two
The Trend Forecaster's Toolkit

> STUFF: NEW THINGS IN THE CULTURE
> CULTURAL BRAILLING
> CROSS-CULTURAL ANALYSIS
> SUMMARY

A REINVENTION of a familiar chair like the Arne Jacobsen Model 3107 series by designer Thomas von Staffeldt as the "Gula" (gluttony) chair can tip a trend forecaster off to the fact that a new mood in furniture may be about to emerge.

"The future is here, it's just not very well distributed."

William Gibson, science fiction writer[1]

AS WE HAVE SEEN, trends are patterns or anomalies that can persuade us to adopt new ways of doing things or expressing ourselves. Because of this, much of a forecaster's time is spent trying to identify new "patterns" or anomalies at their nascent stages. They do this by observing the activities of groups like the Innovators or Early Adopters, and do so within the cities, neighborhoods, and streets where these people are to be found: places, in other words, where many of tomorrow's mainstream ideas are happening today.

In order to detect new anomalies a very distinct set of skills and sensitivities is required. By "skills" we mean practical techniques or processes that need to be followed to identify these changes, and by "sensitivities" a way of looking at and engaging with the world that allows us to examine all aspects of society around us with an open, untainted, and enquiring mind. Too many trends are overlooked, and too many changes in the culture ignored or misread because of preconceptions and prejudices so it is important that you guard against this.

Consider the following: MDMA (illegal), Ugg boots (questionable), Mullet haircuts (a catastrophe), colonic irrigation (puzzling), subdermal piercing (painful). All of these may not appeal on one level or the other, but all are, and continue to be, trends that many people subscribe to. If you are to become a forecaster you need to be open-minded, observant, heterophilous, and able to recognize new patterns or anomalies where and when they happen and, most importantly, why they happen. The following pages explain and explore some of the key techniques you will need to do these things. But before you can do any of them, it is important to consider the role "stuff" plays in this process.

> STUFF:NEW THINGS IN THE CULTURE

"Stuff" can be anything – a car, a pair of sneakers, a music download, a cell phone – but, for the purposes of trend forecasting, "stuff" is a "singular" or "new" object that crosses our visual, emotional, or intellectual field of vision in a way that piques curiosity or commands attention. "Stuff" is important because it can be the first indication that a trend is brewing, or that a new direction in the culture, or the way we live, is imminent.

Here is a random selection of "stuff": Land Rover's LRX car; Yauatcha packaging by designers MadeThought; the interior of a beauty salon in Valencia, Spain by designer Miguel Ángel Llácer; a "Blossom" lamp by Hella

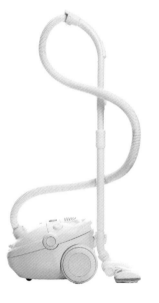

Cross-cultural analysis and its uses

One of the important tasks for the forecaster is what they call cross-cultural analysis, which consists of watching both cultures and industries for signs that an idea or trend in one place is beginning to emerge in another. If such a cross-over occurs, then that trend is very likely to become both long-term and highly influential.

The above images (clockwise from top, left): a detail of a car interior by Land Rover, the interior of a beauty salon in Valencia, Spain by Miguel Ángel Llácer, the "Blossom lamp" by Hella Jongerius, Yauatcha packaging by MadeThought, a power tool by Johnny Shi, and a Pia Wallén Vacuum cleaner, all appear to be random "stuff." But once brought together they collectively take on a new set of values and references. These we shall see add up to a new, more powerful picture about the culture in which we live – the story of a trend called "Eve-olution" (see page 15).

But to identify these products or reference points in the first place, a forecaster has to browse through all the information media on a daily basis, as well as regularly visiting exhibitions and trade fairs for everything from fashion to cars to military hardware. And there now exist ways to make this cross-cultural analysis work more easily. Specialist trend sites on the Internet like Trendwatching, The Cool Hunter, Cool Hunting, WGSN, LifeStyle News Global, the David Report, or PSFK have emerged with free sections that aggregate "stuff" from many sources.

Nevertheless a good forecaster will always have their own, more idiosyncratic resource bank based on the world around them. These "feeds" or "touchpoints" should include a range of sites, magazines, newspapers, journals, books, and reference materials that cover everything like fashion, design, architecture, graphics, technology, clubbing, leisure, music, marketing, science, medicine, finance, literature, the arts, gaming, sociology, and economics. In other words, all aspects of culture where "stuff" is present and where the first symptoms of a trend are likely to emerge.

Jongerius; power tools by Johnny Shi; a new vacuum cleaner by Pia Wallén for Electrolux (see page 35). On first examination, this seems to be a random, disconnected, and arbitrary list. But when we view the objects and products collectively, or cluster them together, their design, finish, surface detailing, and emotional resonance suggest a more telling pattern about changes that are taking place within the lifestyle industries as a whole. There is a new aesthetic – one with a softer, more feminine palette than the colors or shapes found among more traditional and mainstream designs.

But how did this happen? We began with a random list of objects and products from industries with little in common and yet out of this a pattern seems to have emerged – a new style or aesthetic. Is this a happy accident? A coincidence? Something that has happened because of how this stuff was selected, and who it was selected from? The answer is all of the above, and more. This "cluster" has a pattern and a hidden logic to it because of how it was assembled in the first instance. The forecasters who first encountered Pia Wallén's vacuum cleaner, or Johnny Shi's power tools, used a technique to locate them known as "cultural brailling."

> CULTURAL BRAILLING

"Cultural brailling" is a term created by American forecaster Faith Popcorn. Popcorn and her trend forecasting organization, BrainReserve, have been using this technique since the 1980s to detect and track changes in the way consumers live. Susan Choi, TrendTrack director at BrainReserve, explains how it works as follows: "Brailling is a way of communicating language through bumps on a page. We take that same technique here and feel the bumps in culture. The bumps are everything. Again it is about using all of your senses: things that you see, things that you taste, things that you hear. For example, it could be a matter of walking into a retail store and noticing the lighting, the music, feeling the different textures, just fully immersing yourself into whatever environment that you are in."[2]

Brailling is also about being hyper-observant and alert to newness. It is, as Choi suggests, also important to braille a new environment with all of your senses – smell, touch, hearing, taste, and sight. To braille the culture properly, you need to reach out (physically as well as emotionally) and touch anything new in your immediate environment. You also have to reach out for new "stuff" in professions, societies, countries, or industries (automotive, beauty, fashion, architecture, medicine, technology, biotech, stem cell, etc.) that you may have no real knowledge of, or interest in.

Brailling is all-consuming and something you must do wherever you are or whoever you are with. You should be ready to embrace everything, even "stuff" that seems bizarre (spiders that spin steel webs, tomatoes that contain vaccines, material that refracts light in a way that makes the wearer invisible, microscopic engines or nanobots that can repair damaged organs and zap blood clots) and to do so with an open and untainted mind. It is also important to do so by asking the right questions. To understand anything about a trend you need to know "who" started it, "what" it should be called, "where" it came from, "why"

(text continues on page 41)

BROOKLYN

2 - PSFK

Image design by Jenny Beorkrem
www.orkposters.com

Case Study: Piers Fawkes

PIERS FAWKES (psfk.com) is co-founder and editor of PSFK, an online network and offline trend and insight consultancy, which works for a range of clients including Apple, Target, the BBC, and NBC Universal.

For Fawkes it is "stuff" that counts: "Without stuff there is no innovation, and no telltale stepping stones to lead us into the future." Key to the success of his business is how Fawkes and his team of online scouts and innovators convert the "stuff" they upload into the kind of collateral that PSFK's clients need to make strategic and useful decisions about "how they should speak to consumers, as well as the products they should target them with."

Unlike most trend networks, access to the "stuff" Fawkes and his global team collate is free. As he says: "That's the nature of the Internet after all – but what we do charge for are the insights these uploads offer you about consumers, and where the bigger long-term trends are set to come from." These insights are delivered in a number of ways: via the Good Ideas salons, where entrepreneurs discuss trends and ideas with a view to profiting from potential collaborations; from publishing trend books and reports to encourage debate around upcoming trends; and, more recently, through PSFK's Purple List (purplelist.com), an online network of global experts and members where information and insight can be gained on a growing range of sectors.

RESERVED

PSFK founder Piers Fawkes (far left), hosts one of the consultancy's many salon-style events. These are informal gatherings designed to share ideas, create and develop collaborations, and foster a community that encourages debate and a more exploratory approach to understanding Innovators and Early Adopters and how their behaviors impact on the bigger consumer mainstream.

Meetings like this take place in key cities globally. They allow many of the organization's 40,000 networkers to develop their own business contacts as well as allowing PSFK itself to create a powerful group of fractional consultants that brands, businesses, and organizations can call on for support and insight.

Salons like this complement the work created by PSFK's New York team, its growing list of online bloggers, and the increasing number of offices the network has developed globally via salons. It also encourages like-minded people keen to work under the open-source approach fostered by Fawkes and his team.

For Fawkes the difference between information and insight is an important one: "Information can tell you that a market has potential, insight how to make that potential profitable." As he sees it, we are no longer living in the era of the big idea, but instead we are in the time of many niches. To succeed, a brand has to have many ideas in its portfolio, and many experts to advise the brand on how to negotiate this ever-changing landscape. Because of this, global brands are in constant need of local eyes and ears and the Purple List facilities this need. Fawkes also uses his network of global correspondents to work with clients directly and, via consumer-focused networks, to help them more effectively understand the emerging consumer mindset.

Fawkes describes his method of working with clients as "organic": "While some forecasters have very clear ideas of what the overall trends are, and how each client should 'buy' into these, when we work with them we prefer to keep our options open. We look at the brief, identify their issues of concern, and then put this out to our network." In each case, Fawkes and his team in New York can call on experts or collaborators from any number of industries and sectors globally. But members, he says, share a number of underlying characteristics in common: they are tastemakers and opinion leaders – Innovators and Early Adopters who are initiating change – and from within these groups smaller, tighter hubs are assembled when a client wants a more focused and industry-specific response. At this point, Fawkes and his network will survey all the "stuff" that has been uploaded, corralling off anything that suggests a pattern or a potential trend in the making. Once this has been done, Fawkes works directly with the client to identify how this trend can be translated as a product, or as a way to carry existing products into the market. This can be done as an ideas workshop, delivered as a written or visual report, as a series of one-to-one client debriefs, or by Peep Insights and Revelations – a specialist research unit that uses everything from ethnography and video to consumer insight diaries to deliver value to the client.

Anthropomorphic shapes and references to phantasmagorical creatures like Edward Lear's "Chankley Bore" can be found in a recent trend launched by designers such as ding3000 and Maarten Baas, who were keen to evoke a sense of fun, play, and childhood at a time when design itself was becoming increasingly rational and linear. The "Octopus" chandelier by Autoban (see page 10) is also emblematic of this trend.

it is emerging now, and "when" it was first noted. These are basic questions, but without knowing the answers to them it is difficult to ground a trend, or to determine how you can use it when working with clients later on.

__THE WHO: THE INNOVATOR

Although you may find yourself identifying the trend first, it is always important to seek out the "who" – the Innovator. Without the "who" it is difficult to determine the importance or cultural relevance of the "what," and whether or not it is likely to cascade into a trend.

As Malcolm Gladwell, author of *The Tipping Point* (a book that looks at trend mapping in a broader cultural context) explains: "The key to coolhunting, then, is to look for cool people first and cool things later, and not the other way around. Since cool things are always changing, you can't look for them, because the very fact they are cool means you have no idea what to look for."[3]

When we talk about the "who," we are talking about the instigators, the Innovators or, in some cases, the so-called "patient zeros" (as Gladwell refers to them), with which any trend starts. This can be someone such as Bill Wasik, a senior editor at *Harper's* magazine in the United States, who created the first flash mob in June 2003 when he convinced hundreds of New Yorkers to turn up at Macy's department store and tell the sales executives in the ninth floor rug section that they had come to purchase a "love rug" for their commune in Williamsburg. But the "who" can also be a group of can-do, multitasking teens and early twenty-somethings who have been dubbed the "Slash Slash" generation because they describe themselves as DJs/producers/fashion designers/club promoters. These are multitaskers with twenty-first-century style who use the Internet and collaborative possibilities of social networking sites, such as Facebook, MySpace, and Bebo, to allow them to develop and extend their Slash Slash abilities.[4]

__THE WHAT: THE TREND OR INNOVATION AFTER IT IS NAMED

Identifying the "who" inevitably leads us to the "what" – as in the nature of the "stuff," trend, innovation, or cultural shift being identified. In 1994, writer Mark Simpson, in his *Independent* newspaper column, commented on a new type of man about London, the city where he lived. He described him as an urbane male who had a "high disposable income, living, or working in the city (because that's where all the best shops are)" and that he was "perhaps the most promising consumer market of the decade. In the Eighties he was only to be found inside fashion magazines such as *GQ*, in television advertisements for Levis jeans or in gay bars. In the Nineties, he's everywhere and he's going shopping."[5]

Simpson dubbed this protean male the "Metrosexual," a coupling of "metro" used to describe the city and all things associated with it, and the back end of the noun "heterosexual" to flag up the fact that for this man there was a direct link between his sexuality, his shopping habits, and how he groomed and dressed himself.

Simpson, the "who" in this case, recognized the innovation or change – the "what" – and through his column broadcast it to Early Adopters like American writer and forecaster Marian Salzman. She in turn, with a bigger media base and voice, popularized the term and introduced it to advertising, marketing, and media agencies who then used it to target men with everything from make-up and moisturizers to so-called manzilians (a variation on the Brazilian, a pubic waxing treatment that became popular with women in the mid to late 1990s).

Once you know the "who," and can identify the "what," you can then answer the "where." As Gladwell points out, good coolhunters go where the "what" can be found, and where things are found, as we shall see, is invariably on the outer edges of the culture – on that part of the Diffusion of Innovation curve where the Innovators or Early Adopters live.

__THE WHERE: THE PLACE WHERE THE TREND BEGINS
The "where" can be a real, notional, or psychological place where Innovators gather, and new ideas, attitudes, and outlooks ferment and "bubble up." In their book, *The Deviant's Advantage,* Ryan Mathews and Watts Wacker tell us that this happens on the fringe of society or culture. It is here they say that innovation – or "deviancy" (their term for "stuff") – is born. "The Edge is where the innovation builds its first audience."[6]

To ensure you are always in touch with the "where," it is vitally important to cultivate a network of people who can help you maintain this knowledge. We look at networks in more depth in Chapter 4, but, for the moment, imagine your network is a collection of people you are in touch with via Facebook, MySpace, YouTube, etc., who keep you plugged into what is happening in the places where they live. Working online, however, is only part of the picture; many forecasters prefer to operate in the "field" (a term used to describe an area, city, or neighborhood they choose to investigate or live in when shadowing Innovators or identifying or mapping trends among Early Adopters) where they can witness a trend emerging in the "flesh." Every city and every neighborhood has a place within it where new trends and ideas bubble up, and for most forecasters it is important to maintain a presence there, or to visit them on a regular basis and to note and observe these changes.

__THE WHY: THE "DRIVERS" TO CONSIDER
Once you have identified the "who," "what," and "where," it is also important to determine the "why" – as in why a trend chooses to emerge where and when it does. The "why" is one of the most complex questions to answer. Invariably it involves looking at the trend as it manifests itself in the greater culture – the drive to be more austere and careful with money, the move toward buying organic food, the increasing emphasis on the experiential, the need to create products that are more tactile, engaging, and less masculine in finish – and then working back from the trend itself to the underlying "drivers" (or changes) within society itself that may have pushed us along this path or way of thinking.

These drivers are the result of an ongoing and sometimes fragmentary debate within society about issues that inform us psychologically, ethically, environmentally, financially, and socially. These issues can seem marginal at first (debates about the environment, about organic food, about sustainability, about world poverty, or even about objects needing to look less utilitarian and "masculine") but over a period of time, and through exposure in the media and among Innovators and Early Adopters, become issues that concern more and more people.

High-tongued sneakers, ultra-skinny jeans, tight T-shirts, dyed hair, sharp-color silhouettes are all key to the Slash Slash generation look. But this isn't just about fashion, it is about entrepreneurship, as Paul Griffiths, shown here, indicates. Slash Slash, he says, refers to the fact that he is a T-shirt designer/ comic strip creator/ brand creator/party promoter/photographic studio manager. The photograph was taken by Giles Price, who also photographed the contents of Paul's shoulder bag on page 141.

From top: the "Touch Wood" bench by Minale-Maeda for Droog and Front's "Softwood" bench, which were the starting point for a trend in design that used digital printing techniques and faux-wood finishes and graphics to create the illusion of materials that are made from wood, or look hard to the touch, when they were in fact soft and spongy.

Eventually these issues exchange their marginal status for one that is more powerful and profound in terms of how they affect the way we think, behave, and engage with the world around us. Thus they "drive" our thoughts and channel them along a particular route, causing us to think more about the environment, or organic foodstuffs, or even a style of clothing, music, or architecture and, as a consequence, to buy into a trend (if we are part of the Early Majority) or to create a trend (if we are Innovators).

To accurately and effectively map the "why" (and we will explore this in greater depth in Chapter 6) you will need to look at all cultural, economic, civic, political, environmental, and ethical issues that relate to the trend you are investigating. You will need to use these issues, and the many clues they flag up, to define more articulately the overarching drivers causing the trend to bubble up at this particular moment in time.

__THE WHEN: THE RIGHT TIME TO LOOK FOR A TREND
"When" we look for trends is very much tied up with "why" we look for them. In many ways each is interdependent on the other. Trends emerge because innovators are constantly at work stimulating our senses and confounding our expectations. While innovation is continuous and ongoing, however, there are points in time, and in the history of the world, which have been more innovative than others. Consider the Renaissance in the fourteenth to seventeenth centuries, the Age of Enlightenment in the eighteenth century, the Al-Nahda or Islamic Renaissance in the nineteenth century, or the birth of Modernism in early twentieth-century Europe. All were the result of strategic and serendipitous encounters of men and women (Innovators and Early Adopters) who shared ideas through cultural and scientific societies, books, letters, and academic papers in such a way to allow each to develop an idea, while causing others to set out on more profound and unique paths of research.

While these periods within the history of the world seem random, we now know that bursts of creativity or innovation can be tracked back to moments within a society or a culture when Innovators and Early Adopters were more connected and able to communicate with each other than at previous points in history. Creativity and innovation also occurred when there were higher levels of heterophily within cities, clubs, sectors, or social, scientific, and artistic communities.

Richard Florida, Professor of Business and Creativity at the Rotman School of Management, University of Toronto, suggests as much in his book, *The Rise of the Creative Class.* Cities, he believes, with their higher levels of creativity and innovation, also contain more ethnically diverse groups of people, greater numbers of artists, scientists, technologists, sexual minorities, and, importantly, more places and neighborhoods, universities, and institutions (official or otherwise), where all of the above can meet, intermingle, and exchange ideas. This can happen because a city's laws make it easier for same-sex couples to live together, or because city ordinances make it more cost effective for small businesses, new families, ethnic and culturally diverse groups to live in a once expensive area. But it can also happen because high rents drive creative businesses to once forgotten areas where they find themselves collaborating with new people in ways they hitherto never imagined. In moments of upheaval, in a recession, at times of great technological, social, or cultural change, chance encounters are more likely to happen and accidental or serendipitous discoveries to occur. It is at moments like this, and in places where there are high levels of social connectivity, says Florida, that ideas or indeed trends happen.

It is these moments that forecasters are looking for – when a city, community, neighborhood, institution, or university becomes heterophilous and thus more socially, psychologically, or technologically advanced and networked than it has been in previous years. When this happens – when these moments of interconnectivity and cross-fertilization of ideas and attitudes take place – the moment is right for a trend to occur.

By asking the above questions – "who," "what," "where," "why," and "when" – and by doing so in the context of cultural brailling, we are at last beginning to interrogate the world in a way that is useful and strategic from the trend forecaster's point of view. But this process needs to be done across key industries and social and cultural divides, as much as it should be done within a single industry or area of specific concern.

> CROSS-CULTURAL ANALYSIS

"Cross-cultural analysis" is the term used by forecasters to describe how they "graze" across cultures and different industry sectors to determine if a trend spotted in one industry is beginning to emerge in another. If it is, they know they are looking at a trend that is set to become long-term and highly influential. The Hella Jongerius lamp, Land Rover's LRX car, and the Miguel Ángel Llácer salon in Valencia were brought together using this process. In themselves these were random pieces of "stuff," but once identified and assembled by forecasters studying seemingly diverse industries, they collectively took on a new set of values and references.

To identify these products and their significance in the first place, a forecaster has to go through books, newspapers, periodicals, magazines, websites, television programs, and radio shows on a daily basis. He or she will also have to visit exhibitions and specialist trade fairs that preview everything from fashion, furniture, technology, and cars, to military hardware and medical equipment. These exhibitions and trade fairs show products to industry professionals six to twelve months (sometimes two years) before ordinary consumers see them.

A good forecaster will also subscribe to a dizzying array of blogs, cell phone text alerts, online news aggregators (web-based applications that allow you to create your own news alerts) and person-specific Twitter updates (a social network messaging system that allows you to follow, in real time, the activities of a particular person or Innovator). When establishing a "feed" (link) to any or all of the above, the rule is simple: the more random and widespread you make your links, the better it will be in terms of the quality and caliber of the "stuff" you manage to net in your initial search.

These "feeds" or "touch points" you have with the world around you should include a range of sites, magazines, newspapers, journals, books, and reference

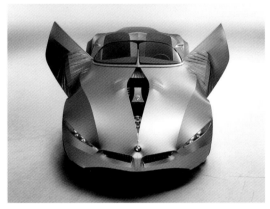

In this version of
"Eve-olution," objects
used on page 35 are
further complemented
by retail interiors,
an experimental car
from BMW, and a multi-
functional technology
pack from Bug Labs to
remind potential
clients that this is
more than an aesthetic
shift – it is one with
a much bigger social
and cultural impact
for design industries
as a whole: (top row,
from left) Beauty
salon by Miguel Ángel
Llácer, detail of Land
Rover interior, paint
cans by Angela Wijaya;
(second row, from
left) salon interior
by Miguel Ángel
Llácer, modular
gadgets by Bug Labs,
"Winds" hairdryer by
deepdesign; (third
row, from left) BMW's
GINA model car
concept, "Two-Timer"
clock by Sam Hecht and
Industrial Facility;
(bottom row, from
left) Yauatcha
packaging by
MadeThought and the
Givenchy Store, Paris,
by Riccardo Tisci and
Jamie Fobert.

Techniques: Global trend forecasting sites

There are over 2,000 trend forecasting and related sites online. All are relevant and all should be bookmarked as a matter of priority. The ones listed below are designed to offer you a cross-sectional overview, and should not be seen as definitive. They are, however, among the most widely used, and are credited by fellow forecasters and bloggers for their ability to collate, interpret, and log trends.

01: Trendbüro (trendbuero.de) is a Germany-based lifestyle and consumer forecasting site with a solid corporate bias.

02: Japan Consuming (japanconsuming.com) is a favorite for trend forecasters keen on emerging trends in key Japanese cities.

03: Cool Hunting (coolhunting.com) is one of the best for aggregating and interpreting "stuff" from around the globe.

04: Iconoculture (iconoculture.com) is one of the better US consumer forecasting agencies.

05: Faith Popcorn's BrainReserve (faithpopcorn.com) is good for "nibble" sized updates on the latest macro trends set to impact on consumer thinking and buying patterns.

06: PSFK (psfk.com) is an online news, insight, and trend consultancy favored by technology and lifestyle brands.

07: Trendwatching (trendwatching.com) is a Netherlands-based forecasting agency which offers free trend updates to subscribers on a monthly basis.

08: Worth Global Style Network (wgsn.com) is one of the best and most comprehensive subscriber-only fashion trend websites online.

09: LifeStyle News Global (Lsnglobal.com) is a members-only consumer-insight, trends, and brand strategy network for the lifestyle industries.

10: The Dieline (thedieline.com) is a must for trend forecasters identifying what's new and next in the world of design, packaging, and promotional graphics.

11: The Cool Hunter (thecoolhunter.co.uk) does as it claims, and helps you source some of the best and coolest trends globally.

12: The Next Big Thing (next-big-thing.net) targets brands and global corporations with advice on how to improve their business edge.

13: Josh Spear's website (joshspear.com) is a rambling blog of "stuff" that matters and inspires.

14: The Trend Hunter (trendhunter.com) is a global resource for the more bizarre and outré trends.

15: Notcot (notcot.org) is dedicated to ideas, aesthetics, and visual amusements.

16: Dezeen (dezeen.com) is one of the most followed blogazines among trend forecasters keen to know more about new and emerging trends and styles in the design and interiors market.

17: Treehugger (treehugger.com) is a fantastic sustainability website which has developed a cult following among forecasters with a specific interest in eco-related trends and themes.

18: Engadget (engadget.com) is the site most used by trend forecasters working in the technology, online, and DIY electronics sector.

19: Gizmodo (gizmodo.com) updates you with the latest technology releases set to create tomorrow's trends.

20: David Report (davidreport.com) is one of the best and most comprehensive trend forecasting sites with a design bias.

Trends can be instigated by technological changes. The way computer screens register colors, pixelate objects, or fragment shapes when a digital signal is blocked have all influenced the work of Cristian Zuzunaga (top), Mike and Maaike (middle), and Studio Makkink & Bey (bottom). This trend has been called "Pixel Nation."

materials that cover different industries and activities. Pressdisplay.com, for example, is a global newspaper portal that offers you access to 700 newspapers worldwide, with search engine facilities and personal page selection tools that allow you to search for new and emerging trends as they hit the lifestyle sections and fashion and business pages of our major newspapers. Trendwatching.com, a forecasting agency based in Amsterdam, likewise produces an online newsletter at springwise.com that does all of the above for its readers on a weekly basis. As Liesbeth den Toom, its editor, puts it: "It is important that you read everything. And that you build up a back catalogue in your head of things happening in as many parts of the world as you can."[7]

You are doing this for a number of reasons:

__to build up a visual and textural library that tells you where the culture is at and where it is going
__to understand and recognize new "stuff" when, where, and how it comes about
__to allow you to place this new "stuff" in a context that makes it more than the sum of its parts
__to begin to detect patterns and shifts that suggest a bigger change or movement is on the cards

__IDEAS DENS AND EVIDENCE WALLS

Much of the research you do at this stage can be done on your PC, laptop, and in your college library. But it is also important to establish a "den" or area in your house, room, lecture hall, or college research lab, where you can paste, post, and capture all this "stuff" in a visual way. Some organizations refer to these rooms or areas as "immersion rooms" (where you literally immerse yourself in the "stuff," ideas, and concepts you are capturing on a daily basis), while others call them "ideas dens." In all cases they are places dedicated to recording, analyzing, and assessing the wider implications of the "stuff" you have captured.

These areas contain books, magazines, Internet access, fabrics, materials samples, concept products, brands, and "objects" collected on the forecaster's travels. All of these are designed to stimulate ideas and allow a forecaster to consider all that "stuff" he or she has collected or encountered against a broader social, cultural, and lifestyle-related context. These rooms should also contain an "evidence wall" – a blackboard, whiteboard, writable Perspex board or any surface on which you can scribble ideas, map thoughts, or stick up or project pictures (see pages 48–49). In its early stages, an evidence wall (or "mapping wall" as it is also known) can look like a fantastic pinboard – rich, highly visual, and over-embellished with magazine clippings, postcards, newspaper headlines, fabric swatches, web-page printouts, Post-it notes, sketches, digital printouts, posters, and color swatches.

As work progresses, these become very ordered, methodical, and specific in the messages they contain. Each of the forecasters interviewed in this book approach their evidence wall differently (some are more visual than others), but the method used for carrying out their cross-cultural analysis hardly varies. To capture the best methods from each, an imaginary trend forecaster called

Evidence wall
Making sense of "stuff"

An we discussed on page 47, an "evidence wall" (or "mapping wall" as they are also called) is anything that allows you to scribble and map ideas, thoughts, and images on to an area that can be constantly replenished and rearranged. Early on this conglomeration of material should be an overstocked, fantastic collage of everything that might possibly have anything to do with the project: from images, clippings, or printouts from the different information media to fabric and color swatches. But as work progresses, they should become less cluttered and more methodical in their arrangement, focusing on specific concepts and messages. Everyone goes through the creating and refining of the evidence wall in their own way, but the process of cross-cultural analysis that lies behind it in fact varies very little. In the instance illustrated above, we are looking at the beginning of a trend that suggests sobriety, austerity, and a new mood of seriousness among consumers.

As the forecaster encounters more and more "stuff," he or she begins to strip

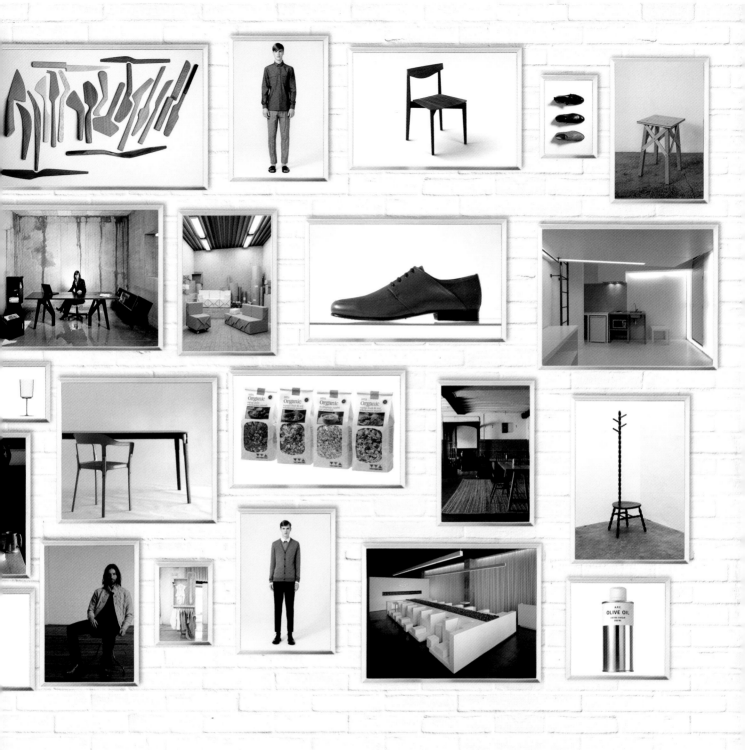

away the less relevant images until they are left with a wall that contains a more coherent collage of "stuff." At this point, the trend begins to take shape. The forecaster will note for instance that the design silhouette looks similar (minimal, pared down, functional, linear), while the look and feel of the objects on the board are austere, serious, and very much in keeping with a mood perhaps he or she is sensing among consumers themselves: the desire to buy brands, products, or furniture that have a sense of purpose and sustainability about them. At this stage, these ideas may be hunches, thoughts, or emotions suggested by the remaining images. Working with his or her expert panel, the forecaster will then test their initial findings via more desk research and then with a panel of experts until they have determined the validity of the trend and its projected impact on the greater culture. At this point, they will also ask themselves if this is an aesthetic trend, one with a clear message, or whether it is anticipating a particular mood or mindset? Either way, the "evidence wall," with its random selection of "stuff," is how this investigation begins.

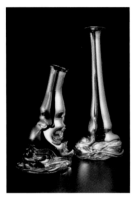

Trends can be counter-responses to previous ones. Here a group of designers challenge a desire among consumers to buy objects that are functional, practical, and "useful." Shown here (from top) "Exhausted Cutlery" by Kathryn Hinton and "Still Life Meltdown" vases by Marie Retpen.

Cassie has been created to take you through a step-by-step method that should become your default for carrying out cross-cultural analysis, if not also the majority of your trend forecasting work from now on.

Imagine Cassie for the moment in her ideas den, a corner of her bedroom that has been commandeered as an area where she can think and be creative. She has a laptop and is surrounded by books, journals, newspapers, reports, magazine and newspaper clippings, and boxes of "stuff" that she has assembled from her library, newsstands, book stores, and from printouts she has selected and downloaded from the Internet. She is here because, like most forecasters, she has a "hunch" that something new and different is in the air – people, she thinks, are becoming less extravagant, less interested in excess, and more interested in and concerned about being less wasteful.

As with many of her forecasts, Cassie doesn't quite know what that "something" is. From her study of "stuff" she knows that there is a change in how people are behaving at the fringes of society and she wants to know what this change is. Working on her laptop, and pinning as many ideas – snippets of text, clipped images, torn magazine pages – as she can on her evidence wall, Cassie catalogs in a free-forming way all the "stuff" she encounters. She is searching for "stuff" that might have something in common, or "stuff" that touches a chord in a particular way. She might see a picture of an organic supermarket in the Netherlands that excites her interest, or recycled packaging she found in a small clothing boutique in the United States that grabs her attention.

__THE FORECASTER'S NOSE

Cassie uses her "forecaster's nose" to search for a pattern, to sense that something new is in the air. On recent trips to Los Angeles, London, Buenos Aires, and Madrid she noticed a growing number of wholefood and organic food outlets in parts of these cities where she wouldn't normally expect to find them. They were also selling seasonal and locally produced products, with pictures of the people who grew them stamped on the packaging itself. Meanwhile in Frankfurt she traveled in a taxi that ran on hybrid fuel, and while in Tokyo visited a store that looked like it had been made from recycled pieces of wood. In Paris, Cassie found a store interior by Riccardo Tisci and Jamie Fobert that was "austere" and "pared back" in a way she wasn't expecting – the store had been created for Givenchy, a luxury fashion brand. Similarly on publishers' book lists and forthcoming catalogs she noticed titles about "cooking from scratch."

All these things are fragments, rarified bits of "stuff" drifting about in the ether and in Cassie's unconscious. She senses a pattern here, anomalous shifts that tell her something is afoot. But what? Something about low-key living perhaps? About being more organic? Living within one's means? About becoming disenchanted with bling, being more determined to live less ostentatiously, even becoming more carbon aware? More clippings go up on her wall and, looking at what she sees, Cassie knows now that the trend somehow relates to the idea that certain consumers are becoming more concerned about what they are buying not only in terms of how it looks and feels, but also why they buy it, and what this means in terms of how they live.

Cassie works on. She sees a clipping from *Corriere della Sera*, the Italian daily newspaper, about the Slow Food movement in Italy; a report from The Future

(text continues on page 55)

Case Study:
Ilse Crawford

FOR ILSE CRAWFORD, principal of Studioilse (studioilse.com), form always follows emotion. As she explains: "It [form] should be about things that make us feel human, and reflect the emotional qualities of what it is like to be human." Based in the UK, her interiors, like the furniture she designs, are emotionally rich offerings that plug into the senses by using materials, finishes, and visual references that remind us of the past.

"You only notice the familiar and the comfortable," she says, "when it is placed next to the new and unusual." Such juxtapositions lie at the heart of Crawford's work, and have allowed her to kick-start bar, club, and hotel interior trends that have since become known as "Heritage Modern," "Rough Luxe," and "Revived Grandeur." For Crawford, all inspiration begins with the space she has been tasked to transform: "To capture the now and the next, it is important to delve back to the roots, to define the soul of the building or space you are transforming."

Once Crawford has researched the physical history of the space, and delved into the many emotional and physical layers it contains, she creates a series of mood boards that set the frame for the project. She does this by combining inspirational images that capture the emotions, fantasy, texture, light, and characters that will bring it to life and create a 360 degreee total experience.

Crawford's studio wall contains a series of inspirational images that allows her to more fully articulate the mood of a place, product, or new hotel development she may be working on. Behind her are initial ideas and visual inspirations for the Villa Budapest - a collaboration with Tadao Ando, including the venue's dining room and one of its public salons.

Villa Budapest, is one of a number of brands that have been created or reinvented by Crawford and her team. Always keen to work with designers that have a love of tactility, textiles, and shapes that are human and familiar, Crawford orchestrates all those references captured on her image wall in a way that creates a harmonious sense of place and purpose for the buildings she works on.

When the concept has been reviewed, Crawford's team will then create models that will further articulate the scale and sense of place she is trying to capture — "it is important to make sure that your initial idea can be realized in three dimensions." The models are crucial tools in winning the trust and confidence of the client.

On Crawford's desk is her iconic Wästberg w084t lamp that she describes as "a sturdy, unpretentious friend, and always there for us." But it is also a product very much associated with her design ethos: the idea that "form follows emotion" which has encouraged a trend for office and household objects that are more inclusive, poetic, and functional. For Crawford, materials are everything, and with her lamp she uses them to tell a particular story. Iron is used for its "feelings of stability, reliability, and trust; wood for its warmth and life; and a glass, chalk, and plastic blend for its intimate glow and tactility."

It is Crawford's attention to detail, mixed with her highly eclectic, but finely attuned, sense of what is new and next versus what is old and worthy that has made her the trend forecaster's forecaster. She attempts to identify and articulate the zeitgeist of the moment, and she also acts as a window through which other forecasters glimpse the future.

Fascinated by what drives us, brings us together and makes us feel alive, in 2000 Crawford started a design department in Holland to bring left- and right-brain values together in design. Shown here (from the top) are the games room at the Kranzbach well-being hotel and spa in the Bavarian Alps, the Matbaren (fast-food bar) at the Grand Hotel Stockholm, for Mathias Dahlgren, and an interior from The Olde Bell Inn, Hurley, England. All of these have influenced a global trend for hotels and public spaces that feel human and welcoming.

There is another component, however, to this kind of approach. While never consciously considering trends, she is, "forever analyzing and absorbing cultural indicators. This happens because I travel a lot, attending trade fairs, but it is also because the Internet has made us more aware of each other, of what we are thinking, feeling, and you absorb and meditate on this." Such meditations have led to to signature brands such as New York's Soho House, the Grand Hotel Stockholm's Matbaren and Matsalen restaurants, the Kranzbach Hotel in the Bavarian Alps, store interiors for Australian beauty brand Aesop, and the design and brand development of The Olde Bell Inn in Hurley, England.

Before her current work as designer and creative director, Crawford built her career on being able to divine what is new and next in her previous roles as founding editor of *Elle Decoration* UK and of *Bare* magazine, one of the first lifestyle and wellness publications. She was also Vice President of Donna Karan Home and DKNY before setting up her own studio, and becoming the founding head of the department of Man and Well-Being at the Design Academy in Eindhoven, Netherlands that has long championed cultural mapping and observational and social research.

Her work, she says, is not about trend forecasting , but a rigorous design process that puts the human being at its center. It is a deliberate and strategic approach: one in which she sets out to create identity and roots, to satisfy an identified need, and then to apply this to create and develop a sustainable idea or business.

Foundation, a British think tank, about people falling out of love with celebrity and seeking people and experiences that are more meaningful; a piece on coolhunting.com about a designer called Giulio Lacchetti, who has produced a range of aesthetically simple knives made from sustainable wood sources; and an article in Australian *Vogue Living* about a new country inn in Britain, designed by Ilse Crawford, that looks contemporary but austere and low key.

By now Cassie (and hopefully you as a reader) can see that there is a pattern forming: yes people are still talking about celebrities and high octane glamour, but in the "edge" news feeds and Twitters, and in the clippings from niche magazines Cassie is looking at, there is a change taking place. Something about people needing less things to live on and be happy with…The suggestion that they are keen on more "authentic" and "real" experiences…That people want clothing, furniture, interiors, and packaging that is less about being flashy and excessive and more about being austere. To determine if this is the case, Cassie now applies a "rule of thumb" used by many forecasters – the so-called "three-times rule."

A growing focus on the home, tactility, and cocooning have all contributed to a trend among product designers for working with materials, textures, and finishes that look homely, while the furniture itself appears lived-in though abnormal and overstuffed. Featured here are the "Memory Chair" by Ole Jensen and Normann Copenhagen, and the "Lazy Bastard" chair by Bertjan Pot for Montis.

__THE THREE-TIMES RULE

The "three-times rule" is used to test the validity of an idea or a trend across a number of industries or cultural disciplines. It is called the three-times rule because it involves identifying three examples of a product (or piece of "stuff") which contain noticeable characteristics in common, within the same industry or sector. You then have to find three different products that share similar aesthetic, social, or intellectual reference points in three other non-related specialisms, such as design, retail, technology, and so on. This is not a "quantitative" process, as in a process that uses statistics or numerically-based "proofs" to justify its relevance, but rather one that offers you a "qualitative" or more subjective and personal way to determine if a trend has "legs" and if you can validate your hunch about a particular trend across a number of separate areas.

Cassie does this. Are there three clear pieces of evidence to support the thesis forming in her mind? Yes. And if there are, does this evidence run counter to the general pattern she would expect to find? It does. But can she find similar clear counter-patterns in other industries which indicate that they too are experiencing similar changes: in design, in architecture, or in fashion retail? She does. A more pared-down aesthetic, a greater concern for sustainability, a more measured approach to fashion in terms of retail and interiors. Excellent. At this point then, Cassie begins to add more and more examples to her evidence wall and sets about assembling a list of experts she can call on to validate her initial hunches and subsequent findings.

__THE EXPERT PANEL

An "expert panel" is a panel, or a loose but selective group, of knowledgeable people or specialist professionals selected to offer you a more coherent and insightful look at the hunches you may be considering, or the trends that you believe are materializing as a result of these hunches. Panel names are usually assembled from the names that sometimes occur again and again when you find yourself delving down into an area of interest: for example, a journalist who has written extensively about a particular topic, a designer perhaps, an economist, a psychologist who has been quoted on a regular basis about recycled products. Some experts will be directly related to the area under review. For instance, if this is a trend about society becoming concerned with living less wastefully and becoming more environmentally aware, experts might include a retailer using recycled materials to create a more authentic look or feel, even the features editor of a magazine writing about the virtues of buying only essentials and brands that are designed to last because of their artisanship and finish.

But your expert panel should also include people who are one step removed from the day-to-day workings of the trend: a philosopher discussing the need for people to have a more ethical understanding of consumption, an economist establishing why people need to have a more measured approach to spending, an artist on why less really is more, an academic or psychologist, like Oliver James, concerned with the origins of terms such as "affluenza."

By the time her list of panelists has been assembled, Cassie will also have a clearer sense about "what" the trend is and some ideas about "who" the key Innovators are in kick-starting it – designers perhaps, a new group of consumers, the author of an influential book. She might even have some vague

Techniques: Selecting your expert panel

The accuracy of your forecast will often depend on the knowledge and variety of the experts in your contact book and on your database. Experts add color, depth, resonance, and new layers of understanding, insight, and credibility to your forecasts and research. Because of this, it is important to choose them wisely.

01: Draw up an initial shortlist of names from the people you encounter as you carry out your cultural brailling and your cross-cultural analysis. Experts can mean those with official titles but make sure you also include ordinary people – those who have an extraordinary knowledge of a particular subject matter or who exemplify a particular trend.

02: Note down the names, job titles, areas of specialism, and attributed works for all your potential experts.

03: Appraise your initial list against the bigger picture of the data assembled on your evidence wall and the questions you believe need to be answered about the trend you are validating.

04: If there are gaps in your list of experts then research additional names. As a general rule, your list should draw from different disciplines and sectors and include experts or analysts who can offer the following: a political overview, social, cultural, creative, and lifestyle perspectives, an economic opinion, and even a philosophical take on the trend you are investigating.

05: Research your shortlist of experts online and make a final decision as to their appropriateness for the work under investigation. Identify addresses, contact numbers, e-mail details, information about their publishers, or the academic or corporate institutions they work for.

06: Before contacting your experts, fully acquaint yourself with their professional biographies and their specialism (as they relate to the areas you are interested in speaking to them about) and draw up your list of questions.

07: Once prepared, e-mail or write to your experts first so that they can assess their usefulness, or not, to your project. Phone after a few days, mentioning your e-mail or letter, and clearly outline the reasons you need to speak to them.

An emerging trend for using natural and organic materials is counterpointed here by a trend embracing the use of industrially polished metals and precisely turned and finished shapes. As forecasters soon discover, every trend generates its polar opposite. Featured are Sebastian Brajkovic's "Lathe" table for Carpenters (top), Richard Hutten's "Cloud Chair" for Ormond Editions (middle), and Ron Arad's "Bodyguard" (bottom).

idea of "where" the trend is coming from – cities like London, New York, Paris, and Tokyo – and the "when." Again, she may have traced this back to a decline in the financial markets or to a more subtle shift taking place among Generation Xers (a demographic now in their mid to late thirties who are becoming increasingly concerned about "quality of life" issues).

___THE TREND THESIS

Cassie uses these notes, comments, and quotes from her evidence wall to formulate a thesis (short outline) of her trend. A trend thesis is a two-page document that roughly sets out the trend as the forecaster initially sees it, perhaps even breaking it into sections roughly marked out under the headings of "who," "what," "where," "why," and "when." A thesis is usually written up as a short concise memo (no more than 500 words) which allows the forecaster, and the people he or she may be interviewing, to articulate more fully and clearly the points the forecaster has captured so far. In itself the thesis is not proof that the trend exists, merely the skeleton of a trend that needs to be further validated or refuted. This is where the panel of experts comes in. Using the thesis (and her assembled evidence wall) Cassie now probes them more strategically about the "who" (the trend innovators), the "what" (its name), the "why" (the factors that have contributed to its emergence), the "where" (its origins), and the "when" (the time when the trend began).

___DEEP DIVING

"Deep diving" is a term used to describe the process by which a forecaster works with a panel of experts to explore further and flesh out his or her hunches about a particular change in the market. It is called deep diving because you are literally diving deep down into areas of concern you wish to know more about. When you interview an expert about their specialist field it is also known as a "depth interview" or a "dive." Depth interviewing is about using a set of strategic but open-ended questions (see box, page 59) to add credence to the thesis you are working on by gleaning third party quotes, facts, statistics, and insights which will help to justify your hunch and clarify your thought processes. Most importantly, it provides you with a richer understanding of the trend you are trying to identify by immersing yourself in the world of these experts and seeing the changes taking place by brailling the trend through their eyes.

With deep diving, however, it is important to seek out evidence from a range of people from across different sectors and from all points along the Diffusion of Innovation curve. Expert interviewees should include:

___Innovators (those who are instigating the change)
___Trendsetters (those Early Adopters who are making these part of their lives – in different industries, if this is the case)
___Trend spotters (other futurists, edge observers, and cross-cultural analysts who are marking these changes at their nascent stages)
___Trend analysts (sociologists, ethnographers, psychologists, etc., who clearly articulate the "why" of a trend)
___Early Majority, Late Majority, and Laggards (to test how far the trend has penetrated to mainstream thinking, and within which areas or social income brackets)

Working across sectors and along all points of the Diffusion of Innovation curve, says trend forecaster Sean Pillot de Chenecey, also allows you to capture a comprehensive and insightful understanding of what the trend is, where it is likely to shift to, and why and how this will impact on consumers tomorrow. But you also need to do this with the experts you are interviewing. In research on energy drinks for GlaxoSmithKline, Pillot de Chenecey found himself interviewing everyone from clubbers, to physical trainers, to Tokyo office workers, to night-shift workers, and members of the military.

When all expert interviews are complete, it is important to add all of the panelists' key comments to your evidence wall. Cassie does this. By now her evidence wall is covered in rich and varied data. This cluster of imagery and reference material is sometimes known as an "information cascade." If you examine it closely you will notice that a number of visual and textural patterns are already beginning to emerge. Certain themes jump out, key patterns, a sense that there is a bigger drama or idea at play. This is your intuition at work and a process called "thin slicing," which Gladwell refers to in his book *Blink: The Power of Thinking Without Thinking*.[8]

"After Hours" is a pair of rotational-molded shoes by artist/designer Marloes ten Bhömer whose shoes are not just sold as footwear, but also as artifacts that frequently appear in museums and touring exhibitions. Fashion as design/art is a trend noted by forecasters that has been developing over the past decade.

__THIN SLICING

"Thin slicing" isn't anything mystical. It is merely an ability our brain possesses to cut through large swathes of data in a way that helps us evaluate all this information more effectively and strategically. As Gladwell proves in his book, too much data or information can become a bad thing if left unedited. This is why a forecaster tends to use thin slicing at this point in the process as a way to swiftly assess all information (visual and textural) displayed on his or her evidence wall and to retain only that which his or her intuition and intellect "suggests" is necessary.

We will look at how this works in more depth in the section on strategic intuition in Chapter 3, but, for the moment, it is enough to understand that thin slicing happens because you have been processing this data subconsciously all the time you have been collecting it and assembling it on your evidence wall.

Cassie will then work from left to right across her wall, removing anything that does not initially fit into the trend as she is "sensing" it. This first edit of the evidence leaves her with a less cluttered wall, but a wall still muddled and unfocused. To make it more rational and strategically useful, she now needs to reconfigure everything it contains in a more meaningful and logical way. This is done by creating a "trend cartogram."

__TREND CARTOGRAMS

A cartogram is a diagrammatic technique used by a cartographer or map maker to capture complex geographic data in a simplified, illustrative but strategically revealing way. A trend cartogram is a more abstract, less formal, or prescribed version of the geographer's cartogram and it calls on a trend forecaster to create a map that visually and texturally represents the trend in a way that:

__identifies the Innovators of the trend (the "who")
__names the trend (the "what")
__assesses the current impact of the trend within society (the "where")

Techniques:
Depth interviewing

The ability to listen and to empathize are the bookends between which all good interviews are placed. Both are skills that you must cultivate from the outset. Below are some useful tips to help with your depth interviewing:

01: Do your homework on the experts you are interviewing. Before contacting them you should know who they are, what they do, and why their specialist area of concern is of use to you in terms of framing your thesis. Be familiar with their most recent publications and areas of study and research.

02: Create a list of short, to-the-point questions (twenty-five to thirty words should suffice). Write these in a way that allows one question to build on, or add to, the insights or opinions extracted from your expert interviewee in response to the previous question.

03: Provide all experts with your questions in advance, together with a succinct paragraph that outlines the thesis you want to discuss with them.

04: Avoid questions that are complex, ambivalent, or "closed" in the way that you pose them. A closed question is one that is asked or written in such a way that it elicits a singular, negative, or abrupt response. Example: "Do you believe that consumers are becoming more responsible in their consumption habits?" Response: "Yes"/"No."

05: Make your questions as conversational and "open-ended" as possible. Example: "Perhaps you can tell me more about the idea that consumers are becoming more responsible, etc..." Interviewees feel less nervous and self-conscious if they can start a sentence that allows them to be expansive rather than reductive in their response.

06: Ask an expert to "comment on" a statement you wish to test or validate. Again this demands a more complex and richer response. Example: "According to a food retailer I interviewed, consumers are increasingly buying food that has a low carbon footprint. Can you tell me why this is the case?"

07: Use "mirroring" – nodding with interviewees when they nod, agreeing with them when they finish a statement, building on the same statement in a positive or affirmative way when they are finished. This helps to put interviewees at their ease and to encourage them to talk more about a subject.

08: Whether you want people to respond to you via e-mail, or to talk on the phone, it is important to limit the number of questions you ask. For instance, five questions will require about twenty-five to thirty minutes of response time from an expert (which is a lot if you are not paying them) so limit the number of questions you ask and be aware of the time while you are asking them. If an interviewee agrees to speak to you for fifteen minutes, be sure that the questions you have set can be answered within this time frame.

09: Listen carefully to your expert's responses and be flexible enough to ask a question that is not on your list if this seems appropriate, or if his or her reply suggests a new vein of thought that is worth pursuing.

10: Take careful notes (even if you record your interview) while your expert is speaking and underline any points or phrases that seem especially significant or revealing.

11: Mark the date, time, and interviewee's name at the top right-hand side of your page, and along the left margin mark Q1 (as in question one), Q2, and Q3, etc., when you ask each new question. This way, when you return to the words you have written down later, you will know which question they relate to.

12: Type up your notes and transcribe your tapes (if you have videoed or recorded the interview) as soon as possible after the interview. Go through all of the notes and highlight paragraphs, statements, facts, statistics, and other qualitative or quantitative insights that relate directly back to your thesis. When doing this, you should look for the following:
– points which further validate your trend and flesh it out
– points that suggest new veins of research you need to follow
– statements that challenge or cast a new light on how you are defining the trend. These can be specifically allocated to the sectional headings you have created on your evidence wall or cartogram.

__reveals the drivers or influences underpinning it (the "why")
__examines the consequences of this impact in the short- and long-
term based on the experts' comments and findings (the "when")
__identifies and articulates what these changes will mean to the society and
culture we live in over the long-term

You can simplify these headings into five titles to place along your evidence wall
from left to right so that they read as follows:

__trend innovators
__trend drivers
__trend impact
__trend consequences
__trend futures

Cassie, because she has repeated this process many times, has already written
them across the top of her evidence wall. Once these headings are in place,
you will need to rearrange all the evidence on your wall to sit beneath them as
comprehensively as you can. Make sure too, as you work across the board from
left to right, that you form these clusters (if they exist) under all the categories,
and ensure you distinguish clusters beneath each heading in such a way that
allows any onlooker to see that a visual cluster which is present under "trend
drivers," for example, has a matching or lookalike cluster under another heading.
   To further validate your trend, and to improve its overall visual and textural
luster, as Cassie does (see box opposite), you should break each heading up into
three or more sectors (fashion, furniture, retail interiors, materials, and finishes,
for example) to show that this is a trend that can be found in more than
one industry.

__TREND FRAMING
This editing, selection, and categorization process is also referred to as "trend
framing." Framing a trend is about imposing a more logical, visual, and
texturally coherent framework around all the data you have collected so far.
At this point, you should be able to define the key characteristics of the trend –
it's about "austerity," a "new sense of sobriety," of "demanding less but better
products," etc. – and to give it a name (the "New Sobriety," or the "New
Seriousness," or the "New Austerity").

__TREND INNOVATORS
If you are assembling material under the section marked "Innovators" and
notice that some of your Innovators look alike in terms of how they dress, or
the technology they carry about with them, then cluster these together.
However, because Innovators tend to be original in their thinking and outlook,
they may in fact share few visual or aesthetic characteristics in common, so do
not be deterred by this. It is important to capture a sense of the idea or the
innovation they are instigating (on Post-it notes, from notebook pages, relevant
images, etc.) and that you include a brief synopsis of what the trend is in terms
of its essential characteristics: for example, it is a trend about a new sense of

New Austerity / No Frills   Affluence

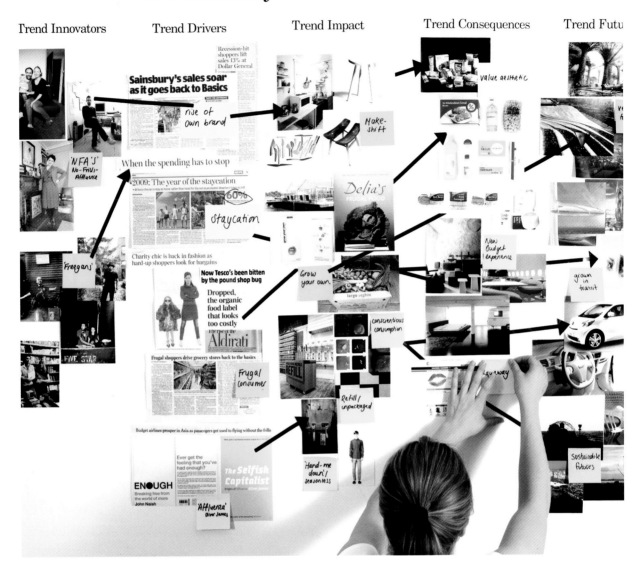

Trend Innovators   Trend Drivers   Trend Impact   Trend Consequences   Trend Futu

The anatomy of a trend cartogram

The trend cartogram above can be seen as a more refined and in-depth version of the "evidence wall" on pages 48–49. There, the forecaster assembled an aesthetic trend that could be categorized as "New Sobriety," while here, after further research, that aesthetic trend becomes an indicator of a shift toward people seeking out products that are sustainable, simple, and austere.

In this instance, a group of Innovators has been identified as "No Frills Affluence": consumers in their mid thirties with high incomes, but increasingly worried about how their spending may impact on the world around them. Our forecaster discovered they were influenced by a desire to be frugal and a growing awareness of sustainability and a mood among the less affluent that people with money should be more considerate about how they spend it (see Trend Drivers, page 63).

When the No Frills were interviewed, they were revealed to be increasingly growing their own food (Trend Impact), recycling, installing solar panels, cooking at home (as opposed to eating out), buying second-hand furniture, and being more ethical about their food choices. Ultimately, the forecaster could identify the brands, products, and services that these consumers (and those who will later imitate them) were likely to buy into as their habits become more focused.

Fragment

Universe

Wonder at the vivid mosaic of the heavens and the great cycles that represent a continuity of genesis. Visions of dynamic waves and veils of saturated, layered colours are studded with starry accents, all set against the beauty of black. This is a versatile and unusually rich palette that delivers real design gymnastics. Use it boldly to inspire multi-colour effects in products that have a light at their source, either through technical innovation or as combinations of rich tonalities. Design something new!

4 : Authenticity

Crafted, heritage, considered, earthed, honest, values

Featured opposite,
from top, Andrea
Dall'Olio's beauty
concept book; *Textile
View*'s autumn/winter
2009/10 fabric
directions for
womenswear; the
*Pantone View Color
Planner*, color palette
for winter 2010/11;
the Chiron textile
inspiration book;
issue 24 of *Viewpoint*
magazine that looks at
upcoming "discreet
destinations"; and a
style board for
Australian denim label
Just Jeans, to be used
as a trend guide for a
new store concept
being developed for
the brand by The
Future Laboratory.
These are all examples
of how different
forecasters explain
trends. Some do it via
a series of books that
contain inspirational
images, fabric
swatches, and
materials that can
be touched to fully
understand the
textures (and the
smells) being
identified, while
others like *Textile
View* magazine, the
*Pantone View Color
Planner*, and *Viewpoint*
magazine take a more
intellectual approach
to the forecasting
process by working
with experts selected
from the world of
color, design,
interiors, and
academia to more fully
interpret the trends
being visualized.

sobriety, of consumers becoming more considered and measured in their purchasing habits, and so on.

__TREND DRIVERS

By examining all the material posted under the heading marked "trend drivers" you should be able to choose at least five key points which, in your opinion, or in the opinion of your experts, best articulate the external sociological forces that have led to its creation (a recession, a growing need to re-evaluate our sense of community, the decline of bling, the rise of a values-driven attitude and outlook, etc.).

These can be bullet pointed and, wherever possible, supported by facts, statistics, and quotes from your experts which underpin the validity of these drivers.

__TREND IMPACT

Under the section marked "trend impact" you are trying to do two things: to find more pertinent examples of how the trend is already manifesting itself, and to do so across as many sectors or industries as you can. Again, this is about using cultural brailling and cross-cultural analysis to root out as many "proofs" as you can that this is a trend with stature and impact. Proofs can include book covers, newspaper headlines, examples of packaging, expert quotes, and relevant product, interior, and retail examples.

__TREND CONSEQUENCES

Under the "trend consequences" heading you need to consider how this trend, especially at its nascent stages, is impacting on the Late Majority, if indeed it has begun to do so. Is it, for instance, affecting how they shop, the kinds of houses they are choosing to live in, the brands they favor, the way they view celebrities, or the packaging they now prefer to buy their food in? You should try to include as many visual and factual examples as you can under this heading to illustrate the point you are trying to make.

__TREND FUTURES

When you are considering the future implications of a trend on a society, a group, or industry sector, it is always important to refer back to the comments and insights gleaned from your expert interviews. Try to distill their comments into five or six key insights into how they collectively see this trend impacting on society as a whole, and then on groups like the Early Majority, Late Majority, and Laggards in particular.

Cassie, as a professional forecaster, will have done all of the above instinctively, rapidly, and logically. She will have created visual and textural clusters under, and across, each heading as well as creating bands of clusters that have key characteristics in common. Her wall will now offer her core and clear insights into how the "austerity" trend she has identified looks visually, and will also provide her with some "buzzwords" (from her expert comments, newspaper headlines, etc.) that she can use to clarify the trend in a more focused and articulate way – words like "austerity," "sobriety," "authenticity," "local," "seasonal," "pared," and so on.

The authentic bicycle

Being cool, authentic, bespoke, sustainable, and bike-friendly has become something of a mania with the inhabitants of cities such as London, Paris, New York, Amsterdam, and Stockholm. The trouble is, few bikes visually demonstrate these credentials in a credible and enduring way. Aware of this, designer Reinier Korstanje decided to create his "OKES" bike that was perfectly "on trend" in that it had an authetic feel to it (the bike's frame is made from high quality French oak), a bespoke finish (the frame is CNC-cut in a Belgian factory renowned for making high-spec, oak interior products), and a name that had a certain hidden allure – OKES derives itself from a Capetown slang word used by teenagers to describe a particular kind of older cyclist, as in "those oakes ride fantastic bikes."

Now much imitated, Korstanje's bike is still regarded as an "innovator" in its class because of its sandblasted frame and matt oil finish that speaks of an attention to detail few bicycle makers can match. Even the frame is made from four oak parts carefully glued together. All of this makes it a bike which Innovators are likely to buy.

At this point, like most trend forecasters, Cassie will work through each section again, adding, subtracting, reassessing, and rearranging any or all aspects of the wall which she feels can be clustered more succinctly, or arranged in a more focused and strategic way. This done, she will now bullet point her findings at the bottom of each vertical column until she reaches the final column of text and visuals that has grown under the heading "trend futures." Before she fills this in, she will check along all of her bottom columns once more, assimilate all of the key points, and use these to clearly and concisely inform and illuminate her final pronouncements. At this point her cartogram is complete, and the trend she originally had a hunch about is now visualized and tabulated in a way that makes it transparent to people who are less adept at identifying and defining trends as they roll out and along the Diffusion of Innovation curve.

> SUMMARY

A trend forecaster's job begins with the identification of "stuff" – the stuff that surrounds us and offers glimpses of a much bigger pattern at work in society. Being able to identify stuff isn't the end of the process, however, as it is also important to judge the caliber of all this stuff and to "braille the culture" to determine if it is the stuff of trends or merely the detritus that constitutes much of the everyday world most of us live in.

By brailling, you are digging and asking some fundamental questions – "who," "what," "where," "why," and "when" – about the stuff you are investigating or the trend you may be sensing. Brailling has to be done across cultures and in a way that is analytical and measured. A panel of experts can be used to question or "deep dive" about your initial findings and a cartogram allows you to visually and texturally map the trend along a trajectory not dissimilar to the Diffusion of Innovation curve discussed in the previous chapter. This cartogram enables you to define the trend's most essential characteristics, determine those factors that are driving it, and, more importantly, to assess its short, medium, and long-term impacts on groups like the Early Majority, Late Majority, and Laggards.

Finally, but more usefully, a cartogram encourages you to exercise parts of your brain that often remain dormant because we have learned to distrust our instincts and to elevate the powers of logic and rational thinking to a position that is higher than, rather than equal to, those parts of our mind that require us to be intuitive and emotional. But, as we shall see in the following chapter, intuition is a tool that can be honed and sharpened to provide us with insights and strategic forecasts every bit as accurate as their more rational and logical counterparts.

Chapter Three
Intuitive Forecasting

IN BRITTANY BELL'S
"Seed Archive," the
planet's supply of
seeds are stored and
cataloged in case of
future ecological
disasters. Although
the archive is still
a concept, forecasters
can nonetheless use
work like this to act
as a prompt or an
indicator for issues
they should be
thinking about in
the near future.

"The only real valuable thing is intuition."

Albert Einstein, nuclear physicist and Nobel prize-winner[1]

FOR ONE GROUP OF FORECASTERS, the ability to detect "stuff" and to braille it across different parts of the social, cultural, and lifestyle spectrum comes effortlessly. They are "naturals" in the same way that exceptional sportspeople, scientists, orators, artists, and performers are, who deploy their physical, intellectual, and emotional skills in a seemingly effortless way and reveal their ability to make the right decision, and to be in the right place at the right time, without using any demonstrable "rational" process. Intuitive forecasters possess similar abilities in that they seem to have an unwavering talent to predict what is new and next without following any of the processes unpacked in the previous chapter. For many organizations and companies, however, this is not acceptable – to arrive at a solution, they believe, requires a trend forecaster to demonstrate rationally and realistically how this solution came about.

Like the star-turn footballer or the genius scientist, an intuitive forecaster has problems breaking down what he or she "feels" and "sees" in a way that is explicable and tangible. For the footballer and the scientist this may be fine: their efforts are self-evident when they happen. But for the forecaster – who may, for example, be predicting that consumers will increase their purchase of GM food over the next two years – more than a hunch is required. Organizations and companies may invest (for that read "risk") millions on the pronouncement of a forecaster, so these intuitive hunches must be underpinned more robustly. For most intuitive forecasters this is difficult as they do not know how they arrived at their conclusion. This is one of the key reasons why, outside of the creative industries, intuitive forecasting of the kind we are looking at in this chapter, is regarded with high levels of suspicion.

Recent developments in the world of cognitive science and in functional magnetic resonance imaging (FMRI) – a technology which allows us to visualize the neurological impact of thought processes within the brain – are, however, changing this point of view. We now know how intuition works and, more importantly, have been able to unpack and better understand the processes the brain goes through in order to reach the solutions it does. These processes, as you will see, are not as illogical, irrational, or lacking in proof as you might initially suspect. Knowing and understanding such processes will help you grasp more clearly what intuition is, how it works, and how you can hone your own intuitive skills more effectively.

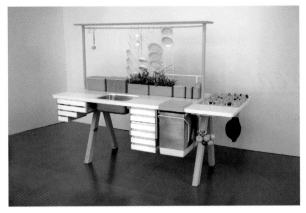

As people spend less money on going out, we are witnessing the rise of a trend that has been dubbed "Homedulgence," as exemplified by the products illustrated on this page. "Homedulgence" is a love of brands, products, and services that turn the home into an active, design-aware hub that feels and looks like a hotel or "third space" that can double as a place to work or hang out in with friends and colleagues.

Promostyl is a Paris-based consumer insight consultancy, with a transglobal reach. Seasonally, teams of designers, visualizers, and trend forecasters produce a range of mens, womens, and lifestyle publications that are designed to inform and inspire clients rather than encourage them to copy or reproduce diluted versions of an original product.

> LEFT- AND RIGHT-BRAIN THINKING

Until recently, many people believed that the left- and right-hand side of the brain utilized different skill sets. The left side, for instance, was associated with rational, logical, and linear activities, while the right side was associated with skills linked to tasks and processes that defined us as creative, imaginative, lateral-thinking, and intuitive in our approach to tackling things. Rational and logical people were thus deemed to be "left brained" in how they worked (and were favored by traditional businesses) and those in the creative professions "right brained." These left- and right-brain distinctions were based on the pioneering work of Roger Sperry[2] and his research into the two-sided brain in the 1980s.

Although brilliant, Sperry's work in many ways forced us to decide if we were left- or right-brained in how we worked; even if instinctively we felt that some parts of our thought processes were rational and measurable, while other outputs were creative, imaginative, and intuitive. Not surprisingly, this feeling proved to be right, as the neuroscientist Eric Kandel[3] discovered when he used axial tomography (CAT scans) and FMRI to show that when the brain is engaged in rational or highly creative tasks, both halves are at work and both are speaking to each other, and to other parts of their hemispheres, in a collaborative and interconnected manner.

> WHOLE-BRAIN THINKING

The intuitive forecaster is tapping into the same reservoir of knowledge as the scientist, although both are outputting it differently: the scientist in a way that requires more facts to underpin it (which makes it appear more rational), the intuitive forecaster in a way that utilizes more adjectives and descriptive processes (which makes it appear softer and vaguer). In essence, however, they are speaking the same language, albeit with a different accent.

Rather than talking about "left- and right-brain thinking," where intuitive forecasting is now concerned, we talk of "whole-brain thinking." This is a process that requires you to "deep dive" into all aspects of the brain to reach your conclusions – brailling the ideas within your conscious and subconscious in much the same way you learned to braille your cultural and social surroundings in the previous chapter. When you are doing this, your thoughts are no longer linear or rational, nor are they lateral or creative, but rather they are mixing and merging and doing so across the many different regions of the brain in a way that is not dissimilar to how we carry out cross-cultural analysis.

In whole-brain thinking our thoughts, if we could photograph them, would look like a rich, shimmering rush of color; each bit of color representing a fragment of an idea, or a part of a solution, that is seeking out other bits it can sit beside in order to form a bigger picture. This interlocking pattern of brain activity, which Kandel noticed, is often called "mosaic memory" because of the patchwork of cross-brain activities that go to make it up. A fellow neuroscientist, Barry Gordon, explains this more clearly in his book *Intelligent Memory: Improve the Memory that Makes You Smarter*: "The dots are pieces or ideas, the lines between them are your connections

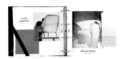

Product, fashion, beauty, textile, and interior trends can come in many forms: as a series of inspirational books with color cards, fabric swatches, and scent strips, or as a more straightforward and pragmatic set of styleboards that leave little to the imagination. Rather than work from one book, clients tend to buy a range of these publications and services to inform their ideas.

or associations. The lines can coalesce into larger fragments and these fragments can merge to form a whole thought. This whole thought may be a visual image, a piece of knowledge, an idea, or even a solution to a problem. Individual pieces, the connections, and the mental processing that orchestrates them generally work together so they appear to be a single cognitive event. That's what happens when ideas or concepts pop into your mind."[4]

Does the above process sound familiar? It should do. Consider the description of how we assembled a trend cartogram in the previous chapter. We began with the "stuff," "dots," or "ideas" that tipped us off to another idea, and then we sought out more examples of these across different sectors and industries. We did this to make "connections" and to create "associations." These in turn pushed us toward larger ideas or "fragments." Using techniques like cross-cultural analysis, deep diving, and thin slicing, we continued to map ideas, and to mix and merge images, until we formed a "whole thought" or to put it in Gordon's words, "a single cognitive event."

In short, the methodology you have learned for producing your trend cartogram is, in reality, an unpacking of how mosaic thinking works at its most fundamental. By practicing this process, and by honing all of the skills used to create your trend cartogram (see pages 58 and 61), you are effectively exercising your "whole" brain in a way that should make you more intuitive and confident in the visual and textural connections you make on a daily basis.

Only once you have practiced this process sufficiently will you be able to do it naturally, invisibly, and seamlessly. Whenever you are undertaking the thought process above, however, you are doing it on a number of different levels, and in all cases using three very distinct types of intuition to arrive at your findings: "gut intuition" (one that is knee-jerk in its reaction), "expert intuition" (one that is more thoughtful and informed), and, most importantly, "strategic intuition" (one that combines both gut and expert intuition in a way that allows you to forward project your ideas and conclusions).

> GUT INTUITION

The first type of intuition – "gut intuition" – can be described as "ordinary," in that it is the one we call on most when meeting new people or when knowing the right "moment" to cross the road. It is also the one you use when identifying "stuff." Sometimes referred to as "gut instinct," it is a feeling that people who work in high-risk professions, such as policing, nursing, the army, and firefighting, learn to work with, trust, and develop on a daily basis.[5] But let us be clear, these people are not jumping to conclusions but are instead, as FMRI scans and cognitive research shows, accessing parts of the brain that contain previous memories and are doing so rapidly and, from their point of view, subconsciously. In this instance, their brain acts as a vast filing system that prompts them when they encounter a situation in the present that may have similar properties to one encountered in the past. They experience a mental "flash" and know the right thing to do.

Conversely, this filing system may prompt these people with an "odd" feeling if they have no reference point for a present situation: in other words, it alerts them to an anomaly, or something that is new, different, and hitherto unknown

The forecaster's notebook can be a simple set of bullet points, or a more visually-inspiring set of images, notes, and explanatory captions that collectively work together to clarify a trend, or to unpack it in a way that makes it usable and intelligible to a particular industry or client base. In this notebook by visual analyst and forecaster Caroline Till, we can see the nascent stages of a trend she has described as "Sin City," because of its dark color scheme, angular shapes, and fairy-tale undertones.

Sin City.

- Designers embrace darker side of imagination
- Fairy tale inspired?
- Black key color for 2010 and beyond - notions of darkness, aspiration ....

Element of surrealism?

Prada Transformer by OMA geometric, harsh structure

Propeller table, Fum 10
- threatening
- masculine

- blue/black the new navy?

Warm, green g... with deepest bla...

holm

| PANTONE® 429 C | PANTONE® 445 C | PANT... Black... |

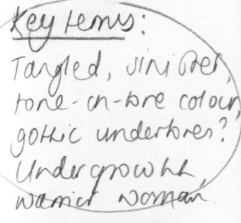

SANDER MULDER

Product & Interior design   T +31 (0)40 - 21 22 900   info@sandermulder.com
Concept development   M +31 (0)6 - 44 76 20 62   www.sandermulder.com

Rubber red,
matt black
surfaces

Key items:
Tangled, sinister,
tone-on-tone colour
gothic undertones?
Undergrowth,
warrior woman

Sander Mulder, Milan 09

Techniques:
Boundary crossing

As a forecaster it is important to cultivate acquaintances and to immerse yourself in places that have no direct relevance to your social life or the way you live. You need to cross boundaries – social, intellectual, physical, emotional, spiritual, sartorial – where and when you can. You can only do this with effort, a strong contact book, and a slightly hard nose. Of all the skills, boundary crossing is the most difficult because it requires you to expose yourself to situations you may have no previous knowledge of, and to be with people you have nothing initially in common with. Without doing these things, however, your work and eye as a forecaster will remain one-dimensional, lacking in analysis, and insular as regards your approach to understanding and embracing the world – the latter being one of the worst characteristics a forecaster can exhibit.

01: Cultivate a contact book or database of heterophilous types – people who are not like you but who are useful to you because they can flood your thought processes with innovative and unusual ideas.

02: Join online and offline groups, networks, threads, and organizations that are affiliated to the areas in which you need to develop a more specialized knowledge.

03: Attend conferences, forums, bars, clubs, or seminars where ideas and viewpoints are being shared and exchanged. When you do this, ensure you have a card or contact details ready.

Always ask for a card or details in return and make sure you contact the person you are keen to develop a relationship with (or add to your network) as soon as possible afterward. Tell the person who you are, what you do, and why you are keen to add them to your database, network, etc. This ensures that people see value in their relationship with you.

04: Create your own social media page (via MySpace, Facebook, LinkedIn, Second Life, etc.) and use it to promote who you are, what you do, and, more importantly, to develop new relationships or contacts with others. To do this, your page (and the people, places, and sites it is linked to) needs to be exciting, useful, and updated regularly.

05: Consider writing and managing your own "blog." Use it to update your contacts on the work you are doing and any upcoming work you are keen to speak to new people about.

06: Keep your blog informative, insightful, and useful to other people who may be keen to know more about you, your thoughts, or the trends you have identified. Do not, however, make it too personal, opinionated, or difficult to read by overburdening it with jargon. If you are using the blog to build contacts and forge alliances, it needs to be as accessible and welcoming as possible.

07: Your blog should also contain links to blogs, sites, or fellow "bloggers" who you respect for their work or the trends they cover. In return ask these bloggers to link their sites to yours – this will increase visitor numbers and potentially add to your overall contact list.

08: Make your blog as visual as you can. Where possible, use an image, sound, podcast, or video clip to replace a word or a descriptive paragraph – when it comes to trends, showing is always better than telling.

09: To maintain relationships and increase your pool of contacts, always communicate with people regularly and thank them when they have been of help. Meet people face-to-face whenever you can.

10: Increasingly, forecasters are keen to assemble ideas in a more formal and tangible way. This can be done via a fanzine, book, or magazine. And it is not costly. Online publishing networks such as blurb.com allow you to create your own magazine or journal online, and have it printed or distributed to any or all members of your network. Disseminating your work like this will also increase your pool of contacts, and place you in touch with a group of people, who, because of their age, design preferences, or need to "touch, feel, and smell" the printed word, may not be familiar with your work or activities, if they exclusively take place online.

11: Finally, the best boundary crossers are people who are out doing and being seen with others – not people who are always online. In the world of forecasting, having a physical presence is more beneficial than having a virtual one, because it invokes and involves all of the senses.

Carlin is a Paris-
based consumer
insight and
forecasting agency
that produces a
range of concept,
innovation, and trend
books for clients in
the fashion, interior,
lingerie, and beauty
industries – the
company prides
itself on marrying
the conceptual with
the practical to
innovative effect.

within their filed range of experiences. An intuitive forecaster, with a vast back catalog of experiences or "stuff," is thus able to use this "alert" mechanism to warn himself or herself that something new and next is in the offing. But his or her instincts can only be as good as the data stored up in his or her brain in the first place. This is why being intuitive is all about being culturally acquisitive and perpetually observant. As an intuitive forecaster you cannot afford to be disinterested or to disengage with the town, city, or country you live in. When you are on the subway, a bus, walking along a street, or in a bar or club, you must observe the three Ls at all times – looking, listening, and learning.

How you do this depends very much on how you like to remember things. It is recommended that the method you use is as multisensorial and as visual as you can make it. You can do it with a camera, an MP3 recorder (for capturing sounds, conversations, new trends in music, etc.), on a pinboard at home, or in the kind of notebooks most forecasters keep – books that contain scribbled notes, Post-its, fabric swatches, fragrance strips, stapled photographs, pasted-in newspaper clippings, even packaging samples still containing fragments of the food that came in them (see pages 72–73). The best kind of notebooks resemble beautiful, in some cases poetic, artifacts but their primary function is to act as a "memory trigger," an elegant but multisensory storage system that helps to capture and catalog the world (or at least those aspects of it that arrest your curiosity) in a way that adds ever more visual, textural, aural, and tactile layers to your catalog of experiences and memories.

The content of these notebooks should also be as random and free-flowing as your encounters in the wider world. The broader and more random your experiences are at this stage, the more wide-ranging your ability will be to trust your instinct across different subject areas and sectors. By being random in the experiences you seek out, you are further reducing the possibility of favoring only those things you like, and conversely opening yourself up to the possibility of the anomalous and the new. As you become more adept at forecasting, and acquire more knowledge of your field or specialism, you will start to draw on a different kind of instinct.

> EXPERT INTUITION

"Expert intuition" is the kind of intuition you develop as a consequence of working in the same field or profession for a protracted period of time. It is an intuition that is informed by gut instinct, but also by the experiences, knowledge, and insights you have gained while studying or working within a particular area.

Expert intuition is an instinct many organizations and companies are happier to trust because they see a discernable value in working with people who have accrued a thorough knowledge of a field or specialism over a period of time. Organizations and companies believe this knowledge can be passed on in the form of actual experiences which are useful (that is instructive or educational) or as "insight" (whereby the experience offers up more profound views on what the knowledge gained can be used for, or can tell us about the world in a more abstract way).

But expert intuition is different from gut intuition because it allows you to develop a very important skill. As an expert you will find yourself speaking to other

Techniques:
Improving empathy

Empathy, a core skill for a forecaster, is the ability to put yourself in another person's position, and to view the world as he or she sees it. Too many businesses are prevented from seeing the changing tastes of their customers, or their potential customers, because of their inability to empathize with them or to see beyond their own prejudices.

Brands like Puma, Adidas, Microsoft, and Nike all work with Innovators or Early Adopters to help them better understand and empathize with current and potential customers. Consumers are happier talking to, and dealing with, people who are like them, which is why good brands and forecasters exhibit highly empathic traits as a matter of good manners and good business practice.

01: Always be an active listener and a sympathetic talker. Never confuse one with the other. Importantly, never talk more than the person you are interviewing! Too many people make this mistake; empathy works when the other person feels you are there to listen, and to learn from what they have to tell you.

02: Try to place yourself in the position of the person you are talking to even if you have little in common with him or her and disagree with his or her lifestyle, beliefs, and opinions.

03: Engage your "presence of mind" and disengage your own views so that you can look, listen, and learn. Your preconceptions of a person, place, or object tend to muddy your view of them, so keeping an open mind isn't just about remaining dispassionate, it is about "breathing in" – taking in details and information without challenge or objection in a way that keeps the flow of information moving and keeps the people passing it on to you "open," communicative, and engaged.

04: Consider your own body language and dress accordingly when working in the field or in areas where it is important you blend in emotionally, intellectually, and physically. People feel more comfortable when you mirror their postures or in some way reflect their dress sense, in addition to adhering to their social codes. As a forecaster, it is always important to blend in. And, as perverse as it seems, forecasters, who spend the majority of their time living with edge groups or in fringe sections of our cities or towns, tend to look quite ordinary and everyday. This is not due to a lack of imagination on their part – it merely reflects a professionalism that requires them to be the least noticeable person in the room or on the street.

05: When a person uses particular words and phrases, repeat these words back to him or her later in your conversation – this subconsciously signals that you have been listening to him or her and, more importantly, that you value his or her ideas enough to remember them. This process, known as "verbal echoing" works because it creates a social bond between you and the person being interviewed or studied; it subconsciously reassures them that you share certain characteristics. In this way, you become part of their homophilous group.

06: If in doubt when speaking to a person and asking him or her to "tell you more about his/her thoughts" or "to explain his/her views in more depth," the trick is to offer the person a non-confrontational way in which to introduce ideas or thoughts that may be different from yours, and to do so in a forum of openness and active encouragement.

07: Finally, you need to accept that people are different and that attempting to change someone, or to harangue him or her over his or her views, isn't the best way to win that person over. However, by introducing words, phrases, and ideas into your conversation that suggest you have been in part won over by him or her, or which indicate that you have been listening in a receptive and fair manner, will inevitably keep that person open to future conversations. By socially camouflaging yourself in this way, you are doing what the best ethnographers do: becoming a silent or invisible observer. In this role, if you remain open and empathic, you will find that more people open up to you, and more clearly explain the drivers that make them behave, dress, or engage with people in a particular way.

Defying conventional tastes, box cars like the Citroën C3 Picasso (top) and the more famous Nissan Cube (bottom) were developed when designers had a strategic "hunch" that a particular type of young urban city dweller would buy a nerdy looking, but iconic, car with a very individual personality despite its squareness.

experts across sectors associated with, or related to, your own. When you do this you "acquire" some of their specialist experiences and knowledge. When this is combined with your own store of personal knowledge and experience, you develop an ability to "infer" something about a part of the culture you may have no actual experience of.

Your brain, in other words, takes what you know and adds it to what you have learned from others to produce an "experienced-based solution" (a solution with higher levels of accuracy because it is based on wider and deeper experiences with higher levels of insights) or an instinctive reaction that is more valued and accurate even though some of the personal experiences used to reach it are not your own.

To develop and hone your expert intuition you need to choose an area that interests you most, and stick with it. You then need to research and fully understand all other subjects that are related to it. If you are interested in becoming an intuitive fashion forecaster, for example, you will need to be aware of the latest innovations and developments in the world of textiles, and to expose your thinking to the most recent shifts in the world of music, art, design, furniture, architecture, and interiors – all of which impact on how we dress.

Your approach also needs to be less random, more focused, and above all open to dialogue, collaborations, and ongoing but strategic conversations about your subject area with other experts and analysts, Innovators, and Early Adopters. This will help you to build up a reservoir of knowledge and experience to draw on, as well as keeping your thought processes and your expert intuition "live" and oxygenated: forecasters who limit their conversations, or who fail to share their ideas with others, tend to produce narrow, rather impoverished forecasts. An expert intuitive forecaster's notebooks, for instance, tend to be more ordered and subject specific and to contain clear-cut case studies and global examples of how other experts have perhaps identified trends or isolated and tracked new and emerging shifts in the culture.

Expert intuition is about making sure that the experiences you have gleaned from others are as rich in detail as you can make them: so detailed, in fact, that they seem real and personal. This is a specific skill which can be developed by using "empathy" where and whenever you can, allowing the thoughts and experiences of the expert to become your own. When we read a book, play an online game, or go to the movies, we do this without thinking: we identify with a character, become immersed in his or her world, sharing, and learning from his or her experiences.

In forecasting, the ability to empathize with others, and to make their thoughts, views, and opinions part of yours, helps you to sharpen and hone your instincts because they allow you to "experience" a vast range of things passed on by others as if they are your own (see box opposite). These skills also help you to boost your imaginative powers and, more importantly, your ability to forward project and to envision what will happen tomorrow. When you do this, you are using your "strategic intuition" at its fullest capacity.

> STRATEGIC INTUITION

As a concept, "strategic intuition" was first identified in 2007 by William Duggan, a professor at the Columbia Business School, after studying key personalities from history who seemed unusually brilliant at developing and executing battle strategies

"Fem-tech" is a term used to describe a range of intelligent, but unusual-looking household products that use slick design cues to show you how the product works rather than telling you. Many of the ideas featured here came out of a flash of inspiration that suggested women had less time than ever to read densely written instruction books on how a gadget should work. Products featured include a dustpan vacuum cleaner by Cha Il-Gu, a folding plug by Min-Kyu Choi, and "Radio Valerie" by Valentin Vodev.

that won them the day on the battlefield.[6] These personalities were unusual and brilliant, because they made split-second decisions of the kind that were imaginative, audacious, and invariably prescient and correct. The men Duggan looked at included Napoleon Bonaparte, the Corsican general and self-proclaimed Emperor of France who dominated much of Europe's politics and history in the first decades of the nineteenth century, and George S. Patton, an American general during World War II (1939–45). Both men were renowned for their ability to anticipate the actions of their opponents and were able to read situations on the battlefield as they emerged "at a glance." "At a glance" is the English phrase for the French *coup d'œil* which, says Duggan, was used to describe Napoleon Bonaparte's almost preternatural ability to predict his opponents' actions and to place his troops in the best and most advantageous position.[7] It is also a phrase used to describe intuitive forecasters who are exceptionally good at their job – you will see it linked to forecasters such as Faith Popcorn (see pages 36 and 46) and Li Edelkoort (see pages 79–82). These forecasters all possess an unerring *coup d'œil* and experience what Duggan refers to as "flashes of insight" – the kind of insight we are used to having "in the shower, or when driving, where a clear thought comes to you when your mind is relaxed."[8]

It is precisely because this insight comes to you in the shower, on a walk, or while driving, that people question its validity. Again, this happens because an outsider cannot see how you tangibly arrived at this solution. As Duggan's studies of the process indicate, however, it is a method that draws heavily on the previous types of intuition mentioned, but with one important difference: if done correctly it allows you to envision answers or to draw results about situations or events of which you may have no previous experience. More to the point, you may never have spoken to an expert with these experiences either. But how can this be? To begin with you are exercising your intuitive processes in a more honed and focused way. As Duggan puts it in his book *Napoleon's Glance: The Secret of Strategy*: "Strategic intuition is the selective projection of past events into a new combination as a course of action that might or might not fit your previous goals."[9]

In other words, you are using what you know from past experiences, combined with what you have learned from the present, to create or envision a future that is likely, if not probable, based on flashes of insight you have when these two are combined. To do this, it is important to understand the three key elements you need to take on board before these flashes of insight occur in the first place. These activities include developing, honing, and listening to your sense of "historic awareness," your "presence of mind," the ability to "suspend logic," and the resolve to follow through on any decision you have taken once all information has been assimilated and insights learned.

__HISTORIC AWARENESS

"Historic awareness" is a term used by Duggan to describe a process we better understand as the ongoing need to embrace, understand, and codify in your head, ideas den, laptop, or trend notebooks, all past examples of "stuff" you believe will have relevance to how you braille and identify trends in the future. As previously stated, this requires you to read widely and deeply and to do so across all sectors that touch on the one you are investigating. Many intuitive forecasters will, at this point, supplement what they know and what they have learned by working with a panel of experts, Innovators, or Early Adopters, whom they will use to further enhance

(text continues on page 83)

Case Study: Li Edelkoort

LI EDELKOORT (edelkoort.com), recently retired chairwoman of the Design Academy in Eindhoven, the Netherlands, refers to trend forecasting as the "archaeology of the future...Found fragments located in discussions, a video, a word, an old lady glimpsed one day on the street, that compels you to think about something bigger, something more profound and insightful." Edelkoort encounters these fragments on a daily basis as she switches from being editor of *Bloom*, a biannual publication that uses horticulture as a metaphor for trends in color, texture, and interiors, to her ongoing role as curator of exhibitions that have ranged from "Armor: the Fortification of Man" to "North meets South," an analysis of the links between Scandinavian design and African craft.

Born in 1950, Edelkoort studied fashion and design at the School of Fine Arts in Arnhem, Netherlands, before working as a forecaster at leading Dutch department store De Bijenkorf. In 1975, she moved to Paris to work alongside names such as Meimë Ardolin, Dominique Peclers, and Nelly Rodi, all renowned forecasters in the world of fashion and lifestyle who helped French and international retailers determine the trends consumers would follow over the coming years.

Edelkoort believes a good forecaster should provide brands with a clear vision and with insights that guide and inspire them. But he or she should also provide them with tangible and emotionally compelling solutions. Products – or ideas, in other words – that appeal to the customer not only because they are on trend, but also because they speak bigger truths about the world in which we live.

The Laurier restaurant and boutique by Edelkoort and Andreas Mavrommatis, at Galeries Lafayette in Paris, carefully reflects an emerging trend for creating environments that are human, tactile, and emotional in how they visually address us.

A trend needs to be interpreted using all five of the senses, says Edelkoort. Considering the smell, taste, touch, sound, and the visual impact of a piece of fabric on the eye is a more meaningful and relevant way to capture the essence of a trend because it relates back to the very things that probably stimulated its birth in the first place.

Magazines like *Bloom* and *View on Color* are seminal reading for any client keen to decode the cultural cues needed to ensure that a new piece of clothing, furniture, or household product hits all the right notes when appealing to a consumer. The trick, Edelkoort says, is to be twenty minutes ahead of the consumer, rather than twenty years – that way the product feels new and fresh, not alien and unfamiliar.

During the 1980s, when fashion designers such as Donna Karan, Ralph Lauren, Giorgio Armani, and Calvin Klein began to create lifestyle brands – selling everything from homewares to furniture and interiors – Edelkoort, sensing the zeitgeist, set up Trend Union, a multidisciplinary studio-cum-forecasting facility, whose aim was to help a range of clients to understand more proactively the key colors, moods, shapes, silhouettes, and materials that would become popular with consumers over the coming year to two years. Unlike most forecasters who concentrated on one sector or specialism, Edelkoort – always aware of how changes in one area impact on another – looked in her predictions at everything from fashion and furniture, to beauty, packaging, materials, and the automotive sector.

A cultural magpie, Edelkoort can be found seeking inspiration, or presenting the fruits of her findings, to audiences as far afield as London, Paris, Stockholm, Amsterdam, Tokyo, and Seoul. Indeed, it is this ability to move between cultures and to sift through the fragments that she finds there which refines and makes fresh her skills as a forecaster. As she explains: "Consciously and unconsciously, you are collecting things, banking them. Then, as enough of these fragments take root, patterns begin to form – signals are sent to the brain that alert you to other ideas and words that seem to push you towards a bigger picture – then there is a flash, and you can see what the new trend is."

If all this sounds slightly mystical, Edelkoort is unapologetic. Science, politics, ethics, the environment, and the mood of the consumer all have their place in mapping a trend, she says, but what matters ultimately is the accrued knowledge and experience of the forecaster, merged with his or her ability to observe, to contextualize and never to be nostalgic. As she outlines: "This is not about your taste, or your ideas, it is about sensing change, and assessing it, regardless of whether it contradicts your sense of the past or not." But experience does matter, she believes, as do training and honing your instincts across a range of disciplines.

It is Edelkoort's ability to assemble myriad fragments that has led her into the world of curating, about which she says: "In some ways this is like 3D forecasting. Things cannot just be objectified, they need to be placed in context. Like trends, the objects we see about us are part of a bigger sentence, or a paragraph that is part of a bigger essay." This, she believes, is what good forecasting is about – exploring contexts, defining relationships, juxtaposing fragments in a way that helps create a better understanding of what the future will hold.

their historic perspective and awareness of the situation they are investigating. So, for example, if a forecaster is asked by a client to look at how people's attitude to non-ethically produced fashion is set to change in the future as consumers become more ethically, socially, and environmentally aware, they will identify fashion brands that have been damaged in the past because of their poor ethical record.

The forecaster will case study these examples and interview a panel of experts (consumers, analysts, etc.) who will be able to place what happened previously in a wider cultural context. The forecaster will also identify companies who overcame these problems and consider how they did this: What were the techniques the company employed? How did they respond to the criticisms leveled at them in a way that made people see them in a more favorable light? At each stage of the research, the forecaster is therefore attempting to build up as full, clear, and comprehensive a picture of what has gone before as possible, with a view to capturing any insights (his or her own or those belonging to other people) that may offer glimpses both into how the current market may change and ways he or she can build this into the forecast.

At this point, the intuitive forecaster is trying to capture the "texture" of what happened as well as the reality. He or she is thus building up a strong visual, emotional, textural, and factual picture of what has gone before, from his or her own perspective, and from other peoples. He or she is trying to see their world through a multiple of views and perspectives. The ability to empathize is essential here, as is your ability to free-associate ideas, or to rapidly assemble a back catalog of ideas, images, and "stuff" that allow you to develop a more complete and coherent historic picture of all essential things which have gone before and which are likely to help you better assess the issue currently under review. This rapid assembly of seemingly disconnected ideas is referred to by forecasters as a "symphonic rush," and the process of rapidly assembling and merging these thoughts into a more coherent picture as "symphony."

Once a sense of historic awareness has been developed – or a context within which the trend you are investigating can be placed – it is then important to develop something forecasters refer to as "presence of mind."

___PRESENCE OF MIND
"Presence of mind" is an ancient concept, and one originally developed by the followers of Buddha to help them suspend belief and remove any sense of prejudice from their mind when encountering a situation that was new or different. Duggan notes this trait in military leaders like Bonaparte and Patton. It is an ability also found in intuitive forecasters – the ability to place what they have learned from previous experiences (their sense of historic awareness) to one side, and to focus on present events without preconception and without prejudicing what they are seeing or thinking with views they might already hold to be true or correct.

If this seems contradictory to what has just been recommended, it isn't. At this point an intuitive forecaster is not ignoring his or her sense of historic awareness, but merely placing it in neutral by refusing to allow it to interfere with his or her present thought (or with the situation they are encountering) in case what is being experienced in the present contains new information which might be rejected on first viewing because it does not sit readily with the historic case studies already accrued.

Techniques:
Using observation

Observation is a vital tool in the intuitive forecaster's toolkit as it enables the accurate mapping of people, places, and things. The vast majority of trends have a social, cultural, or lifestyle aspect to them that can be seen more effectively than be described or explained. It is important, therefore, to mentally, visually, and texturally note the world around you on a constant basis.

Most forecasters now capture trends via their cell phones, or with digital cameras, etc., but it is good to develop a range of methods for noting trends down in a way that can be used to visualize them later. A growing number of bars, clubs, and restaurants, for example, now forbid photography or the use of cell phone cameras, so you may have to resort to using a notebook and a pen or pencil.

But don't despair, for most forecasters, despite the proliferation of technology that allows them to capture trends digitally, the notebook is still the preferred choice in recording their opinions, insights, and observations.

The tips below should be read in assocation with those outlined in Chapter 5 for Cultural Triangulation (see page 137).

01: Use a notebook, camera, camera phone, or sketchbook to record your observations. Unless you have a photographic memory, never rely on memory alone. Trends tend to be identified by, or associated with, very particular details and the forecaster's job is to note these accurately. To improve your ability to do this, always note your surroundings: do this randomly at first – enter a room and make a mental list of the objects it contains, walk into a bar and remember where tables are placed, or what drinks can be found behind the bar. On a street memorize the sequence and dress of the people that pass. Write these up in your notebook, and for each try to recall one single anomaly that sticks out in the room you entered or the people that passed you on the street.

....

02: Record observations as a brief, tight, adjective-friendly list. For example: "a lacquer-finish chair" rather than "a chair"; "a store with a burnished copper ceiling" rather than one with "a metal-like ceiling." Words and phrases that will help you and others "visualize" the object you are describing. It will not only help you more readily understand a trend, but it can also trigger subconscious insights and associations that allow you to see the trend in other contexts.

....

03: Be as specific as you can, layering the descriptive adjectives and nouns you use in the order that best helps you remember what it is you are describing. For example, "a soft russet Harris tweed jacket with brushed gold lining, hand-stitched armholes, and wallet pocket to the left" better captures the jacket you are looking at than "a tweedy brown jacket." The latter gives no sense of the jacket's style or fit – the details in the first description fill out its character.

....

04: When noting what a person is wearing you should always describe him or her from the head down, and from the inner layers of clothing to the outer ones. Remember to note down any jewelry he or she is wearing, all body adornments (tattooing, body piercing, etc.) and accessories being held or worn.

....

05: Some forecasters formalize this process by placing people inside an imaginary "description wheel" or Vitruvian Man style circle which allows them to more accurately pinpoint or record key items of interest along a north, south, east, west axis. But if you can sketch them, do; if you can photograph them, do. Any talent or technology that helps you to get a fix on their image can and should be used.

....

06: Descriptions of a room or retail interior can be recalled in a similar manner. By casting an imaginary grid across the space, a forecaster can assemble a "word picture" of a room, bar, club, or retail interior. By working in a clockwise manner from top to bottom and from left to right of this fictional grid, you can draw an imaginary circle or wheel in the air with your eyes as they pass over all objects in the room. Once mastered, a description wheel allows you to sequentially record, map, or recall any room, etc., in a way that is accurate, logical, and easy to recreate.

....

07: Finally, don't confuse observation, with understanding what is being observed. Observation is only one part of the forecasting process. It is also important to ask questions about what you are observing and noting so that the bigger context of a set of actions or dress codes can be more fully understood. Elsewhere in this book we look at a three-pronged process called Cultural Triangulation, which places observation alongside intuition and interrogation as the three vital points that define and enclose all key activities a forecaster needs to engage in if their forecasts are to be accurate.

....

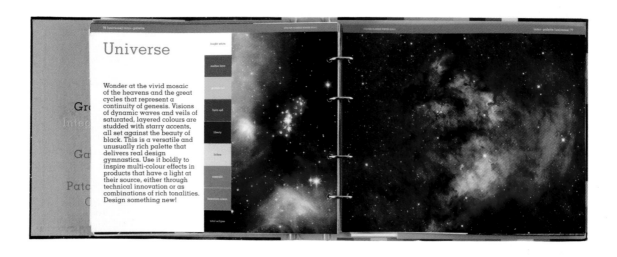

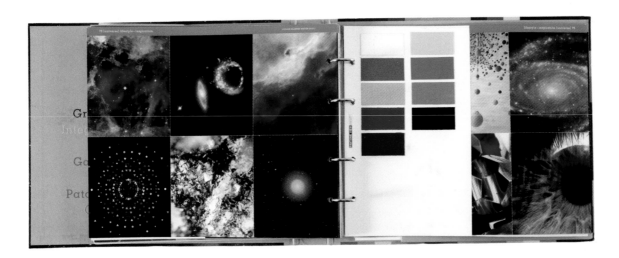

The Pantone View Color Planner

The *Pantone View Color Planner* is one of those rare color, inspiration, and forecasting books that offers designers clear, but directional, insights into what is new and next in the world of fashion, design, interiors, textiles, and automotives. Accompanying color chips, swatches, and tiles then match the colors shown against a particular Pantone number so that each color can be replicated without fault. According to the planner's publisher, David Shah, "Even a color that is fractionally out because of poor printing or bad reproduction can ruin a whole collection because the blue used in the shoot is not the same as the one being viewed by the client on the page. The Pantone system prevents this from happening. But it also means that a client in China can speak to a client in London, Paris, or Frankfurt and know that they are all talking about the same shade of blue or green." As frivolous as this seems to outsiders, the correct shade or luster of a color can make or break a fashion or furniture collection. Forecasters not familar with the requirements of the design, interiors, and fashion sectors can sometimes forget this, only to find out later that their advice to make a product blue did not take into account the subtleties of the particular blue chosen. Simply put, when it comes to making decisions about the shape, color, or texture of a product, nothing can be left to chance.

This tends to happen quite a lot. By nature most of us are Late Majority types and need to see and experience ideas learned through others before we buy into them ourselves. As an intuitive forecaster, you don't have this luxury: you need to know here and now if this is an idea that will become big tomorrow. This is why you should collect and catalog experiences (so that you don't limit your ability to "read" a new idea correctly) and why you should also learn to place these experiences temporarily into neutral in case they, in turn, prevent you from seeing a way forward.

This is why developing your observation skills is also so important (see box, page 84). The ability to see, to take in what is happening around you, and to do so rapidly, accurately, and without pre-judgement, is an essential tool for strategic forecasters to possess and hone. Just as historic awareness can sometimes prevent you from "feeling" what is right, it can also prevent you from "seeing" what is right, especially if the evidence your eyes have seen challenges any fixed ideas you may already have about a situation. Presence of mind demands that you keep your thoughts open, but also your eyes.

This is a vital point to note, believes Carsten Beck of the Copenhagen Institute of Future Studies, one of Europe's foremost forecasting agencies. "Organizations, particularly those governed by willful or strong-minded CEOs, can find themselves in trouble when a CEO or key managers allow their own preconceptions to strangle or prejudice their long-term vision or ability to look beyond tomorrow."[10] When cultivated properly, presence of mind helps to keep your mind clear, your eyes alert, your sense of historic awareness in neutral, and, above all else, helps to avoid being ensnared by other people's preconceptions about the trend under review.

This process doesn't come easily, as our natural reaction is to favor one thing and to dismiss another. But if you are to acquire a presence of mind that is useful in the way a forecaster requires it to be useful, then as a matter of routine it is important to examine, debate, and embrace new (and perhaps "unthinkable") ideas on a daily basis, together with challenging the ones you have previously accepted without question.

If you use historic awareness and presence of mind properly you will create the kind of "fermentation vat" within which flashes of insight have a better chance of happening. Your vat should contain the following: relevant case studies, statistics, data, conversations, and interviews with Innovators and Early Adopters, experiences captured from experts, insights from your notebooks, authored papers, and memories enhanced, jogged, or enriched by either video footage, "stuff," or other trends deemed relevant by your background researches. Once you have assembled these components, it is time to ferment and distill them.

__SUSPENSION OF LOGIC

Logic tells you that fermenting and distilling the components of your vat needs to be done rationally; that it is now time to sit down and appraise your findings in a coherent manner. But if you are to become a good intuitive forecaster, this is actually the last thing you should do. As Duggan suggests, you should now take a walk, have a swim, listen to music, take a shower. If this seems counter-intuitive after all the groundwork you have done, consider for a moment where you have your best ideas. Is it at a brainstorming session where you are forced to come up with a new or original idea within a set time and predetermined framework? Or is it when you are daydreaming and have put the problem under review to one side? Without a doubt, most of us have our "eureka" moment in the bath, or in places where we are mentally

Forecasters can learn the art of suspending logic from designers, who have to do this all the time, especially when asked to envision a futuristic project as here. The work shown includes a 3D printer, an isolation pod, food that is grown while it is in transit, and even a vending machine for luxury products.

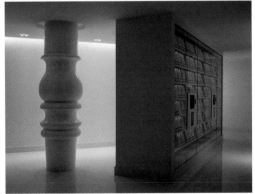

Designers like
Nacho Carbonell are
watched by forecasters
because of their
ability to "think the
unthinkable" when it
comes to reinventing
something as simple
and everyday as a
table and chair. Here
a thin membrane of
elastic is used to
create a desk which
can be stretched to
store things in the
same manner as a
kangaroo's pouch.

relaxed, distracted, or disengaged from the task under review. As recent research indicates, however, far from being disengaged, your brain is actually firing on quite a few cylinders at this point, taking all that historic awareness you have collected and blending it with all that "stuff" you have assembled (using presence of mind of course to rule out nothing), to trigger what is more familiarly called "a flash of insight."

This is something we do quite naturally, aided by a part of the brain scientists have only recently called the "default neural network."[11] This network helps us churn through memories and fragmentary ideas, assembling them into a coherent and future-faced narrative as it proceeds. This part of the brain, researchers have discovered, works more effectively if you try not to place parameters on it or "demand" outcomes. In other words, you need to learn to let go, to relax. To reach your goal or solution you need to give up your goal.

Cultivating the ability to empathize with others also helps achieve this. Sometimes it is impossible to let go because of your preconceptions – about a person, an idea, a place – but by empathizing with (or "becoming") that person you can short circuit those things that may be preventing you from seeing the bigger picture or the new or emerging trend.

Your flash of insight may be your trend in its entirety, or it may be the moment you see the direction the trend is taking, or the routes along which you need to direct your research. For an intuitive forecaster, it is usually the latter: more often than not he or she is building up a vast back catalog of ideas, "stuff," and experiences and adding to them on a daily basis.

As these ferment in the forecaster's default neural network, whole thoughts or solutions emerge which he or she will then – if working with paying clients – have to back justify or "prove" using the cartographic methods outlined in the previous chapter. The process is much the same, except that the intuitive forecaster is now using the trend cartogram to retrospectively prove or unpack a trend that has been fermenting and growing within his or her conscious and subconscious mind.

Some intuitive forecasters can find this process frustrating, but for clients the "resolution process," as in the recording and analyzing of the trend in a comprehensive, logical, and rational way (see page 84), is a further reassurance, if not a measureable proof (and for many clients this, sadly, is always a requirement) that the trend is something that exists outside the imagination of the intuitive forecaster.

Once all of this is done, however, a forecaster still needs to ensure that his or her vision or strategic solution will be acted upon. This isn't so much a skill, says Duggan, but the resolve, willingness, and determination to ensure that the blueprint or plan that you are proposing is adhered to.

In many ways this follows the steps for implementing a plan outlined in Chapter Six (sees pages 153–69). A plan needs an implementation process and, because strategic intuition is more about the intangible than it is about the real and the measurable, this plan needs to be written up as an idea in a clear, logical, and strategic way and one in which all steps used to reach the conclusion are articulated. You then need to say how and by whom the plan will be implemented, how the implementation process will be monitored, and how any new factors emerging during implementation can be assimilated or a new plan drawn up.

> SUMMARY

Unless you are a natural, the best way to encourage and trigger your intuition is to follow through on all the techniques and skills outlined in this chapter until you have truly mastered the different types of intuition that we all possess but which, in many cases, we have allowed to become dulled. These skills can be further stimulated by practicing such activities as symphony, empathy, and cultural brailling. Brailling, as we have seen in the previous chapter, is all about observing the culture and, for intuitive forecasters, seeing is not just about knowing, it is about building up a back catalog of visual experiences as well as emotional ones.

None of these skills, however, can be developed adequately without your ability to suspend prejudice, to set aside preconceptions, and to take a step into new cultures, or to hang out with people who are different from you. As we will see in the next chapter on network forecasting, the skills of listening to your instincts, developing them, and making them more strategic, forward looking, and imaginative, are skills that enhance your ability to develop insightful and strategic networks – the kind of networks which in many ways do the things your brain does when you flood it with "stuff," ideas, and experiences and then leave it to ferment.

Chapter Four
Network Forecasting

FAMILIAR, YET SURREAL
and disturbing, the
work of artist and
photographer Filip
Dujardin has inspired
forecasters to look
at how trends can
be influenced by
technology – computer
graphics, 3D CAD
programs – or
ideas such as
cellular modification
or the notion that
we are entering a
world of science,
technology, and
genetic manipulation
(see also the work
of Stelarc, page 30),
where the artist
takes the place of
the architect or
scientist to help
us more fully
realize our dreams.

"In networks, we find self-reinforcing virtuous circles. Each additional member increases the network's value, which in turn attracts more members, initiating a spiral of benefits."

Kevin Kelly, editor and writer[1]

INTUITIVE FORECASTERS use their power of intuition to synthesize the knowledge of the many into a single view of the future. "Trend networks," on the other hand, harness the collective intuitions of the many to do the same thing. While intuitive forecasters use a single whole-brain approach to arrive at their answers, trend networks use the collaborative potential of a whole crowd of brains working together as a single organism to determine trends. Network forecasting is, therefore, about harnessing the power of the many or, as the author James Surowiecki puts it, "the wisdom of crowds."[2]

To understand how and why trend networks function like this, it is important to understand the hidden properties of networks themselves. At their most basic, networks are created when individuals come together to exchange ideas, products, or services that they have a mutual interest in promoting or knowing more about. Networks can, therefore, be regarded as organic arrangements that last as long as most members benefit in some way or another from the individual or collective activities of other network members.

In network science, members are sometimes referred to as "nodes" because each member is connected to, or holding a dialogue with, one or more members within his or her network. Nodes are, therefore, links through which information and knowledge flows. The more nodes you have in a network, the more information and knowledge flows through it, and the more powerful and accurate in its predictions that network can potentially become. This fact was first discovered by the scientist Francis Galton at the West of England Fat Stock and Poultry Exhibition in 1906. At this country fair, a competition was held

The brands featured
here have one thing
in common — they are
offering consumers
free "stuff" to take
away. The Store for
Tomorrow by Wolff
Olins (top left)
offers up ideas;the
L cafe, Tokyo (top
right), offers free
things to try out and
comment on; Nokia
(above left) has free
downloads to play; and
The Sample Lab, Tokyo
(left) gives products
to test. Even the
Plug'N Drink bar, in
Paris (above), offers
you free refreshments
and wi-fi. This
push toward giving
consumers free
products has been
called "Freesumerism."

annually to guess the weight of an ox after it had been slaughtered and dressed. Galton, who was curious about the accuracy of a crowd's submissions, asked the fair's organizers if he could examine their responses. They agreed to this and Galton noted the following: of the eight hundred or so people who attempted the competition very few of them came close to the right answer. However, when Galton removed the number of spoiled votes, and worked out the average response of the crowd overall, he came up with a figure of 1,197 pounds – one pound off the correct answer. He tested this again and again in other situations and the same thing happened. As Galton put it afterward: "The result seems more creditable to the trustworthiness of a democratic judgement than might have been expected."[3]

Without realizing it, Galton had identified one of the first principles of networks as we understand them today: while individuals within a crowd, group, or organization may not be wholly correct in their responses or observations, the sum total of a group's efforts will always bring you closer to the right answer. One hundred years on, the same principle applies as viewers of the television show *Who Wants to Be a Millionaire?* are apt to notice. In this program, participants have to answer multiple-choice questions, using their knowledge in some instances, but good old guess work in others – a bit like the people at Galton's fair. For *Who Wants to be a Millionaire?* contestants there are three ways of doing this: they can remove two of the four multiple choice questions and take a guess (an okay strategy); they can call a friend (not such a good idea as we shall see); or they can ask the studio audience to guess the answer. This, as we now know from Galton's experiments, is the right strategy to pursue. While contestants' friends manage to get the correct answer only 61 percent of the time, the television audience manage to do it 91 percent of the time. If harnessed properly networks can, therefore, be used to extract more accurate answers from people working collectively, rather than people operating individually, even if all the people within the network are not individually known to each other. Indeed, the less they know each other the better it is for your network.

> THE LAW OF WEAK-TIE NETWORKS

In his research into how knowledge and ideas flow through a network, American sociologist Mark Granovetter[4] discovered that the further away a person is from another person in a network the more useful the information is he or she passes on to this other person. On first sight this seems counter-intuitive, but when you consider it, it makes perfect sense. In the experiment that shaped Granovetter's results, he asked people whom they would turn to if they were looking for a new job. Most said a friend, associate, or acquaintance. As Granovetter discovered, however, this was the wrong thing to do. Those who followed this strategy were less successful in tapping into the knowledge streams that would help them than those who sought out advice and information from strangers, or friends of friends of friends. Why? Because the people we know generally know what we know, and if we don't know something then it is unlikely they will. This happens because we live within

An idea can spread as designers within the same industry, or discipline, note a concept they like and then tweak it in their own way. Here Elements of Islay, the Stockholm Design Lab, Erwin Bauer, and thisislove have all imitated a style and an approach to packaging that is sleek, minimal, and refined. All were pushing against a counter-trend in packaging for overly-designed surfaces and surface finishes.

homophilous groups and thus access the same knowledge pool. On the other hand, the further we remove ourselves from this knowledge pool, the greater we increase our chances of tapping into a new one. In other words, "weak-tie" acquaintances[5] and networks which contain greater numbers of people we don't know, or share only a few things in common with, are more likely to generate new ideas than networks which contain people that are alike. Granovetter calls this the "strength" of weak-ties. Good trend forecasting networks should, therefore, always contain high numbers of weak-ties – people from different countries, cities, and neighborhoods who we are not particularly close to socially, but who we can tap into in order to access their unique knowledge.

> THE RULE OF DIVERSITY IN NETWORKS

Granovetter's research also led to another discovery: the more diverse or heterophilous you make your network, the greater the network will be in terms of the diversity of ideas that flow through it. In other words, your weak-tie nodes – as well as coming from other cities and countries – need to come from different social, sexual, gender, class, and intellectual backgrounds, and from different industries and disciplines. In his highly influential book, *The Wisdom of Crowds*, Surowiecki believes it is important to do this to prevent a phenomenon he refers to as "groupthink"[6] from taking root. Groupthink is a word used to describe how friends, associates, and networks, who know each other intimately, begin to think alike and thus limit their capacity to embrace or explore alternative views, new attitudes, and new ideas. As Surowiecki says: "The important thing about groupthink is that it works not so much by censoring dissent, as by making dissent seem somehow improbable."[7] The point he is making here is clear: networks that have strong weak-ties and which contain high levels of diversity are able to optimize the performance and output of your network, while those that are homophilous tend to limit output and stunt performance.

> THE 80/20 PRINCIPLE

There is also another factor worth considering when establishing your own network. This is called the 80/20 principle. It is also known as the "Pareto Principle," after the Italian economist Vilfredo Pareto who noted during the early part of the last century that 80 percent of all land in Italy was owned by 20 percent of the population. The same pattern occurred, he realized, in how people worked, generated ideas, and owned wealth – in all cases the few (20 percent) did the majority of the work, had the most ideas, and owned the majority of the wealth. Across all industrial categories, and in all social activities, researchers have subsequently noted the truth of this rule again and again. Networks follow the same principle: within them 20 percent of the members are responsible for generating fully 80 percent of the ideas. This is the reason why you eventually see "super-nodes" or "clusters" developing in all networks, as those 20 percent become more visible through the ideas they

Techniques:
Ensuring network diversity

The process of network building is organic and ongoing. In many ways networks are only as good as the last member that has been signed up to them, so it is important that you invite new members to join on a regular basis, and that all new members are recruited from fields or sectors radically different from the ones you have previously looked to for support. Rather than populate your network with like-minded people, be ready to say no to new members if you have to: a homophilous network, while easy to recruit, tends to return ideas that are either too mainstream, lacking in richness, or diluted down from a more original or individual source.

Indeed this is the problem with most focus groups or panels that are recruited on the basis of recording the thoughts and ideas of Mr and Mrs Average – they return ideas that reflect a lack of original thinking. Networks need to be populated with Innovators or Early Adopters – people with new thoughts who are keen to share them with people from equally unusual and diverse backgrounds.

01: Sum up the reason for your network's existence in a single, succinct sentence – a "mission statement." For example: "It is a fashion innovation network established to determine what's new and next in fashion."

....

02: Make a list of all possible fields that are related to the issues you are attempting to address in your network mission statement.

....

03: Use this list to identify the kinds of people you should initially approach to become members of your network.

....

04: If you already have friends in this sector, exclude them from your network (friends tend to know what you know) but do work with them to identify friends of friends who may be useful – weak-tie associates whose knowledge and experience are beyond your immediate field of reference.

....

05: Once you have created your initial network membership list in terms of job types and industry categories, go online and create your own MySpace or Facebook profile outlining who you are, what you are doing, and the kind of network members you are trying to recruit.

....

06: Make sure you include examples of what you are looking for on your site, and that you link it to online resources or special-interest groups that fall within the sectors you need to recruit members from.

....

07: In tandem with doing the above, visit the bars, clubs, stores, streets, and neighborhoods of the areas within which you think potential members live, and hand out flyers containing details of your network, its mission statement, the benefits of membership, and its core and ongoing objectives.

....

08: Make sure you include an ideal list of what it takes to be a network member, and why you are trying to collaborate with potential members who come from different social,

cultural, ethnic, gender, and class-related backgrounds.

....

09: If your network is about answering cutting edge questions, make sure you populate it with as many cutting edge Innovators and Early Adopters as you can. Likewise, if you are using your network to determine how long it takes for a new idea or innovation to filter through to the mainstream, it is important to make sure all Diffusion of Innovation types are included in your initial recruitment process.

....

10: Recruiting members can be as easy as listing the sectors and job titles of the people you are keen to attract or, if job titles are inappropriate or unimportant, the characteristics you believe potential members should have – but keep these positive (i.e. characteristics people are keen to exhibit such as curiosity, inquisitiveness, being innovative, or determined to identify what's new and next in fashion, design, or whatever the core concern of your network is).

....

11: Avoid phrases that alienate or suggest that you are being judgemental, elitist, or scornful of the kind of differences you are trying to nurture and encourage in your network.

....

12: Finally, be collaborative, communicative, and constant in your dealings with your network. Make sure you speak to your network members on a regular basis, and that all network discoveries are shared equally, fairly, and with enthusiasm.

....

A meme can be about a
texture or a surface
detail as well as an
idea, and when
designers like
Fredrikson Stallard
(second from the top)
adopt it, it can
become a trend
championed by other
future-faced names.

generate. When this happens, more people tend to hook up with these people, and thus boost their power, visibility, and potential as connectors within the network. These super-nodes in turn become power networks in their own right, and many are eventually used by brands, businesses, and corporations to monitor new trends, track new innovations, and, in some cases, to seed other network nodes with new ideas or product concepts. All networks to some degree or other contain super-nodes, especially the three most common types of network found in the world of trend forecasting today: "hierarchical," "collaborative," and "distributive."

> HIERARCHICAL NETWORKS

Of the three networks, "hierarchical networks" are still the ones most commonly used among businesses globally to carry out trend, market, and consumer insight research. They are called hierarchical networks because all members of the network report back to a single "node" (or fixed point) at the center of the network (usually the manager, editor, or facilitator of the network) who in turn interprets their findings before passing them on to other members of the organization he or she is working for.

If you wanted to visualize this network it would look like a hub with lots of spokes radiating out from it, with a smaller hub at the end of each spoke representing a network member (see page 100). None of these minor hubs are directly connected to each other in any way, and all information that passes along the spoke to and from them does so via the central hub. Because of this, the flow of information within a hierarchical network is limited. As individual networkers within this system have no direct contact with each other, and as all contact happens via the filtering of the person at the center of the network, the sharing of ideas is controlled. The capacity of the network is thus dampened down in a way which allows only those ideas a network manager is keenest on to influence the overall output of the network.

This method of passing on information does not mean that all hierarchical networks are limited in their capacity to be innovative. If managed effectively, they can be highly creative and future-faced. In structure, trend forecasting networks like CScout (cscout.com) in the United States, Trendbüro (trendbuero.de) in Germany, and Trendwatching (trendwatching.com) in the Netherlands, operate along these lines. Trendwatching and its associated online newsletter, *Springwise* (springwise.com), is perhaps the best known. With its hub located in Amsterdam, it has 80,000 spokes or network nodes (Innovators and Early Adopters) located in seventy countries, all of whom spend their time looking, watching, listening, snapping, and then uploading their findings to Liesbeth den Toom, the site's central editor, who works with a small team of forecasters filtering through all the submitted "stuff," searching out anomalies and ideas that might lead to the detection of a trend in its nascent form.

"To be a spotter, or a networker you have to be in the right place at the most opportune time," den Toom says. "Our networkers are people who are fast-moving urbanites, slow-moving thinkers, frequent flyers: individuals who

Hierarchical networks and how they work

Hierarchical, or centralized, networks are among the most familiar. Traditionally, most institutions, businesses, and even design or architecture studios are configured like this. The central figure or hub – a president, CEO, or senior partner – sits in the middle of the network with the lines of power or influence reaching out from them or back toward them. Used properly, this can be a very powerful system – especially if the hub is an open, creative, and engaged one. But if it is closed and removed from what is original or different in the culture (the case with many CEOs and marketing heads), centralized

networks can be unwieldy, reactive, lacking in imagination, and in the ability to change or to predict change. This happens because the ideas flowing through the spokes of the network are regulated and controlled by one person who decides which ideas, if any, are passed on to the rest of the network.

Decentralized networks and distributive networks actively and organically prevent this from happening. If you are part of a centralized network, however (or if you are the hub of such a network), it does not mean that you have to be dull. Fashion designers, magazine editors, product designers, and architects all operate networks like this – and with few exceptions their work can be inspirational and challenging. This happens because they are open to

ideas, welcoming of opinions, and, as a rule, tend to populate their networks with other like-minded people who are also open and keen to embrace change. Centralized networks also allow you to control and regulate ideas in a positive as well as negative way. For instance, you can modulate them to suit the client base you are dealing with, or use them to hone ideas in a space that is closed off to outside (and possibly negative) influence until they are more refined and ready for the market. As with all network types, hierarchical networks need to be nurtured and constantly stimulated, and this needs to be done by the hub of the network itself.

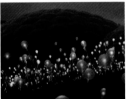

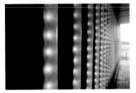

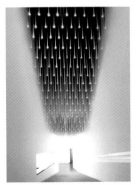

Let there be light: as consumers become more collaborative and ethereal in their desires, the trends that appeal to them have an equally nebulous feel. Light is increasingly becoming a tool and medium of choice for a new generation of visual artists keen to tap into this shift.

recognize a new business idea or initiative when they come across one, at home or abroad. Whether it's a new kind of male grooming lounge in Dubai or a new affordable book publishing service for aspiring writers in Canada."[8]

For den Toom, and for many organizations that want to capture innovation and new ideas in a particular way, the hierarchical network functions best because it allows them to edit, arbitrate, and arrange ideas in a way that makes them easier to manage and unpack. As a system, it is the quickest one to adopt and to run: network members supply you with "stuff" or ideas and in return you supply them with credits or payment. There are no restrictions on what you can do with the members' accrued contributions.

A hierarchical network is also one of the easiest and quickest network types to establish. Consider the notes on creating an expert panel in Chapter 2 (see page 56). Hierarchical networks are assembled in much the same way. Based on the industry or area you wish to explore, you determine the kind of people within it who will be of most use to you in terms of feeding back ideas and the latest updates on the newest and most innovative developments. It is important to have as many, if not more, Early Adopter types in your network as you have Innovators. Early Adopters tend to be more socially and intellectually mobile, and thus will have more heterophilous connections within a community or sector. Innovators tend only to concern themselves with their own specialism, whereas Early Adopters will be interested in lots of different ideas, and will plug you into as many areas as they are interested in themselves. A good percentage ratio of 80/20 (Early Adopter/Innovator) is always recommended.

You can find potential network members in your college (in specialist clubs, general interest groups, college societies), via the growing number of social networks that are now online, or by establishing your own hub on existing social networks such as MySpace, Facebook, LinkedIn, Gaia, Second Life, and Twitter. Once you have found suitable members you will need to outline the areas you want to focus on and then work with respondents to develop a network in which you ask the questions and they feed ideas back to you on a regular basis. If your network is compelling, and of equal interest to the people taking part, very little incentive will be required to keep your members responding and working with you. A good way to keep everybody happy, however, is for you to supply every member in your network with all the insights accrued from other network members.

There is another and much easier way of ensuring that your network is innovative, keen, and mutually useful to all involved. This is a network type that allows the nodes at the end of all the spokes to speak to each other as well as to the main hub. This is known as a "collaborative network," and is the one that a majority of network forecasters now favor, use, and manage.

> COLLABORATIVE NETWORKS

"Collaborative networks" are increasingly the networks of choice of a new generation of forecaster who see the Internet, and the potentials and opportunities it offers in terms of connectivity, as the sensible way to tap into new and emerging trends on a global basis. Collaborative networks contain

A forecaster can use
many ways to explore
and interpret a city
or a place. Here The
Future Laboratory's
LifeStyle News network
has collaborated with
correspondents in
cities like Berlin to
create a sense of how
the culture of that
city looks by viewing
it through brands,
products, graphics,
and found objects
that contain hints
of hidden lives
and alternative
ways of living.

Collaborative networks and how they work

Collaborative networks are more federated in their construction and behavior. While there is still a number of persons or entities through which the flow of information moves, they are never powerful enough to control the overall flow of activity, or the insights these generate. Because of how they are structured, collaborative networks contain within them smaller, more intimate networks, some of which may be connected via a mini hub to the bigger network. This configuration facilitates and encourages a more active and organic flow of ideas that percolate through the system. By doing so, ideas are spliced and merged with others,

connections made, and new insights gained as collaborative thinking is brought to bear on the subject or area under review. In this environment, flashes of insight are more likely to happen, and solutions to problems more readily emerge. This type of network is increasingly favored by online magazines, advertising agencies, and design and product studios where the design output is controlled not by a single designer, but by a creative team who are tasked with developing a look or feel that is innovative without being too radical or avant garde.

It is also an approach used by forecasting consultancies who want to keep in touch with shifts in the market, and to share these changes with other groups or individuals across parallel

sectors, where all concerned have a vested interest in knowing what is happening in sectors they can learn from. There is still an element of control within these networks. As with the 80/20 principle, over time, 20 percent of the people operating within a network like this tend to become the gatekeepers of the information and insights being passed in and around the network. These people are known as "super-hubs," or "super-nodes," and for forecasters they become a powerful extra tool in their battery of watching, listening, and intuiting devices used to survey the future. Super-nodes can sometimes become so powerful that the networks they facilitate become powerful micro-networks, sometimes called power networks.

a higher number of managers (see page opposite), all of whom are connected to each other and to other members of the network in such a way that allows information to flow more freely and, in the process, to be less regulated and controlled by any one person or organization.

Visually, if a hierarchical network is represented by a hub with a series of spokes passing through it, a collaborative network looks like a series of hubs with spokes radiating out from the center that interlock with other nearby hubs and spokes and, in some cases, with the spokes and hubs belonging to other networks. Because of these overlaps, collaborative networks tend to have more, newer, and fresher ideas flowing through them. In terms of reach and influence they also tend to be more powerful as regards the ideas they contain. As these ideas are less regulated and controlled by a single person, they tend to be less tainted by that person's views, prejudices, and preconceptions.

In a collaborative network, information, knowledge, and insight flow across the network as well as up, down, and along it. It is, therefore, a network built on relationships, collaborations, and more intimate and personal interactions between all network members – managers and members alike. Online sites, like PSFK, run a very successful version of this network type (see pages 37–40). Network members – usually Innovators, Early Adopters, and Early Majorities are located in key cites globally and all report back to the network's offices in London and New York. PSFK is a free-access site with over 30,000 users, all of whom are able to comment on the trends, ideas, and insights posted by PSFK trend writers. This allows its co-founder Piers Fawkes and his team to amend trends, verify new ones, or more strategically determine which snapshots from around the globe can be hived off into more relevant business trends which can be used by their paying clients.

As well as talking to the PSFK team, members will have "micro-networks" of their own, which they in turn manage and connect with other networks that may have no direct links with PSFK or its immediate trend needs. Thus ideas will flow out of the network into other non-associate networks, or vice versa, keeping up a healthy flow of ideas and dialogue at all times. Network members are located in different industry sectors and specialisms, as well as in different countries, cities, and neighborhoods – and all are asked to braille the culture for anything that is new, next, or likely to kick-start a new trend.

This collaborative way of tapping into the culture, says Fawkes, is a much better way of understanding consumers than carrying out focus groups and is one of the key and stated aims of the PSFK network. "Focus groups presuppose that there is something that you want to focus on. But what if the issue you are focusing on isn't the issue that you should be focusing on? The PSFK approach, because it is open and free ranging, captures everything – the questions you are asking certainly, but also the answers to the questions you haven't even begun thinking about!"[9] This, explains Fawkes, is always done by talking to the people at the forefront of change. To further boost their online activities, PSFK also organize network events in key cities around the world to bring Innovators, Early Adopters, and Early Majority types face-to-face. "Again it is important for people to talk, to spark ideas off each other – and to watch these grow."[10]

Without realizing it, collaborative networks are the kind of networks more and more of us use on a daily basis. If you are a member of Facebook, MySpace,

Techniques:
Collaborative innovation networks

Networks can be used to harvest "stuff" from society, but managed properly they can also be used to "seed" ideas back into the culture. Networks like this are used by brands or viral marketers to broadcast ideas into the mainstream by harnessing the power of Innovators and Early Adopters, who in turn are connected to Early Majority and Late Majority consumers.

This is known as "piping," literally pushing ideas through a pipeline of influencers to get to the people who have the money to pay for them – but only if they trust the influencer, or are part of what they deem to be a network that is conversational rather than one-way. Networks like this are referred to as collaborative innovation networks (COINs) by the two men who first created them – Peter Gloor of the MIT Sloan School of Management and Scott Cooper, an American writer on innovation and business economics.

01: The Germany-based lifestyle and consumer forecasting site Trendbüro (trendbuero.de) has a solid corporate bias, but it still contains all the characterics of a COIN in that all the ideas that flow through it are shared freely with other members.

02: COINs are collaborative networks tasked to do one thing: to take an idea from one part of the culture and, by actively harnessing the connections between network members themselves, seed or plant it somewhere else.

03: To do this, COINs need to contain higher numbers of Early Adopter, Early Majority, and Late Majority members than other kinds of networks.

04: They also need to have a small number of members within them whose job it is to stimulate or "push" "stuff" through the bigger network in a way that makes its presence more noticeable than it would otherwise be if it entered the network organically.

05: These members are sometimes known as "cool farmers," because they harvest "cool stuff" or ideas from the cultural fringes and use their presence and connections within the COIN to push ideas through it to Early Adopters, who in turn pass it on to Early Majority members, and so on.

06: As a group these cool farmers are closely linked and tightly connected, meeting and talking on a regular basis to share ideas and to collectively agree on which idea or ideas they are keen to promote to other network members via the connections they have with other Early Adopters.

07: Micro-networks like these can be "overt" or "covert" in their activities depending on whether or not they are working explicitly for a single client or for a group of them.

08: If the cool farmers are selling their services as a seed network to brands globally, they may be covert in their activities, in that they join groups, make connections, and initiate conversations in a way that encourages debate and

stimulates interest in a product, without necessarily declaring the fact that they have a vested interest in promoting it.

09: On the other hand – and this is increasingly the case – they may be overt in their activities in that they approach Early Adopters with ideas and ask them to test, try, or talk about them objectively and, if they like the idea, to share it with other members of their network.

10: These micro-networks usually consist of people who are highly connected, highly innovative, and, more importantly, look and think like the kind of people Early Adopters and, by association, Early Majority types are keen to know, talk to, and be seen with. Because they have a vested interest in pushing an idea through a network, they proactively seek out Early Adopters and Early Majority members to speak to and collaborate with.

11: Recruiting COIN members follows the same process as that outlined in the network diversity section (see page 98). You must get the proportion of the mix correct if the network is to function as a COIN. If using the network to target the consumer mainstream with a new idea or to boost a brand's profits, you need to have as many Early Majority and Late Majority members as you can. The membership should be made up of 80 percent Early and Late Majority members, with the remaining 20 percent containing Early Adopters and cool farmers (the latter number of which should never exceed 5 percent of the overall mix).

A trend like "New Seriousness," represented above, is a visual by-product of a shift in consumer desire for brands that are less about bling and excess and more about sobriety, austerity, simplicity, and a no-nonsense approach to graphics and packaging. In this sense, a visual trend can be viewed as a physical manifestation of an emotional or intellectual idea.

YouTube, Bebo, or the hundreds of other social networking sites that appear annually, you are, in effect, part of a collaborative network. By virtue of their construction, these networks allow you to create a collaborative network – via your homepage – through which you can speak to other "friends" in your network who are also running and managing their own micro-networks across any number of social media. A map of these links and overlaps looks like a more complex version of the collaborative network model (see page 104).

Establishing your own collaborative network merely requires you to set up your own homepage (if you don't already have one), outlining on it what you want your network to do (to focus on design trends, fashion trends, food trends, music trends, etc.) and the kind of people (Innovators, Early Adopters, like-minded trend scouts), organizations, and networks you are keen to collaborate with, and link to, in order to share ideas. You will then need to post examples of the "stuff" or ideas you are keen to know more about (using photographs, film clips, sample graphics, short visual and textural pieces, even blogs and links) to identify the range and breadth of the work you are trying to track down. Again, it is important to indicate why you have chosen these examples, and to explain as clearly as possible what you are hoping to do with the ideas, links, visuals, and graphics you are expecting potential members to supply you with.

To ensure that your network functions as a collaborative network (as opposed to a hierarchical one), it is important to recruit members who in turn have a large following within their own network. This is known as testing the "fitness" of a network. You can judge a potential member's suitability (fitness) by examining the content of his or her website, blog, homepage, etc., and by doing the same with a cross section of their "friends." You should also look at the number of friends a potential member has, who these friends in turn are linked to, and, more particularly, how often the site is updated and requests and queries dealt with.

You can have as many hubs as you like on your network, and these hubs in turn can have as many members as they wish, but it is important that you share all views and insights gathered with your hubs on a regular basis. These hubs in turn will make sure that all relevant information passed on is sent to members within their own network. While hierarchical network members are usually paid in credits or money, collaborative networkers are usually paid in knowledge and insight – they will help you, if you continue to help them. This is known as "network reciprocity." The best networks thrive and flourish when the majority of their members – especially those who are deemed to be the hubs within the network – exchange ideas and correspondence on a regular basis.

As the instigator of a collaborative network, you will be expected to be the most active and live member on it. Indeed, in many ways, you will be expected to steer the network, and to make sure that it is fulfilling its original purpose and role. Checking your homepage hourly is recommended – more frequently if you can access it from your cell phone. Networks that are neglected become redundant very quickly or, worse still, attract the wrong caliber of member. If anything, the strength, fitness, and potential creativity of a network is directly proportional to how proactive you and, therefore, your other members are on an hourly or indeed a minute-by-minute basis.

There are many examples of collaborative networks in use today. Some, like the Global Business Network (gbn.com), link a wide variety of Innovators, Early Adopters, and academics together so that they can work on new ideas collaboratively, or act as a cluster of consultants for a single business keen to tap into their collective insights and ideas. Other collaborative networks, like TED (ted.com), that is, the "technology, entertainment, and ideas" network, bring together the most innovative speakers to discuss and offer insights into effective ways of making the present and the future better and more sustainable places to live in.

In other cases, however, collaborative networks are set up merely to answer a single, ongoing question. Who will be the next president of the United States? What film or actor will win an Oscar at this year's award ceremony? The Iowa Electronic Markets (IEM) and the Hollywood Stock Exchange (HSX) are two such collaborative networks. Over the course of the presidential elections in the United States, from 1988 to 2000 for instance, 596 polls were released about how candidates would do. Three-quarters of the time, on the day each poll was published, the IEM (which asked members to collectively work on predicting which candidate would win) came up with results that were more accurate than polls answered by political analysts. Similarly, HSX members have been consistently better at predicting Oscar winners than the small industry of pundits that have grown up around Hollywood's annual rush down the red carpet. Being able to predict winners with any degree of accuracy means the difference between a studio making money or losing it on a film it is unsure about.

So how do these networks function? The answer is in much the same way Galton's crowd worked at that country fair all those years ago. Individually no member of the IEM or the HSX, for example, may have as much knowledge as the experts who are being consulted for their views on who will become the next president, or win the Oscar, but by pooling their resources they become a very powerful brain that mixes, merges, and ferments the sum total of their knowledge together – about an actor's talents yes, but also about his or her private life, sex appeal, celebrity rating, global standing, etc. – in a way that allows the network to have a better collective overall knowledge than individual experts.

There is a third kind of network, however, called a "distributive network," that takes the characteristics of the collaborative network a step further by turning it into a network which contains only hubs. All of these hubs are interconnected and running and managing their own personal collaborative networks at the same time, so that the overall network looks like, and some would argue thinks like, a "hive mind" or gigantic brain.

> DISTRIBUTIVE NETWORKS

A "distributive network" (as the illustration on page 114 indicates) is a network that contains as many super-nodes as its does spokes with nodes and super-nodes attached to them. These nodes in turn are so numerous and so well distributed across the network (and indeed the many other networks they

(text continues on page 113)

Case Study: Sean Pillot de Chenecey

AS TREND ANALYST, product developer, and insight researcher, Sean Pillot de Chenecey (aka Captain Crikey: captaincrikey.com) says: "Less than twenty years ago there was no such thing as a trend forecaster in the way that we understand the job today. Maybe someone in the fashion industry spoke about skirt lengths – but it was all a bit daft! Markets were relatively stable, consumers predictable, and of course brands weren't being impacted on by the digital consumer in the way they are today."

Pillot de Chenecey believes, however, that after 9/11, when the twin towers in New York were struck by terrorist jets, everything changed: that uncertainty became the norm, markets increasingly irrational, and consumers driven by a new sense of self questioning, fragmented in their tastes, hedonistic in their outlook, and more keen than ever on "self actualization." As he says: "For some it was about celebrity and bling, for others debates about environmental ethics and the desire to challenge brands."

A former member of the Blues and Royals cavalry regiment working in reconnaissance, Pillot de Chenecey brought a new dimension to researching the everyday lives of consumers. "For a lot of brands back then it was all about the numbers, seeing people in terms of percentages. But for me it was about

Forecasters like
Pillot de Chenecey
work from home, but
collaborate with a
diverse and global
range of insight and
research organizations
that effectively allow
them to operate as one
of the key hubs in a
collaborative network
of "heterophilous
members": each one
contributing to the
needs of the other
so that each hub, or
member, has a global
database or resource
to draw on for
projects.

The beauty of the
collaborative network
model, says Pillot de
Chenecey, is that it
allows you to be an
"expert" in many
fields. But you still
have to underpin the
work done by others
with your own more
focused and
quantitative desk
research. To do this
you need to have a
good home library, a
handicam, DAT
recorder, and camera
to capture all aspects
of this process.
Research isn't just
about hard data, it is
about the emotional
and visual landscapes
that define it.

Having a home "den"
or office is important
– much of what a
forecaster does is
about considering
the implications of
a trend once it has
been identified. This
requires a certain
level of solitude, and
being able to think in
an environment where
there are few outside
distractions. Such
places encourage those
flashes of insight
that are the hallmarks
of a good forecaster.

observing how real people lived and the trends they bought into, that made this way of living different or potentially profitable to brands... Trend forecasters, because they live in the future, see the world in very exciting terms – domestic robots, 3D printing technology, holographic conferencing, nano-clothing – but the reality for most people is that the future will be mundane: we'll still run out of teabags, still have to clean the house. It is important then that as forecasters we ground things in the familiar and never forget that even if a lot of people have laptops and mobiles, vast areas of the world do not and their future needs to be considered in different terms."

Working for brands like Merrell footwear, Pontiac, Unilever, GlaxoSmithKline, and Diageo, Pillot de Chenecey uses a very qualitative approach to exploring markets, aspects of which include the following: depth-interviewing of consumers within their own environment; spending time living with Innovators and Early Adopters to determine how the trends they are embracing are being absorbed and assimilated into their lives; always focusing on "the edge, the new, and the next, but always being aware of how normal people react to new trends – with suspicion, by adapting it, and, finally, by removing any of its original edge." This process, he believes, takes as much as three to five years: "But a lot of brands want it now. They get into a trend too early, and then blame forecasters when consumers are still catching up. Trends are finely nuanced – and forecasters, and the brands they work with, need to be aware of this 24/7."

This is not a pick-and-mix thing, Pillot de Chenecey believes, but a process that requires subtlety, patience, the ability to observe, intuit, interpret, and above all to unpack the trend in relation to the client or brand you are working for: "Authentic for a food brand, may be about being organic, real, and Soil Association-certified, but authentic for a trainer brand, whose heritage is in performance and innovation may be about synthetics or embracing bio-fabrics."

It is important to analyze the market in relation to your client, as much as it is important to really come to grips with the consumer experience, even if that experience runs counter to the beliefs of the client. "A forecaster's job isn't to bend the truth, but to make sure both sides understand what that truth is – and being prepared to embrace it or not, depending on their own particular views... And the best part of being a forecaster – nothing is 100 percent, people change, brands change – so you need to keep an open mind. That's one of the best talents a forecaster can have – remaining open, watching and listening, and feeling change."

As one group of designers opt for a more monochrome and neutral palette, it is inevitable that another group will develop a taste for the opposite. Here names like Jesse Kirsch, Blind Mice, Oscar Narud at OKAY Studio, and Jenny Gibbs have done just that. In this way trends can simply be a reaction against the norm, or even against the new.

overlap with), that they create a flattened or decentralized arrangement whereby the majority of the members are exposed to much higher volumes of ideas and "stuff" than members of all other network types.

Distributive networks are referred to as such because their construction allows information, ideas, or insights to be scattered or "distributed" across the network at high speed, in the process encouraging and causing high levels of serendipity, and thus facilitating more opportunities for key flashes of insight to occur. By their nature, distributive networks are open, in that anybody can join and use them. Because of this, unless you are monitoring the network twenty-four hours, seven days a week, those flashes of insight, when they occur, may go undetected.

To prevent this from happening, trend forecasters spend as much of their time as possible within distributive networks seeking out the super-nodes so that they can be in the right place at the right time to monitor the appearance of a new trend. A simple way of doing this is to make sure that your network feeds into all key trend forecasting networks (see list on page 46) or that you are brailling these sites on a regular basis to log new ideas as and when they begin to break. Many of these sites are interlocked. Being aware of this, good trend forecasters soon become very adept at noting which trends are beginning to be spoken about on which key sites, and thus can start mapping their movements from one site to another until they make it into sites that are populated in the main by Late Majority and Laggard consumers.

Again, this can be done by creating a whiteboard or evidence wall (see pages 47–49) that contains a listing of the top twenty sites as a series of twenty columns running across the wall from left to right. New and emerging trends can be mapped beneath each trend site title when they appear, and links drawn from one site to another if the same trend, or a trend with the same characteristics (remember each site may refer to the same trend with a different name), appears on another site. The greater the visibility of the trends, and the more frequently they appear on other sites, the higher the rating you give them: scoring them perhaps from one to ten, so that you can create an initial ranking that can be further explored by working with your key network nodes to establish the power of the trend that has been identified (as outlined in the trend thesis section in Chapter 2, see page 57).

As their members tend to come from vastly different industries, distributive networks are among the best at helping you to braille the culture and to do it across categories. The Internet itself is one of the best examples of this kind of distributive network in action – daily more than 1.5 billion[11] people from a wide variety of disciplines, ethnic, social, sexual, and class backgrounds are online, talking, connecting, exchanging, collaborating, and adding to the sum total of the knowledge currently found on the World Wide Web.

Arguably, it is because of the Internet that we have at last begun to understand and appreciate the power of distributive networks, and the many hidden characteristics and potentials they contain. If you continue to add more people to your distributive network you will, because of its size and reach, create a highly "sticky" network which others will be compelled to join because so many people they know (or want to know) are on it, and it is important socially, culturally, or career-wise to be part of that trend. Consider networks

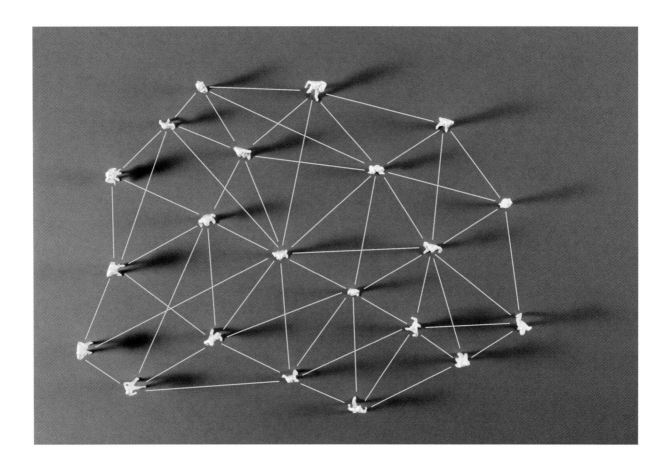

Distributive networks and how they work

Distributive networks function very like the human brain. Each person works like a cell, and each cell contributes consciously or subconsciously to the overall activity being focused on with the network. This happens because there are no single spokes or hubs along which the majority of information flows. All parts of the network are connected, and all parts sooner or later receive the same information, and in addition the accrued insights derived from other members of the network as they add their thoughts and comments to the thoughts and comments of the others. As these collective insights build and flow more readily through the system, other more elaborate and insightful thoughts are added until there is a cascade of energy and ideas that can encourage dramatic flashes of insight to occur.

Distributive networks can be used for identifying new and emerging trends, and for seeding these into more mainstream groups – as with collaborative networks. They can also be used for more complex activities such as scenario planning (see Chapter 6) or to solve a single problem in a unique or innovative way. Although networks like this are not "managed" in the normal sense of the word, within them you tend to find a smaller group of people (20 percent) who assume responsiblity for 80 percent or more of the network's output. Because of this, companies who run distributive networks tend to identify who these people are as soon as they can, and work with them to boost the power of the network by extending their access to facilities they may need to make their jobs easier (e.g. research budgets) and thus to flood the greater network with additional stimuli. Also referred to as power networks, they tend to work best when they are asked to focus on a single problem or question. They are likewise used by brands, businesses, and research institutions to "imagineer" a new product, or to solve a problem faced by one industry which may have already been solved by another. Distributive networks, because of their power, reach, and scope, can usually spot such solutions in one sector and apply it to another.

Images selected randomly by a network may have nothing in common until the forecaster presents them in a different context. Here, while materials differ, a sense of the ethereal lingers – the name forecasters eventually gave to this trend.

like Facebook, MySpace, Twitter, LinkedIn, YouTube: while they initially attracted Innovators and Early Adopters, their membership is now made up more of Early Majority, Late Majority, and Laggard members.

Bob Metcalfe, the founder of 3Com Corporation and the co-inventor of the Ethernet (used to talk to people locally within a protected or secure network), coined the term "network effect" to describe this precise process and principle. "The value of a network," he says, "increases exponentially with the number of nodes you add to it."[12] In other words, the more people the network includes, the more people it will attract, making it ever more powerful as it does so, according to Massachusetts Institute of Technology (MIT) scientist and network specialist David Reed. Writing in the *Harvard Business Review* in February 2001, Reed suggested that Metcalfe understated the real value of adding more and more nodes to your network. He was right, as we now know from studying the power, influence, and the reach of sites like MySpace and Facebook – sites which have transformed themselves from being simply networks to being whole new mediums of communication and collaboration.

It could be argued, therefore, that volume generates its own value. If used correctly you can harness the volume of people found in social networks like MySpace (124 million visitors monthly) and Facebook (276 million visitors monthly) to develop a value-driven tool that allows you to develop your own micro-trend network inside a larger one and to use it initially to attract Innovators and Early Adopters. You can then work with these to deep dive their networks, and the networks they themselves are connected to, in order to detect, explore, and elaborate on new and emerging trends across different cultural, social, and ethnic divides.

For example, in 2008 UK-based trend forecasting agency The Future Laboratory worked with a number of students to establish an "ethnographic hide" on MySpace. Then via links and personal recommendations from other invited networkers on Facebook, YouTube, Bebo, Faceparty, etc., rolled this out across other networks online. The premise of the hide was a simple one: to collaborate with social networkers on these sites – students, clubbers, DJs, designers, video makers, artists, etc. – and to do so to capture a snapshot of new and emerging fashion, music, design, culture, and lifestyle trends of teenagers and students between the ages of sixteen to twenty-one.

The initial hide, managed by five people, attracted 15,000 Innovators, Early Adopters, and via them Early Majority, Late Majority, and Laggard visitors. This enabled the research team to carry out 1,500 unique interviews with all five Diffusion of Innovation types, capturing twenty-five new and emerging trends on the rise. A panel of fifteen experts, including sociologists, academics, anthropologists, authors, lifestyle editors, and urban ethnographers, were then used to underpin and further explain the initial findings of the trend forecasters. An initial report was completed – always referred to as a "thesis" – and shared with a cross section of the networkers interviewed to get them to rate the final content in ascending order of importance in terms of the issues identified, the drivers affecting them, the trends that would be most and least important, and the social groups they believe would have most appeal to them over the coming months.

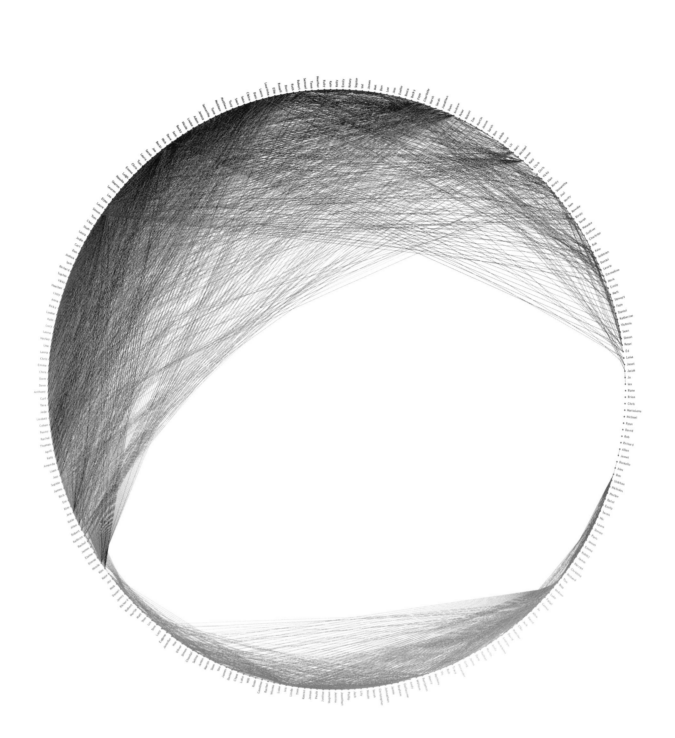

The Friend Wheel

Thomas Fletcher has developed a series of network tools on Facebook including this one which he calls The Friend Wheel, a beautiful and intriguing way to create a visual version of the network of relationships you share with your friends and their friends' friends on Facebook!

More than 25,000 friend wheels are generated on a daily basis. The tool, which is located at facebook.com/friend wheel, can be used to retrieve your friends' links (and all other links) they have created on Facebook. Once this is done, the information is then used to draw the wheel image. Using this tool, forecasters who create their own

networks on Facebook can then generate a visual image of them to determine which "nodes" are the strongest in terms of to whom they are connected, and how these connections relate to the most and least powerful in a particular network.

As happened in this example, once a thesis has been assessed it is then handed back to forecasters to be written up as a final report, using the same headings found when visualizing the trend cartogram in Chapter 2 (see page 61): starting with an overview of the report and its key findings, an executive summary that sets the overall report in context, followed by drivers, the impact, the consequences of the trends or issues identified, and how they are set to play out in the future.

> SUMMARY

Networks allow the many to work for the few – in this case, the trend forecaster, but to do so in a way that benefits all parties involved. Networks – even hierarchical ones – are collaborative and thus need reciprocity to maintain the levels of activity within them and the kinds of outputs we extract from them. "Reciprocity" is the glue that holds networks together, the flow of knowledge and information passing through them, the fuel that keeps them vibrant and alive. It is important to ensure that your network encourages all of these things to take place from the outset.

It is also worth remembering that networks have many hidden rules and properties and it is important to be aware of these when forming and maintaining your own network. The strength of weak-ties reminds you not to populate your network with people you know, while your knowledge of "groupthink" and heterophily should warn you against creating or maintaining small, enclosed networks that are not accessing fresh thinking on a regular basis. Networks need intellectual oxygen to keep their ideas fresh and original.

Networks also require you to be constantly vigilant – monitoring, collaborating, exchanging, and harvesting ideas on a 24/7 basis. In other words, they are always on, live, and demanding your attention. But they are also producing a range of snapshots of the future that are fragments of a bigger picture – the emergence of fuel cells as a new form of energy, the idea perhaps that consumers are becoming more ethical, the suggestion that a new kind of music is on the rise or a new fashion about to hit our stores.

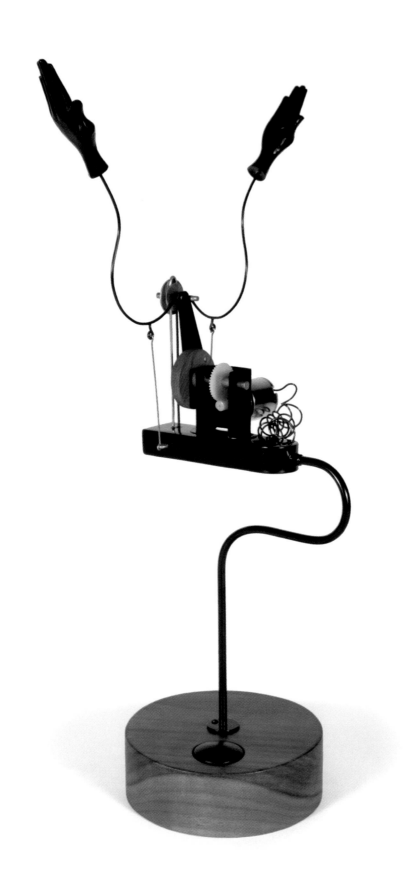

Chapter Five
Cultural Triangulation

MARTIN SMITH'S
"Applause Machine"
is a work of art for
Laikingland, the
creative collaboration
based in the UK and
the Netherlands whose
objective is to design
and manufacture
beautifully-crafted
kinetic objects. This
work and others like
it have influenced a
growing trend among
product designers to
develop household
pieces with an added
kinetic or sensory
element to them.

"What people say, what people do, and what they say they do are entirely different things."

Margaret Mead, cultural anthropologist[1]

AS WE HAVE SEEN in previous chapters, the basic tools of forecasting use a mix of skills that are practical, process driven, and intuitive. For some of the organizations you will work with, however, a more structured and strategic approach is required: one that underpins the "soft skills" of the forecaster (intuition, cultural brailling, cross-cultural analysis, etc.) with the "hard skills" (data driven) of the market researcher, economist, and statistician. This approach – known as "cultural triangulation"[2] – is increasingly favored by global brands, such as Procter & Gamble, Unilever, Nestlé, Nokia, and Microsoft, because it offers them more quantitative ways in which to account for the work of forecasters within a business framework dominated by financial projections, quarterly forecasts, and five-year plans.

Cultural triangulation is a combination of three distinct but mutually beneficial processes, all of which are variations on skills encountered in preceding chapters. They are:

__interrogation: the use of quantitative survey techniques, including household surveys and expert interviews, to poll individuals or groups about their attitudes or activities, with a view to determining the percentage breakdown of these attitudes or activities in relation to the larger population or cultural mainstream.
__observation: the use of a set of qualitative tools such as "ethnography" (a method of observing people at close range) and "visual profiling" to shadow and observe individuals or consumers involved in a particular task or lifestyle activity, with a view to learning more about that task or activity.
__intuition: drawing on your experiences as a forecaster to add a further layer of insight to the qualitative and quantitative underpinnings acquired during the interrogation and observation stages.

Within the context of the cultural triangulation model, all three processes are deployed in a measurable set of steps which organizations, unused to the more qualitative aspects of forecasting, find easy to follow and digest. Cultural triangulation, which matches skills that visually map the culture (cultural brailling, cross-cultural analysis, for instance) with those that attempt to record it statistically, emotionally, and intellectually (through deep diving, expert panels, desk research, and quantitative analysis), is also more robust and

Moving away from the slick textures and highly-polished surface finishes of luxury in the noughties, "Rough Luxe," as a trend and a concept is innovating the world of staid hotel and retail interiors, as well as the product design sector, with its raw surfaces, worn-in qualities, and a look that is all about lived-in loucheness.

accurate in its outcomes – something that makes it a favored method of forecasting with global corporations. Because of this it is a process, like scenario planning (see Chapter 6), that is gaining in popularity with marketers, economists, and market researchers, but also with scientists, technologists, engineers, and industrial designers, all of whom are aware of the gaps in the so-called "hard skill" professions when it comes to investigating the hidden motivations and desires of Innovators and Early Adopters and how these in turn will impact on other groups.

> TRIANGULATION

"Triangulation" is a term derived from the social sciences, where it is used to describe a process by which two methods out of a possible three are used to arrive at the same conclusion, with a view to making sure that the conclusion is the right one. By combining a number of qualitative and quantitative methods and approaches it is believed that forecasters can suppress, if not eradicate, the normal biases found when using only one methodology. Cultural triangulation can also be described as a way of tracing or validating changes taking place in the culture by using one method (quantitative surveys for instance) to test, prove, or validate another method (observation or intuition). So, for example, if you used an interrogative approach you might learn that people like to use their cell phones to do work, etc., but it is only by observing these people that you see how they do this work – predominantly with their thumbs – and thus how you could improve their ability to do so.

Texting, for example, was designed by telecommmunication companies to allow their engineers to send Short Message Texts (SMTs) to each other but was subsequently adopted and popularized by teenagers keen to chat cheaply to their friends. Using interrogative and observational methods, forecasters were able to identify texting as a new and powerful communications tool – as in Short Message/Messaging Service (SMS) – as well as a highly profitable product stream for the companies involved. By analyzing the texts themselves forecasters were also able to identify a new way of communicating: the use of "emoticoms" to visually express what is meant, by combining the functions of the keypad in a purely graphic way – as in (-.-)zzZ or -_-zzZ, the emoticom for sleep.

In many ways, cultural triangulation cherry picks the best methods of forecasting and, because of this, allows you to develop, hone, and further explore processes that can be used individually or collectively to add new skills to your forecasting talents.

> THE INTERROGATION STAGE

To begin the cultural triangulation process it is important to carry out what forecasters using both this method, and indeed all modes of forecasting, refer to as an "information amnesty."

When forecasters ask questions such as "how will food look in the future?" they begin by assembling samples of future-faced foods such as Skin Nutrition's Omega 3 wholefood shake (designed to optimize beautiful skin), along with products like Sip water and Superfruit's Goji, to intuit where the market might be heading for tomorrow.

__INFORMATION AMNESTIES

An "information amnesty" is the term used to describe the initial stages of the cultural triangulation process in which forecasters probe the clients they are working with for all information the forecaster considers relevant to the issue or question under review. The "question" being asked can be anything: from how food will look in the future, to the shape and state of car design to come. Probing the client carefully and strategically allows you to construct a question that more accurately hones in on the real issues that require answering. For example, a global food manufacturer may want to know which food categories they should be investing in over the coming decade. On talking to the manufacturer, the forecaster discovers that some of their money is already invested in the genetic modification of food but, because of the bad publicity this caused in the past, they have decided not to talk about it and indeed to discontinue this as a route of research. From his or her own intuitive knowledge of the market, the forecaster realizes that it is now time to ask a question that relates to genetically modified (GM) food, or at least to include the possibility of GM food in the project parameters.

It is also worth noting here that what the forecaster considers relevant and what the client considers relevant can, in many cases, be two different things, which is why this process can be an arduous one and one that requires a level of diplomacy and a good deal of cross-questioning to ensure all information has been imparted. In the above example, the client having being damaged by bad publicity relating to their forays into GM in the past may be reluctant to do so now, while the forecaster, aware of a change in attitude to GM among a certain age group, might believe it is a good way to proceed.

Marco Marsan, who runs a concept development company in the United States, and does so by working with forecasters using the cultural triangulation method, explains the process as follows: "Get the basics right and you get the bigger picture right as well."[3] Getting the basics right involves seeing a clear and thoroughly written brief from the client upfront, along with all supporting material, documentation, and any other research that has been carried out in relation to the issue you have been asked to look at.

The answers to the questions you may need to ask, and the information for any brief of the work to be undertaken, can come from a number of sources: your client's marketing department, their Research and Development (R&D) team, their brand managers, even the polling and research organizations that they are using to capture a more quantitative snapshot of their target demographic. The key point to remember is that you need to have all the questions answered comprehensively and truthfully.

Incomplete information amnesties can taint the final output of your work. At the beginning of the project you should therefore ask the following:

__what are the overall aims and objectives of the project? In other words, are you attempting to identify a new product idea, a new way to reinvigorate an existing product, or are you focusing on new and emerging behavioral activities or mindsets among a target group of consumers?
__are there any issues that may inhibit this from the outset? Will your target group be happy to take part in your research? Will they require payment?

Are there any issues on your client's side of the agreement that may impact on how you engage with your target group?

__does your client expect to be involved with your work on a day-to-day basis (which many increasingly do) and, if so, what are the implications and impact of this on your work?

__what existing research is available? How tainted is this with your client's sense of what the target group should or should not be. This is important: clients tend to create research questions to validate a product or a view they may already have. If this is the case, you need to be aware of it.

At the information amnesty stage it is important to remember that you are questioning and challenging the company about what it knows, and what it believes to be its failures and blind spots in the market. You have not yet begun to work with their target market or, indeed, to interrogate or observe their market about its opinions or beliefs. Only when you have ascertained all information deemed to be relevant, should you begin to collate information and insights about the market itself.

__SUBJECT FRAMING

Sean Pillot de Chenecey (see pages 109–12) uses cultural triangulation extensively and refers to the project framing stage of the process as "Google bashing." Once you know the question, it is important to identify all external issues (similar to the contextualization process referred to later in Chapter 6) that are likely to influence or impact on the issue under review. As Pillot de Chenecey explains: "It is about doing your homework. About using the Internet and basic research tools and available media and research organizations, including think tanks, to capture a broader sense of the market you are investigating. You tend to do this, after you have interviewed the client and identified what it is they know and don't know."[4]

At this point, your focus is on the trends, and the latest information your research uncovers to determine all of the trends that may be affecting the market or consumer group you have been asked to focus on. You can do this by using information culled from other trend research and organizations (see page 46) or, if you are keen to ensure that your "eye" is untainted by the work and opinions of other forecasters at this stage, you can follow the processes outlined in Chapter 2 under the headings "Cultural brailling" (see pages 36 and 41–44) and "Cross-cultural analysis" (see pages 44–50 and 55–65).

Once this work is complete, and all influential trends or insights have been identified, it is important to draw up an outline overview that identifies:

__any early trends you may be spotting (from the media, websites, television, industry trade journals, etc.) in relation to your initial question

__areas that require further investigation

__expert names that seem to appear again and again in the literature you are wading through, so that you can add them to your list of potential people to interview

(text continues on page 129)

Case Study:
Chris Sanderson

"TRENDS ARE PROFITS WAITING TO HAPPEN," says Chris Sanderson, co-founder of The Future Laboratory (thefuturelaboratory.com), the consumer insight and trends network. Established in 2001 and based in London, The Future Laboratory now works with more than 200 clients globally identifying "what's new, next, and the people that make these things happen" across a range of sectors from fashion to interiors, luxury to automotives, technology to packaging. "We cover over fourteen different sectors," says Sanderson, "all diverse, all significantly different on the surface, but all having one thing in common – the consumer, and how he or she buys into them on a daily basis."

To monitor these sectors effectively The Future Laboratory, with its twenty-five strong team of visual and market analysts, uses cultural triangulation. As Sanderson explains: "This has now become the default approach used by many agencies in this sector. But when we developed it in 2001, it was unique and unusual. Most agencies used one approach over the other – they were generally about intuition, or about observation, and so on, while we decided to bring all three together to offer clients qualitative and intuitive snapshots of the future, carefully underpinned with concrete market data and forward projections."

To facilitate this approach, Sanderson says, the company contains three distinct types of people: trend researchers whose job it is to identify the "stuff"

Style spreads, or mood boards, are used by many forecasting organizations to develop a sense of what a particular trend might look like visually. Once a forecaster "sees" what a trend looks like, they can start developing an understanding of the colors, materials, textures, and social and enviornmental factors of which this trend consists.

For Sanderson, you should never underestimate the power of reading – and reading thoroughly and widely – to understand and appreciate a trend. Forecasters have a reputation for being skittish, especially those who work in fashion. But good forecasting, he believes, is about application, about learning, about deepening and widening your knowledge. "And there is only one way to do that – by concentrating and by always reading beyond the narrow confines of your specialism or area. We have a motto at The Future Laboratory: *sapere aude* – dare to know! Every forecaster should do this."

At The Future Laboratory, trends are mapped in two ways: analysts and senior trend analysts identify what's new and next in consumer thinking in terms of social, ethical, moral, economic, and environmental matters. Then their visual counterparts look at how these identified trends will look and feel in terms of their aesthetic impact. By doing this, says Sanderson, "we are reminding clients that all consumer trends have a design and aesthetic implication and vice versa. This is important; marketing teams tend to negate this, but they do so at their peril. To agree that 30 percent of consumers are keen on organic food or sustainable furniture and then believe (as many marketers do) that this will not affect how these products look is nonsense."

For Sanderson, teamwork and collaborative analysis are the basis for how many of The Future Laboratory client projects are conducted. While quantitative and qualitative research underpins all the identified trends, the instincts and hunches of the forecaster or analyst themselves cannot be ignored. Each member of the team assimilates so many insights during their work, and they are expected to bring these to each project. That way insights are always fresh and unique.

that surrounds us globally on a daily basis; trend analysts who in turn interpret this "stuff" and place it within a broader social, environmental, and lifestyle context; and insight and strategy directors who pinpoint the overarching trends these shifts are creating, and the potential products that may result as a consequence of how they impact on businesses, brands, and the people who consume them.

"Teams are also broken down into visual and data researchers, visual and data analysts, and so on, to make sure that we are mapping these changes in a way that is both visual and intellectual. Too many companies concentrate on the numbers to the detriment of seeing the bigger picture – a laptop is a laptop after all, but when it is designed like an Apple, it becomes greater than the sum of its parts through design, usability, and the impact these have on the consumer psyche. Data alone cannot capture this sensibility," he says.

Sanderson, who trained as a theater director at Goldsmiths College, London, went on to work in fashion PR and marketing before finally becoming creative director of *Viewpoint* magazine, a biannual trends, brands, and insight publication which is now edited by The Future Laboratory. "While I was working on *Viewpoint*, the gap in the market for a trends and consumer insight agency that tied its findings into key consumer needs became more and more apparent and so The Future Laboratory was established as an incubator, a place for experiment, for exploration, and for challenging the average. Indeed we chose the motto *sapere aude*, the Latin for 'dare to know,' to spur us on. And continue to do so."

The Future Laboratory now holds biannual trend briefings in London, Stockholm, Gothenburg, Melbourne, and Sydney, hosts an online lifestyle network called LifeStyle News Global, and runs quarterly network events for creatives, strategists, and marketers working in the lifestyle industries. As Sanderson says: "The process of forecasting is one of continuous sifting; of using people on the ground in key cities globally, to create a mosaic of the world that is then interrogated against client concerns, or how a particular sector will be affected by a change that it may not be anticipating... With this in mind, we maintain a network of correspondents in key cities globally, all of whom work to specific briefs. How will eco-homes look in twenty years time? What are the new entertainment trends teens are buying into? This way, we capture very particular and bespoke views of the future."

These views, Sanderson explains, are translated into a range of insight reports, forums, and strategy documents that visually, emotionally, statistically, and collaboratively map the future, but from the perspective of the Innovators and Early Adopters. "In marketing, people always talk of the average – but if you ask average people what they know about the future, they give you average responses. As Henry Ford once put it: 'If I'd asked people what they wanted, they would have said a faster horse.' This is why it is increasingly important to talk to the Henry Fords of this world – the technologists, researchers, scientists, artists, writers, philosophers, and creative upstarts who are defining our future by deliberately defying all that we understand to be average."

This overview will provide you with an initial direction along which to move your investigations. Based on your question, and the more complex issues you may have identified that surround it, you may now have an idea that fashion-wise, for example, the trends you need to look at might include the growing desire to buy ethically sourced products, a growing demand for trans-seasonal clothes, the idea that luxury is no longer about being glossy and obvious but being inconspicuous and considerate of others in the demonstration of wealth and income.

Undertaking comprehensive background research will also flag up many of the issues and topics you may wish to quiz your panel about. As outlined previously (see page 56), you should ensure that there are a number of academics or research fellows on your expert panel who have made this their area of concern. Academics by discipline and training are invariably neutral and objective when investigating a subject area, and thus their opinions can provide you with a relatively untainted view of what the real issues of concern may be.

Once all these relevant issues have been identified and your panel selected, it is worth e-mailing all of the panel members an outline of your initial thesis with an overview of the questions you are trying to answer. When this has been done it is important to interview them separately (see depth interviewing techniques, page 59) to capture their initial thoughts and insights on whether or not you have identified all issues to be discussed or if there are any areas you have left out.

It is also important to ask the panel members for their best-case and worst-case scenario. This is not the same as including them in a full blown scenario program (as outlined on pages 153–69), but a way of tapping into their valuable, if wholly subjective, insights of how the future will pan out vis-à-vis the area under review, based on the evidence you have collected so far. It is essential that you record the panel's comments, and make sure you flag up any themes coming through, or any ideas that you may have missed out on.

__QUANTITATIVE SURVEYS
When you have fully researched all issues surrounding your initial question and established a clear line on the subject you are investigating – for example, the rise of the organic food movement, the decline of bling – it is time to move to the quantitative stage of the process. At this point you are trying to ascertain the following significant facts relating to the group of people involved in the trend:

__the size of the group affected by this new or emerging trend you have identified, as a proportion of the bigger population (for example, are they part of the Innovator group, Early Adopter group, Early Majority, Late Majority, etc?)
__the relative ages of these people in relation to their adoption of the trend
__the percentage of male to female members within the group
__the income of the people in the group
__the region/town/city in which members of the group live
__the ethnicity and/or sexual orientation of the group
__social/political/ethical views that might influence any or all of the above

Techniques: Successful question framing

When carrying out a quantitative survey it is important to ask your questions in a way that elicits the best results and to do this you need to phrase them in a particular way.

01: Questions that require a simple "yes" or "no" response, for example, should be avoided. Instead, create questions that require the respondent to choose an answer from a menu of suggestions that range from one to ten: one being your base (or default) choice and ten being your most extreme one.

02: It is always better to ask questions that require respondents to supply you with a first person statement which offers up a more emotional and subjective response. For example: "Which of the following statements do you MOST agree with?" – followed by a range of answers written as quotes or personal statements such as:
(a) I eat organic food because it is healthy
(b) I eat organic food because it is fashionable
(c) I dislike organic food

03: Once the overall responses for the above have been tabulated and averaged out, you will be able to say that 35 percent of consumers eat organic food because it is healthy, 25 percent because it is fashionable, and so on.

04: Because of the way surveys are created, most of them allow you to compare answers from different age groups, income levels, regions, and cities. This means you can create a very in-depth snapshot of respondents as well as how each region, income group, or socio-demographic type feels about a particular subject or area of concern. It is therefore possible to draw up a league table of which social types eat more organic food, drink more alcohol, or buy more designer goods than another, and so on.

05: Instead of asking questions, some survey systems allow you to post a series of images – ten different types of house, car, interior, or items of clothing – and then to ask people how they rate. This system allows you to define a group's taste in cars, clothes, or interiors, as well as allowing you to better understand their hierarchies of aesthetic choices in relation to their income, social values, regional or global spread. Increasingly, systems like this are used by design, interiors, and retail researchers to better understand current and emerging trends in mainstream consumer tastes and potential purchasing habits.

06: Quantitative surveys carried out over time – some organizations do this daily – can help determine if a trend for organic food, red wine, or carbonated water is on the rise or wane, and if you plot this on an X/Y axis, it is possible to determine if the trend overall is set to rise substantially or decline. By this means, a good forecaster can more accurately validate their predictions about a market or sector.

07: Other ways of asking questions allow you to create a series of typologies (that is a consumer who embodies the characteristics typical of a particular group of people). For example, this can be done by asking respondents to determine which of the following statements most resembles their attitude and outlook on a particular subject. Food-wise you might offer up the following statements:
(a) I choose my ingredients carefully. I am always concerned about traceability, provenance, the fact that I only eat seasonal and locally-produced products.
(b) Food is about fuel, energy. So I am keen to eat things that boost my system, keep me going.
(c) I will try anything once. And the more obscure and rare the better. Food is about being global, and about tempting and tantalizing the palate.

08: Unseen by the respondent, you can also "embed" a typology next to the above statements. So for the first statement, you might refer to people who click on this as "New Authentics," those who opt for the second statement as "Food Faddists" (because they are keen on foods that are fashionable), and so on.

09: Quantitative surveys have their flaws! Because they tend to poll "average" households in "average" areas in "average" parts of a country, they often return average data with average views. This is fine if you are merely concerned with mainstream consumer tastes. But if you wish to know what Innovators and Early Adopters are doing, then your quantitative survey should be canvassing households from these groups. Most people only know what they know, and what most of us know depends largely on what is written about, or publicized by, the sectors of the media to which we tune in. So, to find out what Innovators think, you need to make sure you survey only Innovators.

· If this seems difficult, it isn't. You will work with polling or quantitative survey organizations to determine all these points, and these questions can be set as standard options which all people taking part in the survey have to answer before proceeding to the next question. Organizations already offering these services include Mori, Mintel, YouGov, Harris Research, Pew Global, Millward Brown, and Carot. It is worth visiting their website homepages in order better to understand the range of survey services on offer. In terms of the number of people you will need to participate in your survey, this will depend on the size of the country you live in: 1,000 is a minimum standard requirement for most clients within European Union countries (although some take this up to 5,000), but in the United States, where the population is rising to 308 million, this can increase to 10,000 or more depending on the level of response required.

You should always exclude participants from the survey who are not actually part of the focus population, and whose answers might therefore taint the survey results. For example, a survey about how people like meat to look, feel, taste, and be packaged will be skewed if vegetarians are part of the polling process. In this instance, an opening question – sometimes called a "screener" or "trick" question – is built in which asks:

Which of the following types of meat do you like?
(a) beef
(b) lamb
(c) pork
(d) venison
(e) I do not eat meat

If (e) is selected, then the potential participant is thanked and asked to leave the survey. Such screener questions, therefore, need to be decided upfront and asked in a way that allows no room for the respondent to "guess" which answer is the right one in order that he or she can proceed to the next question. Planning questionnaires like this becomes an art form forecasters have to learn at an early stage.

With all questionnaires it is important to test and validate the following in relation to the respondents:

__where they sit socially, ethically, culturally, morally, etc., in relation to the issue under review
__their level of knowledge on said issues
__their level of ignorance or "knowledge gaps" on said issues
__the prejudices they might harbor
__their preconceptions
__the gap that exists in thinking between them and your experts
__the typology they nominally fall into – the words and phrases they use to classify themselves

Once you have captured this data, you can use it to determine the overall number of, for example, what has been qualified as "Zeno Youth" (keen on everything) as a percentage of the total demographic of the country you are profiling. You can also divide the overall table up in such a way that it allows you to see how "Zeno Youth" responded to other questions in the survey. This in turn allows you to flesh out your typologies and to develop a richer and more in-depth and useful data-profile of each of the typologies you have identified (as shown on page 130).

The survey will also provide you with those "knowledge gaps" you have been attempting to identify, especially if you ask two to three questions toward the end of the survey that require respondents to gaze into the future and tell you which of the following they believe will happen over a suggested time frame. These questions are usually based on the initial conversations you have had with your panel of experts and are designed to gauge the gap between consumer thinking and how your experts are looking at the market.

As well as establishing gaps in overall thinking, if carried out properly surveys will also allow you to identify the percentage size of your Innovators, Early Adopters, Early Majority, Late Majority, and Laggards. If, for example, the prevailing mood among consumers is "pro-organic," positive toward notions of "natural" or in favor of "free range foods," and your survey identifies a small but significant minority that are keen on GM foodstuffs, you can, if your survey is food related, categorize these as your Innovators, while those that say they are open to trying GM products can be categorized as Early Adopters.

Quantitative surveys can also alert you to the fact that a trend is on the move – moving from being a minority concern to becoming a majority issue. Once you have carried out your survey it is important to identify and to summarize its key findings – known as "topline findings" – and then to send these to your expert panel about a week before you interview them again to allow them time to digest all areas under review.

Your topline findings should be arranged into the initial trends that have started to emerge – a noted shift away from the majority of people consuming convenience food, a higher percentage of people who are keen on "healthy options," etc. You should also flag up any anomalies you would like your panel to comment on. Perhaps you have noted that a small but significant percentage of people in urban areas are now growing their own vegetables. This, with input from your expert panel, could indicate a new and more important trend: one not just for eating organic food but for the rise of urban farming, the return in popularity of community gardens, organic food consumption as an increasingly female activity, and the rise of a new generation of health conscious teenagers.

Once your panel has been presented with your topline findings you should interview each member again independently noting his or her comments. In each case you should ask to discuss the implications of the survey findings in relation to the initial question being investigated. Your experts should also be asked to comment on any of the anomalies you have flagged up.

All comments should be incorporated into a much larger document which combines your quantitative survey findings and desk research with expert quotes in a way that adds significant layers of additional knowledge, insight, and forward projection to your growing snapshot of the trend.

Fieldwork can involve visiting a bespoke retail store, an experimental office, hotels, even niche beauty and fragrance outlets to look at how their layouts can be used by more mainstream retailers to maximize customer interaction, encourage footfall, and stimulate sales. Inevitably what is found on the fringes of culture ends up influencing less risk-averse stores in more diluted formats.

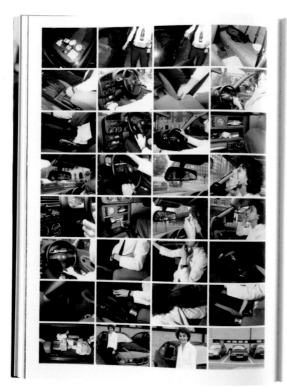

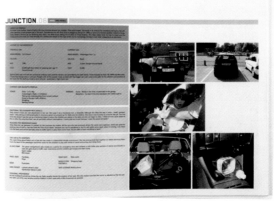

Observational work can take many forms: as a detailed study (top) of how a driver responds to turning in a hard-to-navigate situation, or a portrait-style look at how another uses her car as a "third space," a place in which to work, drive, and rest (bottom). Both projects were carried out by The Future Laboratory for BMW.

> THE OBSERVATION STAGE

Quantitative and qualitative in nature, the interrogation process is at all times about interrogating people, experts, or data tables to determine the significance of a new trend on the rise, or the size and scope of its eventual impact on the mainstream. But interrogation of this kind only reveals part of the picture: for a trend forecaster it is important to go behind the percentages and to see, feel, touch, smell, and braille the trends firsthand by mixing with the Innovators or key typologies in a way that allows a forecaster to minutely observe the lifestyle of these groups, and to use these observations to gauge how this lifestyle in turn is set to impact on other groups – a process known as "ethnographic mapping."

__ETHNOGRAPHIC MAPPING

"Ethnography," which roughly translates from the Greek as "folk writing," is a process used by anthropologists to carefully and sequentially map the behavioral activities of an individual or a group with a view to better understanding their motivations. In its more commercial form it is a method increasingly used by forecasters (sometimes known as "ethnographic forecasters") to help them unlock the behavioral attitudes of the Innovator or the Early Adopter, with a view to mapping how the rest of the groups will behave tomorrow. To do it, a forecaster may work with a photographer or an ethnographic video maker who is trained to carefully observe and track a person's behavior in situations that directly relate to the trend under investigation: for example, how teenagers shop.

Through his observational work within retail environments, Paco Underhill,[5] has become one of the foremost authorities in this area. Underhill, who runs Envirosell (a consumer insight and ethnographic forecasting agency based in New York), uses video, store walk-throughs, and customer movement mapping techniques (printouts of a store plan on which a customer's movements and activities through the store are completely and methodically recorded) to help him and his team of retail ethnographers coin phrases and unpack insights that have now become the retail ethnographic buzzwords used by forecasters everywhere. These include phrases such as:

__"clustering" – when stores with the same lifestyle aspiration are grouped together in a mall or on a street they attract people with similar value sets and thus drive up the overall pricing potential of the stores in that cluster
__"human parking lots" – the idea that if comfortable benches and chairs are placed near a store targeting women, the footfall in the store will increase because their partners, usually men, now have a place to "park" themselves while the women (less stressed now) can get on with the shopping
__"the sunlight effect" – the idea that department stores with natural sunlight can demand higher prices from their shoppers than those with artificial lighting, because customers feel better, more vital, and alive when encountering natural daylight

The point Underhill makes, however, about these discoveries is that if you asked shoppers what they were doing – as in "clustering," or being attracted to

and revitalized by natural light – they wouldn't be able to tell you. In other words, their activities must be observed to be defined and understood.

The same principle applies to the process of trend identification and monitoring. People are invariably better at showing trends to others then they are at describing them. Consider how we tell the time for instance. Ask somebody over fifty the time and he or she will consult a wristwatch. Ask somebody under twenty-five and he or she will consult a cell phone. In essence then, the invention of the cell phone, a tool for communication, has altered our relationship with the tools we use to tell the time. It has also altered the universal gesture we use to ask for the time if we are in a different country and do not speak the language. In the past a Parisian businesswoman in London would simply have to raise her right or left hand and point to her wrist, and the gesture would be understood. Now, especially when asking a teenager, this is no longer the case. A person has to try one of a number of options, most of them involving a cell phone rather than a wristwatch. By recognizing and observing these changes in how we do things, cell phone manufacturers and watch brands, for example, can see new pathways of opportunity: a watch like the Cellwatch M500 wristwatch phone (which looks pretty much like a standard Swiss style watch with leather strap but offers Bluetooth, video playback, and GPS access) or a cell phone with a vintage Swiss watch face display have proved hugely popular.

You can carry out ethnographic studies in a number of ways:

__by identifying a "typology" you are keen to shadow or track
__by asking your target group to keep diaries or activity logs that capture a sense of their day in relation to the area or subject under review
__by asking your target group to record, photograph, or digitally capture (via their cell phones, the movie function on their cameras) key highlights of the activities you wish to observe
__by uploading diaries, visuals, texts, footage, etc., to a designated social networking site you have been granted access to

In all cases, you are trying to understand better what they do, how they do it, and what this means to the trend under review or to the question you are attempting to answer. Images should be studied and diaries analyzed for any insights that may suggest ways in which the mainstream are set to become influenced or infected by a trend.

At this point in the cultural triangulation process you will have completed:

__your desk research – background facts and statistics that contextualize your initial question or the focus of your initial research
__your panel interviews – done to supplement your desk research, but also to add a new layer of insight, direction, and context to your initial question
__your quantitative research – helps you to add context to your expert insights and to identify ways the potential trend may be impacting on the consumer
__the identification of your key typologies – this helps you to identify the core characteristics of consumer types vital to understanding the trend and to encouraging its spread

Techniques:
Undertaking photographic
case studies

Observational analysis of the typologies (see page 84) is often supplemented with a number of typology case studies which more artfully and visually unpack the lifestyle or key behavioral traits of the typological group you are honing in on. These case studies usually consist of a portrait of the people who represent the typology under review in the place, space, or zone most associated with the trend they are being profiled for. Case studies should also contain a number of other crucial and visually revealing elements:

01: Room sets – it is important to capture a sense of how the people live by photographing the main rooms within which they work, rest, play, and sleep: the living room/family room, the bedroom, the bathroom, the kitchen, etc. are an important focus of study and research.

02: Intimate spaces – case studies must contain detailed close-ups of those areas most related to the subject under review: details of bookshelves, DVD collections, magazine racks, etc., found in the main living or work rooms. Also include close-ups of food cupboards, fridges, kitchen work surfaces, wardrobes, and bedside tables – places where people tend to leave personal and revealing items out on display.

You should try to make these as ethnographic as possible. They should be as rich in detail as you can make them. But also make sure that you include studies of the people found in these places: their dress, their hairstyles, the accessories they carry, what they drink and eat. It is important that each picture is loaded with the kind of visual detail you can use later to create a thorough and multi-textured narrative of the typologies you may have to report back to clients. Remember that these pictures are not meant to be atmospheric or intriguing: they are meant to capture a true, accurate, and useful snapshot of the place, person, or activity you are profiling.

03: Technology/personal kit – increasingly we are defined by the technology we own or use, so most photographic case studies hone in on this. Objects can be photographed individually or collectively by laying them out on a bed or table. Brand names should always be visible.

04: Handbag/backpack contents – we have become a culture always on the move, and consequently carry a lot of what we value and require for comfort in a bag, backpack, handbag, or wallet. It is important to photograph the contents of all of these and to ask the owner to explain their significance and the emotional as well as commercial value they place on them.

05: Obscure objects of desire – there are objects and products we treasure and covet regardless of how much they are worth: an old teddy bear, a dog-eared book, a piece of coral, plastic flip-flops, pictures taken on a cell phone of a long-forgotten night out. It is important to capture these and to make sure you get the owners to tell you what makes them so meaningful.

06: The places and spaces they visit – the stores, bars, clubs, cafés, restaurants, and public spaces people visit can also tell you a lot about their tastes, values, outlooks, and how they would like other people to see them. It is important to photograph these places and to capture within these shots any details that may prove revealing about the typology.

07: Your case study should leave no issue untouched in its visual attempt to truthfully and accurately pin down the typology in terms of how they live. All visuals should be accompanied by clear, precise, and explanatory captions or with short, concise interview-style statements (see page 84) that explain what is being noted in the photographic essay (and why), and the insights it is offering you about the typology in question.

08: Some forecasters use still photography, while others will use the moving image made with handicams, cell phones, or digicams to enrich our understanding of a case study. All are equally valid. But remember that the same rules apply – all footage must contribute to a clear, precise, and accurate understanding of the subject under review. You are not testing your abilities as a documentary maker but rather your skills as a reporter, or ethnographer – accuracy comes before artistry, and truth before poetry.

09: Video diaries can also act as a valuable insight tool when assessing what people themselves think about as a group. They are easy to do and can be recorded on a cell phone, or on a PC- or Mac-mounted camera.

A customer typology should offer you a visually revealing, in-depth, and insightful snapshot of how a particular type of consumer lives, where they shop, the brands they buy, the rooms in their home they most frequently use, even the basic products they keep in their cupboards, beneath their sinks, or in their handbags.

139_CULTURAL TRIANGULATION

__interviews with your key typologies – these allow you to get beneath the numbers and to unpack the landscape of the people driving the trend you are attempting to identify

__photographic case studies of your key typologies – these help clients to see as well as understand what this group is about

> THE INTUITION STAGE

When all sections of the above are complete, it is time to write a first draft of the final report to be submitted to your client. But before this happens, there is a final layer of insight to be added by the forecaster – the "intuitive wrap" – an added layer of context, insight, opinion, and speculation derived from the forecaster's own extensive knowledge of the broader issues set to impact on consumer behavior.

__ADDING LAYERS OF INSIGHT

At this juncture, you should read through all your notes and interviews, and go through all of your quantitative data, typologies, typology interviews, and the assembled photographic evidence or visual diaries assembled by interviewees and ask the following:

__how does all of what you now know relate back to your original question or area of concern?

__how can you use what you now know to better inform your client in terms of what they need to understand about the present?

__how will all of these changes impact on your client's future prospects?

__are there aspects of your findings that haven't been factored in by your clients?

__if the answer is "yes," what are they, and how should they incorporate these changes into their current strategy?

__have you identified new revenue streams and, if so, what are they?

__have you identified new threats and, if so, what are they?

__based on your current knowledge, and on what you know about your client, have they all the necessary tools, resources, and facilities to cope with the changes they need to cope with?

__if not, can you alert them to this?

As you sift through all the evidence you should, as we have learned in Chapter 3, use your wider knowledge of the culture to better interpret the facts, statistics, comments, and opinions you have collected (your historic awareness), but doing so with a strong presence of mind that requires you to test what's new and next, quantitatively and qualitatively. To do this, you need to suspend your everyday sense of logic and try to identify the hidden forces that drive people to do what they do and, more incredibly, to buy into trends that on face value may seem illogical, dangerous, silly, or puzzling. The ability to do this plays an important part in the final writing up and tabulating of a trend.

Paul Griffiths' visual portrait

In this pen and photo portrait, forecaster and writer Sarah Bentley has collaborated with photographer Giles Price to "describe" UK Internet entrepreneur Paul Griffiths. Note how Bentley balances the use of first person quotes with biographical details supplied to her by Griffiths. "I wear my sunglasses at night. I am constantly on my BlackBerry. I party until I collapse."

It was with such tongue-in-cheek comments on a MySpace profile that the ultimate Slash Slasher was born. In less than a year, Paul Griffiths became an Internet phenomenon. Since March

2007, his Babycakes T-shirt line has sold 15,000 units (that's US$230k revenue); under the Club Kids moniker he runs a hugely successful club promotions company. He receives up to 2,000 MySpace friend requests a day, runs a successful photographic studio, and employs a staff of five, including his mum. "The business runs itself now," he says. "I delegate as much work as possible, but I'm still working all the time."

Babycakes design is based on a series of star-shaped cartoon creatures, including PlushieCakes, KyleCakes, and MeanieCakes, but the center of the brand's success is Griffiths' own image and personality. He models the

Babycakes range himself and uploads blog posts, film footage from the Babycakes office, and personal pictures onto the brand's MySpace page. "The blog's had 1.2m hits," he marvels. "It's ridiculous – there's not much on it."

He aims to make Babycakes "as big as Hello Kitty – in every shop, known by everyone." And he has no qualms admitting he is driven by the desire to get "Richard Branson-style rich." There is no such thing as a work/life balance for Slash Slasher kids, says Bentley commenting on Griffiths' overall ethos: "their life is their work and their work is their life."

> WRITING UP YOUR REPORT

The writing up of your final report can be a complex affair as there are many different layers, comments, quotes, and opinions that need to be incorporated into the final document. The following approach will help you to unpack your findings in a logical, sequential, and insightful way.

__INTRODUCTION

Always open your report with an introduction that outlines the overall aims and objectives of the research document and the key question originally posed by your client. It is important that you do this as a client may forget the specifics of the original question or brief. It is also important to outline your research methodology – the quantitative, observational, and qualitative aspects if applicable – and to highlight all the experts you interviewed, and all key sources quoted if these are not apparent in the subsequent text.

By listing your panel of experts, along with their relevant credentials, you are adding an early and vital element of reassurance for those clients who can sometimes be sceptical about the forecasting process and who are made more comfortable when they see a list of names that number among them their peers, respected colleagues, competitors, academics, authors, and market analysts they hold in high esteem.

__EXECUTIVE SUMMARY

You should always follow your introduction with an executive summary of the report's overall findings. This should be short, succinct, and stand alone as a document which can be read by parties who need to absorb the essential facts and insights of the report without wading through all of the proofs.

__REPORT DRIVERS

Following the executive summary, the report should open with a "drivers" section that once more states the question being asked upfront and then unpacks the key social, cultural, economical, and environmental drivers that are likely to impact on the outcome of the question being asked. Here, wherever possible, it is important to validate claims, or gauge the impact of said drivers, by using quotes, comments, and insights gleaned from your expert panel. This is also the section within which most of the statistics gleaned from your quantitative survey will be deployed. These can be used to do two important things: to underpin and validate claims being made by your experts and to show the gap between your expert thinking and that of mainstream consumers.

__TRENDS SECTION

Once you have identified your drivers, it is important to articulate the trends that have been ushered in on their coattails – the rise of authenticity, of organic foodstuffs, of user-generated content and social networking. Trends are the by-products of the drivers and how they interact, respond to, or indeed work against changes that are abroad in the culture. In response to any question, there can be any number of trends or counter trends and it is again important that you annotate all of these in an articulate and comprehensive manner.

Jammer's visual portrait

In this photographic and textural portrait of Jammer, the photographer Giles Price and forecaster and writer Sarah Bentley have perfectly captured the essence of his character, via words and visuals. Says Bentley, "Jammer is a one-man grime brand who has reached top boy status. He is a DJ, producer, engineer, record label CEO, MC, and merchandiser with his Are You Dumb line of T-shirts, hats, hoodies, jackets, and underwear."

Jammer has been working on music "seriously" since he was eighteen and for the last four years has been renowned and respected as one of the leading lights of the grime scene. He compares the feeling of a crowd finishing his lyrics when he's performing to being "like a drug," yet would never leave production and managing a label to focus solely on being an artist.

"I'm a one-man army. It's only now, after eight years in the game, I've got a few people helping me out with stuff. I like doing everything myself. It can get a bit intense at times, juggling studio, performances, meetings about merchandise, managing my diary, and what-not, but I love it. If it was all taken off me, I'd miss it."

Jammer regards his Apple Mac G4 as the key to his operations, with his Samsung D950 phone, MySpace, and YouSendIt accounts next in line. "YouSendIt's a godsend for musicians – no more waiting on CDs." Jammer's aim is to build and run his own "empire," and get his record label to such a healthy position he won't need to sign over to the majors the young talent he finds and nurtures. He believes his success is down to hard work and "not relying on other people – financially, equipment-wise, skill-wise – to get anything done." The fact that he is well known outside grime circles is down to "presence," he says. "When I'm in a room, you know it. But at the same time, I'm not an asshole."

For typology and fieldwork, portraits speak volumes about a person's tastes, attitudes, and aspirational needs. Here, three very different people within the same attitudinal demographic, demonstrate just how aesthically and socially different their lifestyles are. Shown are Liz Hancock and family, Tim Guthrie, and Rachel Rae. Photographs by Emma Hardy.

__TYPOLOGIES

When you have outlined the drivers and the trends, with the help of your quantitative findings and any ethnographic work or fieldwork you have carried out, it is then important to identify and unpack the key consumer typologies that may be associated with these trends and the changes they may be ushering in. Details about a typology can be built up from field research, consumer interviews, and from the facts and statistics gleaned from your quantitative study. In all cases, however, it is important that the study of your typology offers your client a fully fleshed-out picture of the group's emotional and attitudinal state, as well as capturing details of their tastes, the environment within which they live, how and where they socialize, what they eat and wear, and the major pieces of technology they own.

__CONCLUSIONS AND RECOMMENDATIONS

Once you have completed all of the above sections, you now need to look at what they mean to your client and to the question that was asked at the beginning of the project. This is a vital and must-do final step, but it is invariably one that many forecasters forget about. In many cases this is what your client is paying for: what the research means, how it is set to affect their current and future strategy, what opportunities it contains, how they can and should move forward, etc.

This is only the first draft of your report. To ensure that it is watertight, and that all questions have been answered, it is important that you revisit all sections to make sure that:

__all figures and statistics used are correct
__all references and quotes have been cross-checked for accuracy, spelling, etc.
__approvals have been sought for all copyrighted materials being used
__all sources and academic references are accurate and attributed
__all visual material has been cleared of copyright issues for use and publication in your report
__all expert names, job titles, and academic qualifications are correct and that you have secured all the necessary permissions to use quotes within the context of the report
__the titles of all books, academic reports, articles, and cited journals are included (including names of authors and editors, place of publication, publisher, date, volume, and page numbers)

Only when these issues have been ironed out, should you begin your final draft, a process that involves repeating all of the above stages.

> SUMMARY

Cultural triangulation, as we have seen, is a methodology that involves using more specific and, in some cases, more intense versions of the skills and processes – interrogation, observation, and intuition – covered in previous chapters. It is a good overall approach to use if a client requires more tangible proofs that your predictions are worth considering.

The first stage of the process is to gather as much information as possible from your client and then to contextualize your subject or opening question through desk research and interviewing an expert panel. To make the qualitative aspects of your work more robust, a quantitative stage is now added to provide you with the necessary data a more corporate client may require. As we have seen, quantitative surveys are an effective way of doing this as they provide the percentage breakdowns of a trend's impact, as well as insights into the current and potential behavior of consumers. For the forecaster to fully understand who these people are, it is important to capture and frame them visually through ethnographic mapping, and to use those visual portraits to unpack the spiritual, emotional, textural, and more personal and intimate aspects of their lives. Only when you have been through these processes can you start to record your findings and write and tabulate them in a way that is strategic, but also quantifiable and measurable.

There are, however, limitations to the cultural triangulation process. Because quantitative surveys require you to ask very particular questions, they can sometimes prevent you from harvesting more complex and insightful responses from the consumers. Likewise, because you are interviewing a large body of "average" people to establish how they sit in relation to new and emerging ideas being fed to them by Innovators and Early Adopters, you are potentially missing out on less visible, but more profitable, trends that are set to impact on the culture long-term. Scenario planning, a qualitative process that uses strategic and measured approaches to imagine the future in tangible yet multiple ways, can allow you to do this and is explored in the following chapter.

Chapter Six
Scenario Planning

> THE ORIGINS OF SCENARIO PLANNING
> SCENARIO PLANNING STAGES
> SUMMARY

"BAD INNOVATION in the name of protection" is a bulletproof glass, camouflage, and painted steel artwork by Kristof Kintera that knowingly comments on the growing trend for bulletproof cars, tinted windshields, and accessorized "body guards" that are becoming familiar sights in our cities as "blingtastic" celebrities and their offspring become the target of kidnappers on the one hand, and a growing band of consumers who are falling out of love with their hitherto celebrated lifestyle excesses on the other.

"The future is not written, rather it remains open. The future is multiple, undetermined and open to a large variety of possibilities. That which will happen tomorrow depends less on prevailing trends or any sort of fatalistic determinism, and more on the actions of groups and individuals in the face of these trends."

Professor Michel Godet, Laboratory of Innovation, Strategic Foresight and Organization (LIPSOR)[1]

IF TREND FORECASTING is about identifying the new and the next, scenario planning is about anticipating how the new and the next might impact on the way we live tomorrow. "Might" is the operative word here: for scenario planning is all about what "might" happen, rather than what will happen. Scenario planners, as the opening quote suggests, accept that there are many futures, and that the best way to anticipate these futures is to envisage all of them in as much detail as possible.

So, while a trend forecaster may use his or her skills to identify the rise of a new sense of austerity within consumer buying patterns, a scenario planner will carefully map out how this shift is likely to change the social, cultural, ethical, and environmental framework of people's lives on a day-to-day basis. In this sense, scenario planners have much in common with intuitive forecasters. Both draw heavily on their intuition, sense of historic awareness, presence of mind,

Callebaut's "Lilypad"

The "Lilypad" is a "floating Ecopolis for
Climate Refugees," created by architect
Vincent Callebaut, to address the
ongoing issues of climate change, and
how we might address it in a way that is
both practical, but also beautiful,
imaginative, and dreamlike.

Callebaut's project, slated to be built
off the coast of Monaco, is one of a
growing number of so-called
"dreamtelligent" projects that have been
mooted around the world as scenario
planners, architects, designers, materials
specialists, and imagineers work with
more traditional property developers to

scenario-plan buildings, or to create
climate-change solutions that are long-
term and far reaching in their vision.

This process, which uses scenario
planning at its heart, is designed to force
traditional brands, businesses, and
corporations to "think the unthinkable"
when problem solving, and to consider
ways and means of doing this that
deliberately test, challenge, and
confound accepted practices in how we
broker solutions or tackle problems in
the first place.

While much of this thinking is now
being applied to climate change and
sustainability, it is also becoming more
prevalent in business as consumers

themselves, once happy to purchase
"average" products from "average"
companies, become more irrational,
adventurous, and imaginative in the
demands they now place on the brands
with which they do business. Scenario
planning, and "what if" approaches to
problem solving are just some of ways
brands can stay on top of their game.
But they are also working with futures
panels, visualizers, and storytellers to
formulate what these possible futures
might look like. Using this approach, a
brief is set by the forecaster, a narrative
developed by the storyteller, while the
visualizers will work with both to create
the world that has been described.

"What if" is a very good way to start any simple scenario exercise: "what if we needed to utilize the space a dam takes up by turning it into a hotel, like the Songjiang Hotel, Shanghai (top); what if we wanted to re-use the dead areas around a former mine or oil well (middle), or develop a hotel like the Bird Island project, Kuala Lumpur (second from top and bottom), with an eco-footprint that rested lightly on the landscape. Here Atkins Design Studio, visualizers dbox, and Graft have done just that.

and ability to suspend logic as a way of envisioning future possible scenarios. Scenario planners, however, also utilize a range of quantitative tools and envisioning techniques developed by corporate, social, and military planners since the 1950s and these add an extra and vital layer of strategic and analytical underpinning to their work.

> THE ORIGINS OF SCENARIO PLANNING

A key scenario planner from the 1950s was Herman Kahn, a member of the RAND Corporation, a United States government body that specialized in strategic military research and development (hence RAND). In the 1950s, the United States military was seriously considering the idea that all-out nuclear war was the only response to any imminent threat from the Soviet Union, a country whose expanding military ambitions they feared. They believed that America could emerge as the overall victor from such a war, as devastating as it would be. In Kahn's policy work, and in his subsequent book *On Thermonuclear War*,[2] Kahn explored this idea in-depth and reasoned out an alternative, but far more devastating, outcome or "scenario" as he called it. The world he envisioned would not be a happy or simplistic one, but one where the many separate scenarios considered by strategists at the time – nuclear fallout, radiation sickness, food shortages, food riots, radiation storms, a breakdown in civic order, mass emigration to safe zones or regions, etc. – would be synthesized into a single overall "doomsday scenario" as frightening as it was potentially accurate. Kahn's book courted instant controversy, but the methodology he used to underpin his reasoning has now become the backbone for scenario planning strategy today.

At its heart, Kahn's book promoted the idea that the consequences of our actions should not be considered or imagined in isolation, but in concert with those bigger social, cultural, ethical, civic, political, and environmental factors that influence our lives –whether we admit to them or not. He also understood that the choices we make are highly dependent, interdependent, and influenced by the choices made by other people. Finally, and perhaps more relevantly to the way scenario planning needs to be conducted today, he asked his readers to do the one thing few of them were willing to do: to "think the unthinkable." In other words, to use their creative and imaginative abilities to add flesh, depth, and a new perspective to how the future could be. Kahn's ideas were further refined by pioneer strategy planners such as Peter Schwartz, Arie de Geus, Michel Godet, and the economist Pierre Wack, the latter of whom used them to predict a shift in the balance of power between the West and the oil-rich Arab states in the early 1970s.

___"BREATHING IN"
Pierre Wack, together with his Strategic Planning Team at Shell (which included de Geus and Schwartz in its ranks), engaged in a process he referred to as "breathing in" (his term for an activity now known as "cultural brailling") in which he researched everything that could be known about the attitude of the leaders of the Organization of the Petroleum Exporting Countries (OPEC)

to oil production at the time. He did this by taking into account the social, ethical, geopolitical, and religious mindsets that dominated their thinking. But he also analyzed the mindsets of the key organizations and political leaders in the West, creating emotional and intellectual profiles of them in a way that was unheard of at the time. More unusual still, he encouraged his team to empathize with the key players by each one "becoming" one of them – role playing in other words – so that they could fully understand and appreciate their motivations.

Wack then created six scenarios or "pathways" the future could take if certain factors – what he referred to as his "long-term drivers" – were taken into consideration. In Art Kleiner's book *The Age of Heretics* Wack's process is described as follows:

"The twenty-odd members of the scenario team spent much of 1972 plotting out the elements of six stories about the future, weighing them according to what would 'really make a difference.' They overlaid these scenarios with a 'triangle,' as they called it, of the most significant energy factors: the oil-producing countries of the Middle East, the oil-consuming countries of the West, and the oil companies. They picked the most promising combinations and then they role played them – taking the part of every significant player on the scene. What would the Shah of Iran do? How would Richard Nixon react? How about Qaddafi? And Exxon? As they played out the results, sometimes shouting at each other in character across the conference room table, they listened for contradictions."[3]

The results, when this process was complete, were staggering. Using the above approach, Wack and his team were able to predict the ensuing oil crisis in the mid 1970s and Shell, then ranked eighth in the world of oil production companies, was able to move to the number two position because of the insights it gained from the scenarios created about the changing marketplace.

If Kahn instilled scenario planning with a sense of drama, Wack brought to it a more articulate and transparent process. This was added to further by fellow Shell Strategic Planning Team member, Peter Schwartz. His work and book, *The Art of the Long View*,[4] artfully unpacks many of the stages now used by scenario planning teams today. According to Schwartz, these stages – nine in all – can be called on to anticipate the impact of anything from a new product arriving on the market to the election of a new president. Each stage is designed to add an extra factual, statistical, emotional, psychological, and intellectual layer to the process, so that the final scenarios are as textured and as complex as real life is when it pushes us toward a particular path or course of action.

If these nine stages are done well, you will find yourself with a set of key scenarios that are most likely to contain all of the elements which will impact on the overall success of a product launch or, if you are attempting to test the impact of a trend, all the issues that will affect how people accept or reject it. To reach this point, it is important to keep an open mind at all stages of the planning process. Scenario planning requires you to be imaginative, creative, and collaborative in your approach to asking questions and seeking out answers.

The European School and the American School of scenario planning

In the twentieth century, two schools of scenario planning emerged, one based on a methodology developed in the United States, and the other on work carried out by European scenario planners mainly located in France. Among the latter, Michel Godet, the director of LIPSOR, is perhaps one of the best known. Godet is also the planner most associated with the so-called "European School" (favored by Europe, but excluding the United Kingdom) of scenario planning or, as it is better known in France, *la prospective* ("foresight"). Godet describes *la prospective* as an "art" combined with "rigor and methods designed to enlighten our actions and direct us towards a desired future." Below are some key points which highlight further the differences between the two schools:

01: The American School places a stronger emphasis on keeping scenarios simple, strategic, and focused on clear and definable outcomes. It also places more emphasis on the power or impact of the individual on the scenario plan itself than the European School. This emphasis on how individuals (as opposed to institutions) can have a greater impact on the future also means that more time is spent on role playing within American School scenario planning exercises.

02: While both schools emphasize the need to research all social, ethical, and environmental drivers in a way that is rigorous and thorough, the American School allows these drivers to be framed by the opinions of individuals from a non-academic and populist (even controversial) background – with a view to capturing the dissenting voice or the minority opinion.

03: Intuition also plays a stronger and more vital part in the American School's way of working up a scenario plan. In part this has its roots in the fact that many scenario planners in the 1960s and early 1970s were avid supporters of the Beat and hippy movements, but also because scenario planning in itself, according to Michel Godet, became even more simplistic after the Vietnam War (1959–75). "The war created a deep mistrust of rational methods of system analysis. The Americans had failed in their efforts to analyze conflict scientifically so they threw the methods, like the proverbial baby, out with the bath water."

04: Because it has developed out of a more rigorous academic tradition, the European School tends to take a more scientific, structured, and, some would argue, bureaucratic approach to scenario planning. Godet insists, for example, that seventy or more drivers need to be considered if any plan is to be successful, while exponents of the American School recommend no more than ten to fifteen.

05: The European School also argues that before you ask the key question upfront it is important to first ask "who you are" and "why you are asking it." This approach, while adding a layer of philosophy and introspection to the proceedings, can also add a lot of time to the overall process of developing and implementing the plan. While a typical American School scenario plan can be completed within a month, Godet believes that a year to five years is an acceptable amount of time for a European School plan to be fully fleshed out and embedded into an organization or municipal structure.

06: The European School also uses a technique called "intellectual impertinence" which requires those taking part in the process to deliberately ask questions that "upset" regardless of the consequences. Intellectual impertinence, Godet believes, is about probing, challenging, and tackling drivers or threats, regardless of political incorrectness.

07: Finally, to cope with the sheer number of components within the European School's methodology, a series of analytical tools have also been developed by Godet and LIPSOR researchers some of which are summarized here:

__MICMAC (Impact Matrix Cross-Reference Multiplication Applied to a Classification) – which allows the high number of drivers these plans require to be identified and managed.

__MACTOR (Model Actor) – a software package that calculates the impact each role-playing member of a scenario planning team has on another.

__MORPHOL (short for "morphological analysis") – which is used to analyze all possible futures that can result.

__SMIC-PROB-EXPERT – a cross-impact probability program that is used to identify and isolate the most plausible scenarios.[5]

External drivers such as climate change, sustainability, and a growing need among consumers to immerse themselves in more exotic, experience-based holiday locations have led to the development of James Bond-style resorts such as Zira Island, Baku, Azerbaijan, by BIG (top and middle), and the Tree Top Villa in Cay, Turks and Caicos by Chad Oppenheim (bottom).

> SCENARIO PLANNING STAGES

__STAGE 1: DETERMINING THE QUESTION

As simple as it sounds, making sure that you are asking the right question at the outset is one of the most difficult parts of the scenario planning exercise. To be able to define the question is to know the subject, but this is exactly what many brands, businesses, and organizations concerned with the future fail to do.

The correct framing of the initial question is vital to the integrity and accuracy of the outcome of any particular scenario. The question then should be singular and clearly honed. To achieve this some planners follow a very straightforward "what if" approach. For example: "What if the temperature of the planet were to rise by one degree per century?" "What if one of our competitors were to create an engine that ran on electricity rather than petrol?" "What if consumers only bought products that were proven to be sustainable?" Questions like this keep your outputs focused and reflective of the question being asked.

Another frequently used method is the big opening statement followed by the "little" question that relates this statement back to how it impacts on what it is you are trying to anticipate about the future. For example: "The Planet is Dying" (the big statement) followed by "How does this affect my business's ability to sell stuff that is environmentally damaging" (the little question). The trick is to strip the big statement down to its most basic components – subject, object, concern – and to keep the question responding to it equally focused and strategic.

__STAGE 2: CONTEXTUALIZATION

Before you attempt to answer an agreed question, it is important to understand the context within which that question is being asked. Two factors govern this: internal drivers (forces) and their external counterparts. Internal drivers are those factors within an organization that require a question to be asked in the first place (for example, declining performance, slow response to competitor activities, a de-motivated workforce, inadequate budgets, poor leadership, etc.), while external ones are those broader cultural, social, environmental, and market forces that directly impact on, or indirectly create, those internal forces in the first place.

An initial probe of the key people involved in a scenario planning exercise – referred to as "stakeholders" because they own a "stake" or a "share" in the project being undertaken – will illicit details about the nature of the internal and external drivers involved as they see them. The leader of the scenario planning team will usually interview the stakeholders individually at the outset of the exercise, making careful notes or recording each interview as he or she goes along. The leader will probe the concerns of each stakeholder, discussing with him or her the nature of the question being asked, why it is being asked now, whether he or she thinks it is the right question, and, more importantly, if he or she thinks it is worth asking. The leader will also ask the stakeholders to list the external drivers, as they perceive them, which need to be considered in answering the initial question.

Radical economic and social shifts, such as the recent recession and a realization that our global resources are fast running out, can lead to scenario plans such as the fifth, or rogue, scenario, which poses the question: what if cataclysmic change became the norm? How would we cope? Could science save us, and genetic or robotic modification be used to make us faster, more efficient, and better human beings? Scenarios like this are designed to "think the unthinkable."

Ethical drivers can also influence trends in very particular ways, from the growth of door-to-door organic food companies like Abel & Cole, delivering to the home, to the rise of brands like Duskin's pure apple juice or fair-trade chocolate from mainstreet brands like Marks & Spencer in the UK.

At this point, the team leader is attempting to identify all internal issues that are relevant, including those that are likely to lead to conflict or confusion later on in the scenario planning process. These issues can be anything from stakeholders who are not keen on the process in the first place (and thus can become disruptive, prejudiced, or biased in their thinking), to a group of stakeholders who are not fully embracing the enormity of the internal, or for that matter the external, forces about to swamp them.

The team leader is also attempting to identify the external drivers which stakeholders deem to be most important, so that these can be compared to those people outside the business believe to be of relevance (see stage three). This ensures that the correct drivers impacting on the company's performance are being measured. To make sure you are identifying these drivers, list the ones that matter internally, getting people to rank them according to the most and least threatening, and then compare these to a list of external drivers as determined by the independent analysts, academics, and experts you interview at stage three.

__STAGE 3: EXTERNAL DRIVERS

If stage two is about establishing the context within which the initial "what if" question is being asked from an internal perspective, at stage three you are carrying out a very similar exercise, but doing it in a more systematic and objective way. At this point, expert input is usually required. Some organizations refer to this as their "star chamber," but in essence it is a panel of experts (see page 55) who have a thorough knowledge of the company or the sector under review, and an equally thorough understanding of the drivers that are most likely to impact on the outcome of the question being asked. Budget permitting, this star chamber may be on hand, or at least be available to be called on, at all stages of the exercise. They are always brought in at stage three and stage eight to validate, challenge, or to make further contributions to the scenario plan before it is finally agreed on by all stakeholders and written up. The size of a star chamber varies, and new members can be added at any time if, and when, issues arise that require third party explanation.

Depending on the nature of the question being asked, the research carried out at this stage will encompass many disciplines and sectors, but as a default requirement most organizations will carry out a thorough analysis of the following external drivers in relation to the question under review:

__Cultural: the prevailing climate toward issues and matters relating to leisure, lifestyle, and inner-directed activities or experiences that govern our sense of well-being, personal esteem, aspiration, and social position
__Economic: the prevailing climate in terms of market buoyancy, or how consumers sit economically in relation to changing market fortunes
__Civic: the prevailing social and civic mindset of the culture generally. Are people more or less disposed toward notions of civic engagement? Are they becoming more or less ethical or socially aware in their daily activities?
__Social: what is accepted socially among friends and associates and in the wider community. Is our sense of what is socially acceptable changing and, if so, how?

The underlying principle at Le Laboratoire in Paris, is for their thinkers and designers to dream and create the unthinkable in an atmosphere that encourages this process. Walls, rooms, even objects within them, are designed by Mathieu Lehanneur to stimulate debate, capture thoughts, and encourage visionary thinking.

__Political: the state of political involvement locally and globally. Are governments, for example, more legislation prone, increasingly right wing, left wing, concerned about health, equality or welfare issues, etc?

__Technological: the changes in technology by intention or by accident that might be imposing on a business. The Internet, for instance, was established as an academic and military router for vast lakes of data, yet now it permeates all aspects of our lifestyles from shopping and dating to how we consume, create, and distribute media

__Environmental: our changing attitudes and outlook to sustainability, a brand's carbon footprint, or how a product is sourced and developed within a problematic global framework

__Ethical: the prevailing stance people are taking on a range of civic, social, sexual, corporate, and moral issues that would suggest an overall shift toward a more judgemental, fair, indifferent, or concerned public

__Competitive: competitor activity and the new and emerging products or services they are planning to bring to market that might impact on the brand, product, or service being looked at

__Known unknowns: as irrational and contradictory as it sounds, there are always "known unknowns" (left-of-field innovations, discoveries, or changes in attitude) that you may not consider because they seem too wild or weird, but nevertheless should be considered for this very reason. For example the World Wide Web, the iPhone, the Nintendo Wii, and the Dyson vacuum cleaner were all considered too weird by the Late Majority and Laggards when first mooted.

For each external driver, it is important to establish a true and comprehensive picture of how people are feeling, and why they are feeling as they do. This is done by assembling all key facts, statistics, and market commentary that has been published about the sector you are focusing on in relation to your identified drivers. This is referred to as "desk research" because it is usually done online, or culled from existing documentation.

Armed with this research, you will collaborate with the project stakeholders to assemble an initial list of experts who will be asked to delve deeper into the default list of drivers and to refine them even further. Although these drivers are generic, once they have been judged in relation to the question being asked, and discussed and debated by the star chamber (who do this with the stakeholders), they take on a new relevance and meaning as some become more important than others and some change from being a general driver to one that is very significant or potentially more threatening than previously believed.

Much of this debate takes place in the scenario planning room, a room similar to the ideas dens and evidence walls looked at in Chapter 2 (see pages 47–49). This room needs to contain blackboards, whiteboards, pinboards, Post-its, Internet access, projectors, and break-out areas or tables where small teams can work together. It also needs paper, pens, notebooks, reference books, and a "base knowledge library" where all previously researched material is assembled, alongside the books, papers, reports, surveys, etc., put together by the scenario planning team.

__STAGE 4: RANKING AND RANGING

Having established your internal drivers and their external counterparts, it is now important to rank them all in order of relevance and immediacy, but also in terms of the levels of uncertainty they may introduce into the scenario planning process.

To get this right, and to keep things simple, it is always best to rank the most important or influential factors first – the ones that are most likely to affect the outcome of the question. This is done by assessing all drivers with the star chamber and the scenario planning team present, and talking them through until there is a majority agreement on how they should be ranked. Once drivers have been assessed and ranked, it is then important to test them against the initial question to make sure that the question being asked is in fact the right one. If it is not – and this can sometimes happen – do not hesitate to change it. After all, this is why you have asked your star chamber to take part in the scenario planning process in the first place: to ensure you are on the right track but also to identify any gaps in your knowledge that might detrimentally impact on your overall research.

As you rank and group the drivers, you will also notice a particular pattern or emphasis emerging. If, for example, civic, ethical, social, and political drivers rank more prominently this infers that issues impacting on the question are very much the concerns of people (as opposed to issues relating to the economy, market forces, or a competitor's activities). If this is the case, this must be factored in, or the question reframed. If, on the other hand, economic, competitive, and technological drivers are on top, you can probably infer that threats are mainly market-centric and competitor ones.

__STAGE 5: NAMING AND FRAMING

You are now at the pivotal point of the scenario planning process. Here you begin to flesh out the scenarios that are now starting to suggest themselves from the fog of data, evidence, drivers, and star chamber quotes appearing on the mapping room wall or the work areas around you. Up to this point you have assembled all kinds of empirical evidence and logged both an objective and subjective view of the world in relation to the opening question. Likewise you have listened to and used your star chamber to flesh out an understanding of the key issues under review and of the drivers that are likely to impact upon them.

From now on you are trying to reach a situation where the drivers are showing you a number of ways forward: a question perhaps that proceeds along a predominantly civic and social route; one that sees technology as a key and overriding threat; or one that is dominated by environmental questions. Once this ranking is complete – and the best way to do this is to draw up your final list of drivers as agreed by all parties and then call for a vote on the most and least important – you will find that you now have a list of drivers that are also suggesting a list of very clear themes: a civic and social theme, a technological theme, an environmental theme.

These themes provide you with the underpinning for five basic scenarios developed by planners since the 1950s. Each scenario is subtly different, but each has been designed to accommodate some overlap and also to move the

(text continues on page 163)

Case Study:
Carston Beck

FOR CARSTEN BECK of The Copenhagen Institute for Future Studies
(cifs.dk), scenario planning is not just about predicting "anticipated futures,"
but about creating awareness of the future by highlighting its importance to the
present. The Institute does this through its extensive scenario planning
programs, its future clubs (in which these scenarios are debated and
discussed), and via its magazine, newsletter, presentations, books, and members'
reports, many of which interrogate the world in a more cerebral and socio-
political context. For Beck's clients this is vitally important: unlike most
forecasters, who work predominantly with global brands, Beck and his team
also work with a growing number of public sector organizations who
increasingly use scenario planning as a way to map out "what if" social scenarios
on a national and global scale.

Beck refers to these as "megatrend scenarios" – that is, scenarios that embrace
"big themes, human-scale issues, concerns that are epic and philosophical in
scope." Recent work by the Institute has included large-scale scenarios on the
future of happiness, work, religion, and family life in 2017, along with more
notional and cerebral reports such as "Between Individualism and
Communities," which focuses on the growing tensions between the rights

Much of Carsten Beck's work is done by collaborating with other futurists and forecasting organizations internationally. As he puts it, "we are not trend forecasters in the traditional sense of the word — but rather we look at what is being predicted and then help our clients develop strategies to better cope with these changes." But to do this, he and his team produce a range of online tools, books, and their in-house magazine, *FO/futureorientation*, that more accurately unpacks the key issues being focused on by other forecasters.

The difference between "information" and "insight" is an important one, believes Beck. "Information allows you to assemble the present framework within which your scenario plan can be built, while insight allows you to take that framework forward into the future in a way that is meaningful and revealing. Information, in other words, equips you, while insight prepares you." This is why, in his opinion, it is important to have a very diverse group of experts working alongside your core team of planners — they need to reach out far, wide, and deep and make you aware of the world in ways you are perhaps incapable of seeing.

For Beck, when
producing a scenario
plan, it is vitally
important to strike a
balance between what
is rational and what
is possible. One is
not always the same as
the other, nor does
adhering to a rational
argument or hypothesis
always bring out the
best results in a
scenario plan.
Consumers are
irrational — driven
and dominated "by
emotion and needs and
desires that are not
always definable" — or
credible when
considered using
classical economic
theory. But if you
accept that behaviors
are irrational,
erratic, and governed
by emotion rather than
logic, then this can
be a better way of
fleshing out a
scenario involving
people. "We are, in
effect, defined by
what we feel, as much
as what we know and
believe to be true."

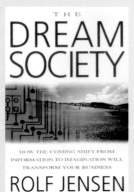

of the individual and the collective responsibilities we have and share as members of a local or global community.

"The crucial aspect about scenario planning," says Beck, "is to use it in a way that makes people consider new possibilities and routes to, and through, the future that previously they were not at all considering." To do this, Beck and his team use a method he refers to as "criss-cross scenarios," which propose four possible scenarios that include, as he puts it, the usual suspects: "One very good scenario, one tough one, and two in-between, where things are neither bad nor good, but complex and less black and white – companies tend to know that this is how the future will in reality shape up, but they are trained to see things in very linear and black and white ways (to suit the accountant in them) and thus shy away from these as potential paths, unless you usher them along it, in a meaningful and reassuring way."

Unlike most forecasting organizations, Beck and his team do not produce their own forecasts. Working with a range of forecasters, they synthesize all trends identified into a number of overarching "megatrends" (trends with a global impact) and look at how these will affect change within a particular sector, or area of public or business concern. They also work with a range of professionals – from sociology, political science, mathematics, technology, philosophy, ethnography, and economics, who in turn "work within interdisciplinary teams to ensure that there is a cross-fertilization of ideas, and that we approach the future with openness, intelligence, and a very lateral mindset."

All scenario work begins, says Beck, by interviewing key stakeholders, followed by desk research to identify the trends set to impact on the sector in question. Avoiding reports that are too text heavy, Beck and his team then engage stakeholders in a series of dialogues, designed to tease out the issues of concern, and the potential scenarios that will need to be followed. Expert witnesses are brought in to provide context and additional insights, while Beck and his team map out a framework for the scenarios that unfold as this happens. Role playing, Beck believes, is also a vital and important part of the scenario planning process.

A trained economist, Beck believes that scenario planning is vital to a company or a country's long-term health: "We have tended towards the short-term for the past decade, with short sighted CEOs and short-term business plans, but now with the future being so uncertain, and the Internet changing everything from how we trade to how we assess breaking news events, the only constant thing we have in our arsenal is our ability to envision, and to imagine that which has not yet happened. Thus, the one tool that nature has equipped us with becomes increasingly important. Scenario planning gives us a framework within which to allow our imaginations freedom to roam, yet to come back with insights that are unique, useful, and actionable."

collective work of scenario planners and stakeholders along in a way that allows them to envision most eventualities. As Carsten Beck explains: "When working with scenarios we are not talking about actual futures, but about potential ones. Ways the world may change as a consequence of other seen or unseen forces that may push a brand or business along a route hitherto unimagined, or indeed unwelcome."[6]

The five basic scenario frameworks used to do this are as follows:

__Scenario A: is the "base case proposition" – a scenario that suggests that the future, with minor variations, will be more or less the same as the present
__Scenario B: is the "best case proposition" – a scenario that suggests a future that will get better and brighter if all current drivers continue along the direction they are going, and all variables are taken into account
__Scenario C: is the "worst case scenario" – one that suggests things will get worse in terms of competitor activity, but also with regard to all social, cultural, economic, and civic drivers, etc.
__Scenario D: is the "cross case scenario" – a scenario model that accepts things are never black or white, but mercurial and less pure
__Scenario E: is the "rogue scenario" – a scenario model that requires you to "think the unthinkable" and which challenges all participants to be lateral, imaginative, and progressively whole-brain in their thinking and insights

At this point you should also be naming your scenarios, so that each one develops a distinct personality. Using ideas suggested by your drivers, and by your original question, your titles should be clear but compelling. For example, for a scenario dominated by civic, social, and ethical themes try a name like "The New Moral Order"; for one dominated by technology and the Internet "The Silicon Cascade"; for one governed by environmental themes "The Eco-Wars." Titles need to be memorable, but they also need to be short – there will be five to remember, debate, and hold in mind at any given time.

__STAGE 6: LOGIC AND NARRATIVE
When mapping out these scenarios it is vital to ensure that each one contains its own internal logic, rationale, and narrative that seems real and true. While scenarios are possible future realities, in each case they need to be constructed as if they are real. In this way, they are like good works of fiction: while the story itself may seem fantastical – J.K. Rowling's *Harry Potter* books (about teen wizards and witches), Stephanie Meyer's *Twilight* (about teen vampires) – the logic and texture of the worlds created within them are entirely real and believable. The scenarios should, therefore, be written up to resemble the plot of a good film, book, or television series. To focus your mind, it is best to block out each scenario as follows:

__Question: for example, "What if I am a newspaper editor and my readers start reading all their news coverage for free online?"
__Scenario title: for example, "The Digital Threat" [Scenario C – the worst case scenario]
__Scenario synopsis: based on the key drivers that dominate this particular

To test a concept
on consumers, some
scenarios need to
be fully visualized.
Here dbox, a multi-
disciplinary brand,
visualization, and
design consultancy
in New York, create
a series of futuristic
holiday and leisure
scenarios based on a
brief that asked them
to consider themes and
trends such as zero-
impact resorts,
underwater vacations,
the return and rise
of the airship,
and the idea that in
the near future pods
could be dropped into
remote travel spots,
and later removed
without leaving
a trace.

scenario: for example, for "The Digital Threat" these might be wireless broadband, 3G, touch screen navigation, free content, readers who no longer see newspapers as the most convenient way to consume news, the rise of e-readers, e-ink, and e-newspapers.

___Full scenario narrative: here you map out a fuller picture of your worst case scenario as outlined above, using as much data and statistics, and as many expert quotes and analyses to create a scenario that is credible, believable, and rich in detail and scope. The full scenario narrative can be done as a series of written bullet points, but it is also recommended that you write the scenario up as a fully fledged "story" that describes this future in some depth.

Scenario planning at this stage of the proceedings should, and usually does, involve a lot of acting out or role playing. Each scene should be played out as a drama, and each member of the team should assume a role or a point of view which they must articulate, defend, argue over, and so on. Doing this will help you to flesh out the scenario. Such role playing will also help you to understand and empathize with your competitor or the people behind the supposed threats to your business. The more you do this, the richer the full blown scenario narrative becomes.

You need to follow the above process with each scenario type until you have pinned down and written up all five scenarios in a thorough and comprehensive manner. The time taken for the scenario planning process up to the point of a fully annotated scenario document does vary, but can be completed within the following time frames:

___one week with your key stakeholders to determine the internal drivers
___one week with your star chamber to assess the internal drivers against the external ones as they see them
___one week carrying out desk research to underpin all drivers and issues raised by stakeholders and the star chamber
___two days to meet in the scenario planning room with the star chamber and stakeholders to agree on the final drivers and to begin the scenario planning write-up process
___a minimum of five days to work up each of the scenarios to a point where they are credible and usable for the remainder of the scenario process (done with your key stakeholders and, where required, relevant members of your star chamber)
___one week to ten days writing up the scenario plan into a final, fully annotated document

___STAGE 7: DISTILLATION AND DIALOGUE
When all five scenarios are complete, you need to revisit them again from the beginning, carefully combing through them for ideas that they may now share in common. For example, are some of their themes similar? Could you fold one into the other to create four master scenarios rather than five? Could you reduce these four even further? For scenario planners the ideal number of scenarios to work with tends to be three. Experience suggests that this is the number most people can manage over a sustained period of time without losing

Techniques: Successful role playing

Role playing is one of the most engaging and immersive components in scenario planning and allows you to utilize the facts and statistics collated at the desk research stage in a way that brings them to life. It is done to help you better understand, assess, and anticipate a competitor's actions and their underlying motivations. Role playing requires imagination, the ability to be creative, flexible, responsive, and empathic. If executed correctly, it also develops a player's ability to listen, learn, and adapt quickly.

Role playing is not just about playing a character or "becoming" another person; it is also about becoming anything that encourages and helps you to better understand the underlying drivers of change. A player then may decide that it is important for them to "become" the latest cell phone handset in order to appreciate the world from a handset's perspective.

In medical scenario planning it is not unusual for stakeholders to assume the role of a flu virus. By doing this, they can more readily imagine the virus' motivations for survival and the methods it may use to resist any attempt to kill it off. Activities like this only work, however, when all key data about the subject, object, or person being impersonated is assembled and fully digested.

01: Assessing the question – it is vitally important to understand the nature of your opening question and the context in which it is being asked. This context provides you with your underlying motivation as a player or object.

02: Agreeing on the context – when each scenario has been fleshed out – usually by stage six – the context of the scenario, and thus the impetus for your concern as a player, will become increasingly clear. As a player you will be "worried," "afraid," "cynical," "curious" – the context in which your character exists. You can be any or all of these depending on the scenario you are working within and, more importantly, the drivers impacting on or contributing to the overall framework of that scenario.

03: Choosing a role – choose a role, become a character, or assume the characteristics of an object to better understand what motivates, inspires, or drives that character or object to do what it does, or to become what it wants to become.
__Role playing a person requires you to fully immerse yourself in his or her world, or rather the world as he or she sees it.
__Role playing an object requires you to fully immerse yourself in its world, or rather the world as it occupies it. It is important to role play without prejudice, preconception, or reservation – your task is to fully immerse yourself in a world you may have no prior understanding of, or sympathy with, so that you can fully understand the consequence of another's actions.

04: Building a character – you need to fully mine, embrace, and articulate the personality of your character if you are to truly understand him or her. To do this it is important that you look at a person's motivations as well as his or her actions.
Use all the desk research you have accrued to give your character a voice or a way of looking at the world that is colored by his or her point of view – and make this as true to his or her previous actions and motivations as you can.

05: Enacting the scene – your character requires a drama as well as a motivation, one gives impetus to the other. This is why it is important to fully flesh out your scenario at stage six. As you map out each scenario, and the drivers and conflicts it contains, questions will arise as to how these changes affect the key players. This is where role playing comes in, and where stakeholders determine the scene of their drama.
__Your scene can be hypothetical: an imagined round table discussion between key players who have agreed to come together to thrash out their differences, a chance encounter in a public space, even a summit or trade fair in which all parties are likely to meet.
__Your scene can be real: a documented meeting that has taken place but as new evidence comes to light a meeting is now held that may have a totally different outcome. Both scenes need to be played out in real time and with a real commitment to each player staying in character and fighting his or her corner.

06: Character impact analysis – as your role is played out, and you engage with other players, you should record any comments, points, decisions, actions, insights, or "flashes of inspiration" that occur during the course of the exercise. At the end of the session these should be further analyzed and added to the overall thrust of the scenario under review.

Having a clear vision is vital to the scenario planning process. But so too is keeping up-to-date with the new visualization tools, algorithmic software packages, or rapid prototyping technologies that allow you to utilize and bend these to the needs of your will and vision as design visionaries like Brittany Bell, Zaha Hadid, and Fletcher Priest Architects have done in the projects illustrated above.

focus, or confusing one scenario plan with another. To simplify things even further, each scenario should be given a color – red, amber, and green – to distinguish their key characteristics.

A "red scenario" is a scenario that is turbulent in that it contains high levels of change, challenge, and a need to react quickly and strategically to incoming forces. This scenario also calls on you to thoroughly assess all possibilities, including those that may seem on face value improbable, if not impossible.

An "amber scenario" is a scenario where there are medium to low levels of risks involved and one or two major changes that could suddenly, but not irrevocably, impact on the answer to your question. It is a scenario which advises caution but also assumes that if you proceed carefully, all will be okay in the end.

A "green scenario" is a scenario in which you have factored in every possibility and are assured that the question being asked can be answered in a way that is positive and beneficial. Yes there might be one or two adjustments to make, but overall all issues can be resolved.

Distilling your five scenarios down into three workable and all-encompassing ones is a painstaking process. A very effective way to do this is to allocate a color to each of the three new scenarios – red, orange, green – and to use red, orange, and green highlighter pens to mark up points on your five scenarios that are relevant to the red scenario only, the green scenario, and so on. When this task is complete you will see red, orange, and green color fields on all five scenarios. These now become the basis for drawing up your three new master scenarios. To do this you need to repeat the steps laid out in stage six – stating your question, scenario title, scenario synopsis, and full scenario narrative, and filling each of these in accordingly.

This time, your full scenario narrative should be even richer in content, context, and expert quotes. Each narrative needs to offer a very clear and separate snapshot of the future. Each, although answering the same "what if" question, is doing so in response to separate drivers and a completely different set of influences and ways of reading the same situation. If the scenarios are too similar, it is important to rework them again, so that there are three clearly defined plans to follow when moving forward: a plan that calls on the business or organization you are working for to "think the unthinkable" and deal with it; a plan that flags up their weaknesses and suggests ways that these can be managed; and a plan that calls on them to make minor adjustments rather than to panic.

A key function of all scenario planning is preparedness and the more encompassing each scenario is the more prepared the business or organization you are working for will be. While the question asked should be as simple as possible, each scenario should have within it elements of complexity – drivers that are not as clear cut as would be liked, threats that are more gray than they are black or white. All threats are caused by people, or at least instigated by them, and people by nature are not simplistic. Each of your scenario plans should, therefore, remain as true to the human condition as you can make it – embracing wherever possible all those frailties, passions, quirks, vanities, and needs we have as people, and weaving them into the framework of your scenario wherever possible. For example: if the threat to the business you are working for

Good scenarios –
even amber ones –
can embrace more
than one concept:
clothing label Ami-
e-toi, markets
itself as a luxury
label, but is
actually run by
Mode Met een Missie
(fashion with a
mission), a
charitable concern
for vulnerable
women. The store's
ethos embraces two
seemingly opposed
concepts – luxury
and philanthropy –
but does so in a
seamless and
successful way.

is an ethical one, and it is an ethical one spearheaded by a need among consumers to penalize brands that are damaging the environment, you should ask yourself who is driving this, how do they think, what are their motivations? Are the consumers passionate, cynical, misguided, or lead by someone else? If so, what is she or he like? The more "color" like this you add, the better, more vibrant, passionate, and compelling your scenario plan will become.

__STAGE 8: VALIDATION AND REFINEMENT

When you have completed the above stage, it is always a good idea to ask your star chamber to rejoin you, with a view to assessing and commenting on your results. They should be asked to choose which scenario they feel is most likely to answer the question being posed, and the one least likely. Some scenario planners will also present the five original scenarios to the star chamber along with the three new ones, to make sure that nothing vital has been discarded in the distillation process. If the chamber has any queries about the new scenarios, or is in any way unhappy, it is important to question them closely and to understand their reasoning. At the end of this session, if your mind is in any way altered, or if the chamber has brought up issues you were deliberately or unconsciously ignoring, it is important to factor these back into the equation. Again, scenarios must be true to the market realities (no matter how unreal these realities may seem) and not to your desired outcomes.

At this point of the scenario planning process you should now know the following:

__the nature of your question
__your scenario title
__the key drivers defining and dominating it
__the key weaknesses in all social, civic, cultural, ethical, and technological areas, etc., which are set to impact on it
__the key weaknesses within the business or brand that the above drivers have alerted you to
__the key items you now need to arm yourself with if you are to answer the question that has been posed in a positive and proactive way

__STAGE 9: INTERPRETATION AND IMPLEMENTATION

Once you have plotted each scenario and provided yourself with answers for the above bullet points, you will now need to look at the strategic implications of your answer. In many cases, even the most comprehensive scenario plans are unsuccessful because stakeholders themselves fail to implement the agreed plan in a way that is measurable and transparent.

In the United Kingdom and the United States, where the methodology of the American School prevails (see page 152), once the plan is created it is up to the stakeholders involved to implement it. The European School follows a different route. Drawing very much on the techniques and processes developed by Michel Godet at LIPSOR, once the scenario planning process is complete, stakeholders and the scenario planning team leader must appoint a committee to agree a time frame for delivering the plan, as well as a set of independently assessed benchmarks against which the success of the plan itself is measured.

Plans also fail because the people who implement them fail to include new ideas or to restructure their original plan in an organic and ongoing way. It is important, therefore, to make sure that all plans incorporate a feedback mechanism, or have a number of people working on their implementation whose sole purpose is to update them as and when new data or insights become available.

> SUMMARY

As we have seen, scenario planning is all about preparedness, so it is important that all of the above stages are followed assiduously: determining and contextualizing the question, monitoring and assessing such contextualizations against all inside and outside drivers, and using these drivers to create a hierarchy of issues that are most and least likely to impact on the question originally asked. Once these issues have been ranked, your scenarios should be fleshed out in a way that is rich in detail. When this task is complete, and all aspects of each of the five agreed scenarios mined so that you understand and appreciate them thoroughly, it is important to revisit the planning exercise to distill the scenarios down to three – a number that is more manageable to work with when finally implementing the results of the exercise.

These three scenarios need to be fully fleshed out and assessed against the previous five to make sure that nothing useful has been culled. Role playing is key at this stage and it is important to empathize with those people who may be driving the changes. Once you have fleshed out your plan, it is then important to implement, monitor, assess, and re-calibrate the implementation process in an ongoing manner. Doing this will require resources but, as we shall see in the next chapter, it also involves a further set of strategies and tools to build the products envisioned.

Chapter Seven
Insight, Strategy, and Innovation

THE TOASTER PROJECT
by Thomas Thwaites is
a humorous reflection
on one of today's
burning issues –
climate change. In
many ways Thwaites'
work is a predictive
metaphor for how
global corporations
will have to make
their products in the
future – by sourcing
them from sustainable
resources, but also
by telling customers
where those resources
are located, so that
they can validate a
manufacturer's claim
for themselves.

"The future belongs to those who prepare for it today."

Malcolm X, black activist[1]

IDENTIFYING A TREND is not the same as identifying a brand, product, or service that results from a particular trend impacting on the social, cultural, or lifestyle landscape. Although techniques like intuitive forecasting and scenario planning can be used to identify trends, such techniques are not designed to identify actual brands, products, or services. To do this, a forecaster must add an additional set of skills to his or her toolkit: skills that help unpack the components of an identified trend in a way that allows him or her to translate them into future-faced but very market-specific and consumer-friendly products. The process used to do this is known as "ideation" – a contraction of the words "ideas" and "innovation" – and is a term used by industry practitioners to describe a process that is about taking ideas and turning them into workable, tangible, and profitable products via the following four distinct stages:

__an inspiration stage
__a translation stage
__an immersion stage
__a product development stage

There are a growing number of ideation, design, and brand strategy companies and forecasters who use this approach. Among the best known are design consultancies such as IDEO and brand strategy and innovation organizations including Innosight, The Future Laboratory, and Swedish trend forecaster and design innovation strategist David Carlson. All are at the forefront of a new kind of company – one that combines the work of the forecaster with the hands-on processes and activities familiar to designers to develop products created by collaborating directly with the client or end user. Carlson puts the process in context thus: "Once you identify trends in terms of their cultural relevance, it is then important to work with clients in a very hands-on way to help them translate these cultural shifts into tangible and saleable products."[2] He uses his background as a designer to engage with clients in this way, working with them to identify the trends first, then directly with their brand, marketing, and innovation teams to develop products that are "on trend" – as in products that will have a direct appeal to consumers and a visual style that makes them easily recognizable, relevant, and appealing in terms of the consumer they are targeting.

(text continues on page 177)

Case Study:
David Carlson

DAVID CARLSON (david.se) is a multifaceted, multi-disciplined creative who best exemplifies a new breed of forecaster. Blogger, lecturer, consultant, DJ, and lifestyle writer, he is also a fashion and product designer who works with a range of clients including Ikea, Audi, Sony Ericsson, and household product brand Iittala.

This ability to move from one field to the other, explains Carlson, is underpinned by an understanding that an incoming trend affects all aspects of the culture, rather than one particular area. "The job of the forecaster is to identify these changes, but also to know when they are most likely to affect the area under review. If you do this well, you have the advantage over competitors," he says.

Like trends, Carlson believes design offers brands a competitive advantage: "Some see it as an added extra, but if you are on trend, and use this to inform the design process itself, you are on to a winning product, as well as creating a brand that is seen by the consumer as culturally relevant."

Carlson uses his talents as a designer, and skills as a lecturer, to take clients on a journey that helps them see and feel these processes for themselves. As he says: "You take them through the trends, look at how these are impacting on

Unlike most forecasters, David Carlson already enjoys a reputation as a product designer in his native Sweden. He has found his ability to visualize the world in three dimensions makes him a better forecaster. "When people speak of tomorrow, they tend to do so in one-dimensional terms — but the realities of envisioning the future are far more complex, textured, and mercurial. People don't conform to neat patterns, or fit into neat, pre-determined boxes. They have edges, angles, corners that are sharp and dangerous — and this is what a forecaster must take into account."

Carlson's blog, the David Report (davidreport.com) is written at his desk, where all of the things that matter (including his children!) can be found. But for him the beauty of a blog is that it can be written live — at a fair, a conference, or while walking along a strange street. It is this sensibility, he says, that good forecasters need to cultivate — the ability to be reflective and to able to reflect and comment on the real and the "live" as it happens. "Later, you find that these things congeal into something else — a new way of seeing a brand, or of creating a cocktail, or of solving a problem. But to do that, you first must observe and absorb these things."

While some forecasters use data to determine what is new and next, Carlson prefers to use the sights, sounds, smells, and stimuli accrued by his senses to do so. "Opening yourself to new stimulus online is fine, but doing it in the flesh is better. For the moment, the Internet cannot capture a smell, or how a smell activates another sense like taste, for example. My advice then is simple; if you are a forecaster, you should try to experience as many things as you can in the real world.

Carlson's recent projects have included developing a range of glasses with designer Konstantin Grcic for Absolut, the La Chapelle table line with designer Inge Sempé, and acting as co-writer of Designboost's "Sharing Design Knowledge." Carlson also co-runs a design store called Carlson Ahnell, in Skanör, Sweden.

the consumer, or on the designers that are perhaps at the vanguard of the change – sustainability for example, a new understanding of luxury – and then you look at how this can be interpreted by the brand in question... To the forecaster this seems logical, but to many brands, used to working in silos, where strategy, marketing, design, and retail teams seldom talk, this can be a revelation. But it can also be a problem."

The David Report (davidreport.com), and his daily blog, are two of the ongoing ways Carlson uses to address those people who cannot readily understand and appreciate how changes in attitude and taste affect the emotional, aesthetic, and material aspects of a product. While the David Report offers his clients a more focused, insightful, and strategic understanding of a range of sectors from sustainability, to luxury and retail, his blog is a freewheeling roll through design, packaging, graffiti, marketing, media, fashion, and branding, which offers them a collection of visual semaphores from the future.

Through his blog Carlson also organizes tours of design shows such as the Salone de Mobile in Milan, a biannual trade fair where design, product, furniture, and materials innovations for the upcoming year are exhibited. As he says: "Here you can see the designers that are set to make an impact, but if you work this show properly, you can identify the trends that are set to contextualize them, and to give their work momentum."

He also uses a process called "immersion" to "show" rather than "tell" his clients how the world is changing. To explain to brands such as Plymouth Gin and Cruzan Rum how global definitions of luxury were altering – from being about bling and excess, to becoming more understated and sustainable – he organized a retail safari to Paris, the center of the luxury industry, taking his clients to the bars, stores, and retail spaces where this new sense of luxury was being embraced.

Carlson believes, however, that trends in themselves are not enough to "inform change, or indeed to drive it." To instigate change it is important, he says, to have an underlying philosophy: "Increasingly my work as a trend forecaster tells me that all aspects of what we do must be holistic, sustainable, and collaborative."

With this in mind, Carlson has used insights accrued as a designer, forecaster, consultant, and brand concept developer to co-found Designboost (designboost.se), a knowledge-sharing design collective that places sustainability at the heart of all its outputs and solutions, whether they are exhibitions on the future of energy, collaborations between designers such as Konstantin Grcic and brands such as Absolut, or the establishment of a social network that allows brands keen on sustainable solutions to speak to designers who can help them achieve such ends.

"In a way it all comes down to this," Carlson believes, "reading the future, and then making such readings into a philosophy – this is what happened with globalization. It became more than an economic activity or trend, it became a mantra, a philosophy. It is now time to change direction, and to take all those trends that are telling us sustainability is the next big thing, and turn these into our new mantra and philosophy."

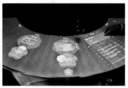

Reinventing food, or eating out for that matter, can be a difficult exercise if the clients involved say that the two things you can't change are the space, and the food! But innovation is all about constraints – and using the latest interactive, overhead, and visual display and sound and light systems to create an experience and a trend that has been dubbed, "Dining 2.0."

> THE INSPIRATION STAGE

To determine the correct aesthetic, or to create a product that perfectly mirrors the trends consumers are influenced by, it is important to note these trends from the outset. It is also vital to make sure that the client you are working for understands that products do not exist in isolation, but are created in response to a consumer need or cultural change which pushes them away from one product or way of doing something, toward a newer, more acceptable product or way. Any of the trend forecasting techniques covered in previous chapters can be used to determine what these trends are, but whatever method you use to identify your key trends your trend report (as mentioned in previous chapters) must do the following:

__identify the key trends relating to the sector under review
__outline the key drivers underpinning them
__define and explain any sub-trends that relate to the above
__identify the key consumer typologies associated with them – those creating the trends or adapting them earlier than other groups
__identify new and emerging brands, products, and services associated with these trends
__outline how these trends are likely to impact on the client's brand in terms of its tone of voice or way to market

At the inspiration stage, it is also important to make sure that all stakeholders in the work you are about to embark on receive copies of your trend report at least a week before everybody meets to discuss its contents and any ideas it may contain in terms of generating future product streams. Stakeholders include all the key people likely to be involved in the development of these products such as the company CEO, heads of market research, brand strategy, planning, and consumer insight, sales, and brand managers, the product design team, the trend forecaster, "visualizers" (mock-up artists or designers who work onscreen to create visual mock-ups of the products suggested), and a workshop facilitator (different from the trend forecaster).

__IDEATION WORKSHOPS

Once stakeholders have had an opportunity to study the report, they will meet formally in a workshop setting to discuss the contents, and then to identify more strategically which trends are relevant, how they will affect consumers, and how in turn this impact can be used to create and develop products.

Marco Marsan, a concept and product developer, who runs and organizes many such workshops for a range of clients producing drinks, breakfast cereals, and household products, suggests that all stakeholders "should be provided with a sheet containing a brief outline of the workshop in terms of content and running order – where it is being held, aims and objectives, key tasks that will need to be executed, timings for each task to be completed, any materials attendees may need to bring with them, expected outcomes."[3]

To ensure each workshop runs smoothly, work is evenly distributed and ideas are generated by mixing and merging the many talents of those taking part; it is

At the Inspiration stage, workshops play a vital part in creating team cohesion, exploring a wide range of ideas and allowing many different minds to come together in a heterophilous manner.

Teams should work in groups of five to seven, and wherever possible use circular tables to do so. This makes it easier for groups to talk, share ideas, and perform complex tasks together. Cabaret-style room layouts also discourage any single person from dominating a table or group.

Leave plenty of physical space between each group and make sure that everyone has room to stand and to move freely around their tables or work areas. If workshop participants are cramped, or feel that competing teams are eavesdropping on them, it can have a detrimental impact on the quality of their output.

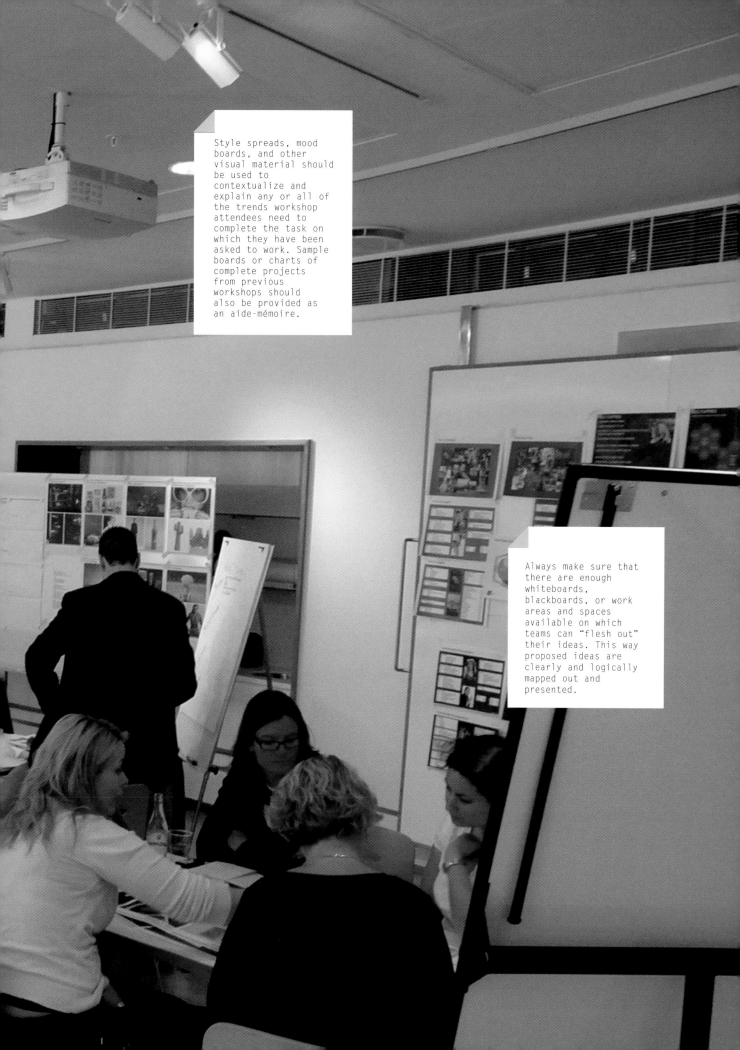

Style spreads, mood boards, and other visual material should be used to contextualize and explain any or all of the trends workshop attendees need to complete the task on which they have been asked to work. Sample boards or charts of complete projects from previous workshops should also be provided as an aide-mémoire.

Always make sure that there are enough whiteboards, blackboards, or work areas and spaces available on which teams can "flesh out" their ideas. This way proposed ideas are clearly and logically mapped out and presented.

It is important that visual material is supplied to ensure that all ideas can be clearly articulated; some workshop attendees find it easier to "show" something rather than to explain it.

also common to preselect groups of people (five or six) who will work together in teams for the duration of the workshop. Again, as with all teamwork it is important to put together teams that are heterophilous in make-up, rather than groups that are homophilous. The best way to do this is to create teams from people who do not work in the same department or within the same discipline (for example, marketing, planning, strategy). Teams should be in place at the beginning of the workshop, with a team leader appointed to ensure that all members of his or her team have all the equipment needed to carry out the tasks in hand. Team leaders should also be tasked with keeping things running smoothly and on time. Workshops can be digitally recorded, photographed, or written up by an appointed workshop monitor who will also summarize all workshop sessions and key findings for later analysis.

Marsan also suggests that each stakeholder should be tasked with bringing something to the workshop that is a by-product of one of the trends identified in the trend report. This is done to remind stakeholders that other companies are already contributing to the growth of these trends (and are, therefore, ahead of the game), but also to reassure them that the identified trends are indeed potential profit streams waiting to happen. "They can be products from their own sectors, but we encourage people to choose something from any industry they feel might have relevance,"[4] says Marsan. Bringing products to the workshop from other sectors stimulates ideas and reminds people that solutions developed for one industry might equally be applicable to theirs.

__THE IDEATION ROOM
Workshop settings and layouts are not unlike the ideas dens or immersion rooms encountered in Chapter 2 or the scenario planning rooms described in Chapter 6. In each case, these rooms are designed to stimulate ideas and to act as a buffer between those using them and normal day-to-day distractions. In the case of an ideation room, however, there tends to be more visual material for stakeholders to use in a hands on way than is found in a room used for scenario planning (which tends to contain more text-based reports, market surveys, books, journals, periodicals, etc.). As in a scenario planning room, an ideation room needs to be an isolated area or room within an organization that can be prepared in advance for what is usually a two-to-four day event.

In terms of basic requirements, the room should contain a laptop to run a presentation from, a digital projector, a screen, flip pads, white boards, Internet access, and work tables and benches where stakeholders can work separately or in teams without feeling cluttered or having their discussions overheard. Materials-wise there should be notebooks for all delegates, pens, pencils, a pack of highlighters, tabloid-size worksheets, letter-size blank pages, tape (or other forms of adhesive), enough scissors for all the teams, Post-its, scalpels, metal rulers, cutting boards, and thumbtacks.

The room should also contain multiple copies of the trend report – at least one for each of the teams involved in the workshop – and wall-mounted boards summarizing the macro or micro trends that have been identified as key and crucial to the organization's future potential. In tandem with all necessary reports and trend boards, each team should be provided with a visual inspiration pack containing 100–500 images that have associations with the

(text continues on page 185)

Case Study:
Marco Marsan

"IDEAS THAT SHIP" is how product developer Marco Marsan (marcomarsan.com) describes the kind of products that can be developed by brands when trends are used to shape their look, feel, and position in the market. And Marsan should know. Working with a range of trend forecasting companies in the United States and Europe, he and his team of visualizers have created food, packaging, and drink products for a range of brands including KFC, Quaker Oats, Kraft, Pizza Hut, and Absolut.

Noting a trend toward families eating and playing together, Marsan created Pizza Hut Cheesy bites, a pizza with a cheese-in-dough base segmented into "poppable" kid-size bites. At a time when connoisseurship and the lure of the designer object was in vogue, he developed Absolut 100, a super premium vodka still sold in its now iconic black bottle. Other concepts he has worked on include Vapor Shots, a steam-based cold remedy that appealed to consumers increasingly keen on self-medication, and the now familiar "gift windows" used in Honey Nut Cheerio boxes that allow parents and children to choose the toy inside.

Using trends to kick-start innovations is not as easy as it seems, Marsan says: "To do it effectively, you must be collaborative, inquisitive, and involve all

For Marsan, Innovation workshops require leaders who are dynamic, insightful, and able to fully articulate and explain the trends that have been previously identified by forecasters. "Brands sometimes confuse a trend with a product these trends suggest. This is a common problem in workshops. It is therefore vital to have a leader or facilitator who can strike the right balance between encouraging collaborations and clarifying confusions or misunderstandings when they arise."

Before designing a concept, or fleshing out an innovation, a facilitator may have to interrogate a panel of experts or work with his or her core team to more fully understand what the planned innovation is to be used for, including the target audience, proposed price point, even the way it is to be deliverd to market – online, in a brick-and mortar-store, or a combination of both. "All these things," says Marsan, "can impact on the final look, feel, and emotional texture of the product."

In Marsan's opinion, Innovation teams don't fail – but if a client fails to disclose all aspects of the market being targeted this can have a detrimental effect on the success of the overall product. "It is therefore important to begin an innovation or concept workshop only when you have fully explored all areas of a product's development cycle as laid out in my patented COMBAT methodology." Marsan says that if these guidelines are followed, innovation teams have every chance of succeeding.

An author, thinker, blogger, and innovation specialist, Marsan also sees himself as someone whose job it is to "empathize" with the other guy so that he can see the world from their perspective – "this is the best way to begin any innovation program – to think like the customer, not like the client."

stakeholders within an organization. There is also no point in being too far ahead of the consumer in terms of an idea – it's a case of being twenty minutes ahead of their thinking and needs – you are trying to target the Early and Late Majority, and to use the Early Adopter to do this."

Marsan uses the acronym "COMBAT" to describe this process. As he explains: "The 'C' stands for the consumer, and the fact that you need to understand them first – everything from their needs to the bigger changes in the culture that drive them." It is also important, he says, to understand how the brand you are working for operates (the "O"), how the marketplace (the "M") impacts on these assets in terms of the trends it contains, and, more importantly, how the brand (the "B") and its values should and could respond to these changes. "You then need to look at what assumptions (the 'A') people will make about a brand if, and when, it does change direction and, finally, you need to look at what tactics (the 'T') a brand needs to use to take advantage of the incoming trends and how these are likely to impact on its core customer."

The ideation process for Marsan is a careful, creative, and highly collaborative one, much of it distilled from insights contained in his self-help novel, *The Lion's Way: Why We Haven't Won the War on Poverty, Drugs, or Terror*, and in his business books, *Who Are You When Nobody's Looking*, and *Think Naked: Child-like Brilliance in the Rough Adult World*.

As Marsan outlines: "Being collaborative is the best way to get what you want – but as my book, *The Lion's Way*, suggests, ego is your biggest hurdle, empathy your best asset. That's especially true of the innovation process. Brand owners believe it's all about the brand, without realizing that the brand is nothing without the customer, or the cultural or social changes they in turn may be subject to or creating."

A veteran of the United States air force, where he worked as an intelligence specialist, Marsan is also a citizen of Canada, the United States, and Italy, from where his father emigrated in 1956. This rich and diverse background, he says, forces him to think outside the box on a daily basis: "People get pigeonholed, and this can work two ways – it can box you in or you can enjoy, explore, and learn from the diversity of your background. This is how the best kind of concept or product developer works; by embracing diversity, by being willing and able to draw on experience, but most of all by listening and collaborating. If you do this you end up creating a product that is shaped to, and by, the voice of the consumer. And that's what makes products that sell, that mean something to the consumer, because they already think about these ideas, or at least the need for them, when you take them to market in the first instance."

Ideation spaces need to inspire you, but they also need to contain "break-out" spaces for small teams to work in and to be surrounded by furniture, objects, colors, and a design sensibility that stimulates creativity. Spaces like One Alfred Place and Eight Moorgate in London, or Amsterdam's new CitizenM hotel all provide backdrops that do this.

trends identified and the sectors targeted. Again, good forecasting companies make sure that this kit contains a substantial number of new and emerging product ideas that have been carefully chosen to stimulate debate, kick-start new idea streams or "jobs-to-be done" solutions.

For instance, if the brand you are working with is a fashion brand trying to create a new store format the workshop area and pack should include images of new inspirational stores and retail interiors, fashion and packaging samples, competitor products, color and material swatches, influential magazines, books and newspaper articles, key designers and architects to note, materials to give a sense of smell, taste, and texture.

According to Marsan, stakeholders should also find quotes or statements from the key consumer groups – those identified in the typologies section of the trend report – in the ideation room to help them hone in on the "need states" of these groups. Need states are the key words, product qualities, lifestyle references that attract consumers to a product or brand and the key words consumers associate with a particular trend in a way that is positive, enabling, or affirmative. These can appear as slogans on the wall, or they can be printed out on cards and left at appropriate points around the room. In short, there should be enough stimuli present to allow participants to create visual mock-ups of their new product concepts by the end of the workshop.

No matter how much the stakeholders have been prepared in advance, it is always worth beginning each workshop with an outline of the key aims and objectives of the day, the running order, and, more importantly, the expected outcomes – whether it is a product idea, a new target market, or a new brand or service category. A workshop should kick-off with a stimulus session in which all key trends being used by stakeholders are fully explained and visualized.

It is at this point that all typologies to be targeted are also "unpacked" in a way that reveals their attitudes, outlooks, mindsets, and key social and personal habitats (bars, clubs, home). This should be done using as much visual stimulus as possible, from ethnographic case studies and visual diaries, to quotes, samples of the products, and clothing these typologies already buy. Only when all of the above have been fully explored and explained, should you move to the translation stage of the process.

> THE TRANSLATION STAGE

At the "translation stage," the discussed ideas captured as notes, paper tears, images from magazines, jpeg printouts, annotated scribbles, and inspirational collages are used to construct a more formalized picture of potential products being considered. Some organizations prefer to do this as a wall chart that outlines each of the chosen trends and then cluster around them a set of products and ideas from other industries that might work (perhaps with a few tweaks) within theirs. If the brand you are working with is keen to compete in this way then creating these "trend relevant clusters" (TRC) are a good way to ignite the ideation process.

If you are working with brands that want a solution that is unique, copyrightable, and relevant to their brand DNA, pushing the identified trends

As gyms defined the
hotel experience in
the 1990s, and spas
in the 2000s, we are
now seeing the
emergence of the
spiritual retreat —
a concept defined
and developed by
forecasters and brand
innovation teams
within the hotel
industry keen to
create the next big
guest experience.

Techniques: Running a successful workshop

All workshops are different, depending on their aims and objectives. It is important to follow an overall format that is familiar, focused, and which contains clear goals and measurable outcomes. Below are some useful tips to help with running a workshop:

01: It is essential each workshop begins with the following key components:
__an outline of the key aims and objectives of the day
__detailed notes on the running order of the day, including an outline of the times at which each of the tasks being tackled should be completed
__a breakdown of which teams are taking part, their relevance, who their leaders are, and what is expected of them in terms of their individual team efforts, aims, objectives, and expected outcomes
__the overall outcome of the day itself whether it is a product idea, a new target market, or a new brand or service category, etc.

....

02: Once the overall aims and objectives of the workshop have been explained, the workshop leader should open the session with a "stimulus" presentation which outlines the following:
__the key trends that have been identified as relevant to the day's aims
__the drivers influencing them
__the typologies these trends have created
__examples of the brands, products, and services Innovators or Early Adopters have already created to cater for these new and emerging markets and expected cultural shifts.

....

03: At the end of each workshop stage, a question and answer session should be encouraged to ensure that all stakeholders understand and fully accept each of the trends they are about to work with, and all of the issues previously debated or discussed. It is also important to make sure that each stakeholder chooses more than one trend to work with:
__a trend that is likely to appeal to the stakeholder's core target consumer in a way that is immediate, but not necessarily challenging or too future-faced – this is about creating a brand, product, or service category that has immediate relevancy and appeal rather than one that is too confrontational or difficult to market or assess.
__a trend that seems to be more left of field (fringe-like) so that there is always a minority choice – a brand, product, or service, in other words, that tests boundaries, challenges preconceptions, and deliberately targets a more fringe and niche consumer today with a view of becoming a mainstream product leader tomorrow.

....

04: Doing the above prevents people from choosing the trend they like (or feel safe and familiar with) rather than the one that is most applicable, or perhaps contains the kernel of a more innovative, original, and challenging idea. Use visual stimuli at all times to prompt debate, encourage discussions, and determine the overall direction of the workshop, or each team's contribution to it.

....

05: If in doubt, use an image or a series of images to define or clarify what it is people are trying to articulate. For example, while most of us have some idea of what "an authentic product"

should look like, when probed about this word definitions vary – for some it can mean "organic, real, local, and natural," while for others it can simply mean "that which is true to its original roots and essential characteristics."

....

06: By the end of the inspiration stage of the workshop each team should be able to agree on the following:
__the two key trends (the majority trend and the minority one) that they believe are set to have a sustained and long-term impact in their market
__the two key sub-trends (one from each of the above) that are impacting or about to impact on consumers
__some initial ideas (from the material provided) on the kind of brands, products, or services these trends are likely to create in their wake

....

07: At this stage, these trends can be written up and captured – using visual stimulus, key words, notes, quotes, inspirational phrases – roughly on tabloid-size sheets by each team involved. The look is free-form, the effect a mental aide-mémoire to capture the essence of the trend in a way each team best understands it.

....

08: Once this is complete, the opportunity cartogram can then be used to determine the kind of brand, product, or service these trends are likely to produce.

....

through something called a "trend funnel" is a better way of doing things. This is used by fashion brands such as Mexx clothing and Marks & Spencer, and alcohol brands such as Absolut. If executed properly, a trend funnel (see diagram, page 197) allows you to be more creative, collaborative, and less prescriptive, and to develop a map or a cartogram designers and product developers find easier to read and understand.

__THE TREND FUNNEL

As the name suggests, a trend funnel encourages each team to work through a series of stages, or zones, that will attempt to filter out extraneous ideas until the lowest zone of the funnel is achieved. Although trend funnels vary in the number of zones required for a trend to pass through (anything from five to ten), all are designed to be visually stimulating and to allow each team to capture the visual and emotional qualities of a trend as refracted through the lens of a particular brand. Teams should also appreciate and understand how ideas put in at the top of the trend funnel can create opportunities and new product streams at the bottom as each trend is filtered, refined, and reassessed in each zone of the process. To do this effectively, trend funnels need to be divided into carefully-defined zones. What follows is a six-zone funnel, each zone of which is designed to push the team using it toward making a more refined and less open-ended decision. Each zone should be completed within blocks of forty-five minutes duration.

__ZONE 1: TREND IDENTITY

In this zone, teams need to use the data and images to identify the trends most relevant to their brand in terms of the retail/product or marketing ideas they could generate. Two trends should be considered: one most likely to appeal to a brand's target demographic in the short term, and one more left of field but likely to appeal in the medium- to long-term. It is important to identify these trends in two ways:

__a twenty-five to thirty-five word description of the trend's key characteristics – for example, "as consumers increasingly order products online they now want retail stores to be more about an experience rather than a white box that sells product"

__a visual storyboard that contains five to eight images from the stimulus pack that attempts to define what the team means by "experience retail" and how this sense of "experience" might look or feel

The above exercise should be completed for both of the trends.

__ZONE 2: TREND DRIVERS

In the second zone, it is important that teams bullet point all of the key drivers associated with each trend, especially those likely to affect how consumers will see, or engage with, the trend. This should be completed as follows:

__a hundred word description or bullet point breakdown of the underlying drivers associated with each trend being reviewed – for example, "the

Internet is making it more convenient to shop online," "stores need to work harder for consumers' cash," etc.
__sample visuals that might prompt you to think about these drivers in the context of the trend being reviewed

__ZONE 3: TYPOLOGY/TARGET CONSUMER GROUP
In this zone, the consumer typology that is most likely to "buy into" a trend or a product needs to be identified. Each team should be encouraged to keep their descriptions short, and to bullet point the consumer's mindset or general outlook wherever they can. The zone should be completed as follows:

__no more than twenty-five words should be used to capture the emotional essence of the typology being targeted – for example, twenty-something shoppers who want to experience a brand as a live, engaging event
__a series of images should be assembled that offers all stakeholders a clear and unequivocal "photo-montage" of who this typology is, what they look like, the stores, bars, clubs, etc., they visit or empathize with

__ZONE 4: ASPIRATIONAL TOUCH POINTS
Having focused on each trend, its drivers, and the typology it should appeal to, it is important to use all of the above to articulate the key brand, product, or service the typology currently favors. Teams should attempt to do this by:

__writing a one hundred word description using the kind of words that best describe the nature of the products they are currently keen on seeking out – for example, "showy," "artisan," "tactile," "premium," "understated," "bling," "organic," "synthetic," and so on
__working with the supplied images to capture a sense of the products these consumer typologies aspire to buy or are likely to buy

Visuals can be accompanied by notes on the look, feel, texture, or finish of the product(s) being featured. At this point, teams should also be encouraged to restyle or rework visuals in any way that makes the products they are working with more relevant and on trend.

__ZONE 5: TREND LOCATION
In this fifth zone, it is important that teams make notes on where each trend is happening – locally, nationally, or globally – how and where it is likely to impact first, and the effect it is set to have on the typology identified. It is important to carry out this exercise as accurately as possible. For example, while the notion of experiential shopping might be a trend that has been noted within an urban-based population, it may not be a trend that is relevant, or indeed sustainable, within regional, rural environments. Consumers living in rural areas may not have the same ultra-fast Internet connections, and it may instead be easier for them to travel to the nearest town to shop. It is important, therefore, to place the trend and typology within the culture it is generated by so that the team can determine whether or not the trend is a global, urban, or rural one and, in the process, gain a better understanding

Brands like Absolut will employ a range of visualization and storyboard techniques (above) to capture the essence of a trend. These are then used in a workshop situation to equip marketing and design teams with the visual and emotional imagery needed to define and develop a product.

of the potential investment it may require and how long it may last in terms of profitability.

__ZONE 6: BRAND/PRODUCT/RETAIL OPPORTUNITIES

Finally, in the sixth zone, teams should be encouraged to use all of the above visual and textural data to suggest two product concepts/retail formats/service opportunities that could work within the markets defined and the consumer groups identified:

__a defensive one – as in one that needs to be produced quickly to capitalize on the strength of a trend the team believes is soon about to pass on from Early Adopters to the Early Majority and Late Majority
__an offensive one – as in an idea that still appeals to Innovators but will in the medium- to long-term become a viable product that can be used to target consumers over the next two to five years

When articulating this idea, teams will need to complete the following:

__a brand/service or product concept: a succinct name for the product – for example, "The Retail Club"
__a concept description: a short, focused sentence or "strapline" that can be used to sell the concept to other workshop participants – for example, "a place for brand loyal customers to party, hang out, and express themselves in a club-like environment"
__a more focused summary of the typology identified in zone three – for example, "New Experientials," as in young, first time jobbers keen to party and meet new interesting people
__the product opportunities: a brief outline of how this concept could be developed, extended, or used in other parts of the team's business – for example, an event-based concept that could be used as an effective marketing tool for the brand nationally

By working down through the trend funnel, and by discussing, debating, and synthesizing ideas as they go, workshop teams are using their accrued knowledge, collective insight, and collaborative skills to hone in on a set of trend ideas, typology groups, and underpinning drivers to create a final set of visual and textural prompts as outlined in zone six. This, in essence, is a concept brief, which is then used to inform and kick-start the immersion process.

> THE IMMERSION STAGE

At the "immersion stage" teams are working with the concept ideas identified through the trend funnel and once more pushing down through a new series of zones, known as an "opportunity cartogram" (see page 193), to develop a more coherent and articulate product concept. This concept will then be mocked up and tested on a group of consumers who represent the targeted typology.

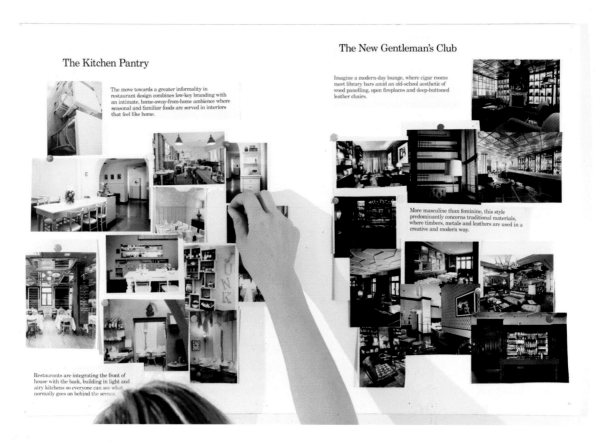

The Kitchen Pantry

The move towards a greater informality in restaurant design combines low-key branding with an intimate, home-away-from-home ambience where seasonal and familiar foods are served in interiors that feel like home.

Restaurants are integrating the front of house with the back, building in light and airy kitchens so everyone can see what normally goes on behind the scenes.

The New Gentleman's Club

Imagine a modern-day lounge, where cigar rooms meet library bars amid an old-school aesthetic of wood panelling, open fireplaces and deep-buttoned leather chairs.

More masculine than feminine, this style predominantly concerns traditional materials, where timbers, metals and leathers are used in a creative and modern way.

Style boards are sometimes used to suggest a mood or an ambiance that is later used by an interior designer or architect to act as a brief or blueprint to develop the actual space. Shown on the right are two projects that could have been inspired by trends such as "The Kitchen Pantry" (The Modern Pantry, London, by Jump Studios), and "The New Gentleman's Club" (Kitchenette Bebek, Istanbul, Turkey, by Autoban)

Defining your target
market is very much
like defining your
target typology — and
because of that it is
important to start
with people who
represent the variety
of attitudes or
mindsets that we tend
to find within any
single market. From
this point, you can
more clearly "map"
their lifestyle
tastes.

__THE OPPORTUNITY CARTOGRAM

The opportunity cartogram encourages teams to take the concepts they have arrived at in zone six of the trend funnel and to refine them even further into product prototypes. As with the "trend funnel," each zone requires teams to discuss and consider carefully all points that are recorded and visualized. Teams should spend no more than forty-five minutes completing each of the following zones.

__ZONE 1: BRAND/PRODUCT/CONCEPT

In this zone each team is asked to look at the two concepts articulated in zone six of the trend funnel and to change, refine, or hone down each one in terms of its key characteristics. It is important to articulate and lock down the essential details in the description.

__ZONE 2: CONCEPT MOOD BOARDS

Once each team has described the two concepts they wish to champion, they now need to visualize them in terms of a mood board – a set of images used collaboratively to suggest an overall mood or feeling of how this concept should look, feel, and be visually interpreted. Images for these mood boards are usually chosen from the visual stimulus kit provided, but if the workshop happens over a number of days they can be collated from magazines, trade publications, architecture journals, coffee table books, etc. Mood boards can be simple or detailed depending on the teams involved, the time allocated, and the nature of the work being undertaken. It is important, however, to make these mood boards as useful as they are inspirational. A mood board for a retail club might, for example, include the following:

__five/six images of existing interiors that capture the essential design qualities of the intended club
__five/six images that hone in on the design or aesthetic details of existing interiors by designers the team is keen to reference
__images that focus on the type of props and furniture wanted to articulate the space
__color swatches (added to lower right-hand side) to capture the key colors to be used to define the mood and overall impact of the club

__ZONE 3: TARGET MARKET

At this stage it is vital for the team to pin down the core words and sensibilities of the key consumer group that the concept is targeting. Teams should be encouraged to act out the characteristics of this consumer if they can, and to fully flesh out all aspects of the consumer's life such as the job he or she does, the type of house lived in, where he or she shops, places visited, favorite drinks, music, books, and so on.

Some of the information can be culled from previous work carried out in zone three of the trend funnel, but it can also be taken from the case studies and more in-depth typology work done during the cultural triangulation process. It is also not uncommon at this stage for team members to invite a cross-section of their "target group" to the workshop and to collaborate with

The trends on the
boards shown were
part of a workshop
on the future of
consumption, and were
meant to help the
teams more readily and
visually understand
the trends that were
about to impact on
this sector over the
coming decade –
trends such as "Neo-
nonsense," "Heritage
Modern," "Womenomics,"
and "Hometainment."

them to capture more accurately a sense of who they are, what they do, the places they visit, etc. Other organizations – those with greater vision and a stronger belief in the collective and creative powers of their key teams – prefer to keep consumers away from the project at this stage of the operation, relying instead on the accrued knowledge and insights of their teams.

__ZONE 4: VISUAL CONSUMER PROFILE

In tandem with the above, it is vital that that each team creates a thorough and comprehensive visual mood board of their consumer's lifestyle. Again, this should show (as opposed to tell) at a glance how this consumer lives in terms of his or her home, key tech products, favorite drink, bar, club, holiday destinations, and so on. This mood board is the visual equivalent of the word portrait, but is designed to give a sense of the products the consumer surrounds himself or herself with broken down into the following headings: home, leisure, shopping, holidays, play, favorite things. Some workshop facilitators recommend that the mood board is created so that moving from left to right are images relevant to the consumer's lifestyle as it is, followed by more aspirational images (as in the objects the consumer desires, would like to have,

Techniques: Working through the innovation process

It is important to remember the following when working through each of the processes outlined in this chapter:

01: The trend funnel is there to filter trends into concepts, while the opportunity cartogram is there to help teams turn these concepts into specific and tangible products.

....

02: A "concept" is not a product in itself, merely an idea or a notion derived from a specific set of circumstances that in turn must be refined further into an actual product – the point of working it through the opportunity cartogram and the usability testing stage.

....

03: Even when a potential product has been identified, it must be further tested and refined in the field.

....

04: Fieldwork can require the creation of different versions or generations of a product. Factor this process into the overall cost and time frame of your workshop, and its aims and objectives. These "mock-ups" can be as simple as a balsa wood shell, or they can be fully funtional prototypes. Either way, they need to offer potential users a relatively truthful version of how the final product will look, perform, and feel.

....

05: There is no point in creating a mock -up that requires further explanation, or is without a vital component as this will affect the quality of the feedback you receive.

....

06: Finally, some products might fail the prototype stage because the vision of the designer is more advanced and intuitive than that of the consumer (even those categorized as Early Adopters). If this happens, bravery, intuition, and a belief in a company's overall ability to determine the market is sometimes required. As Henry Ford once famously put it, "if I had asked consumers what they wanted, they would have said a faster horse." Bill Stumpf's Aeron chair for Herman Miller is also a classic example of this: now the most recognized and bought office chair in the world. The inital impression it gave was of ugliness and impracticality until actual usage revealed its ergonomic brilliance. Miller, believing in the design, ignored the early feedback on the grounds that consumers would come around to Stumpf's way of thinking eventually. Which they did.

....

Trend Funnel

1: Short description (25 words) of trend, and 5–8 images that visually define it.

2: List all key drivers determining this trend and add sample visuals.

3: Describe the target consumer and use 5–8 images to illustrate him or her.

4: Visualize and describe the products he or she currently buys.

5: How is this trend affected by the territory in which he or she lives?

6: Use the above data to suggest two products or actual concepts that could work for your market.

Artist-designers such
as Patrick Jouin are
sometimes used by
brands like W Hotels
Worldwide to visualize
a hotel of the future
which is then
exhibited or toured to
key cities globally to
test the concept among
Early Adopter
consumers. The Extreme
Wow Suite is one such
project and features
a room with 3D
projections, ambiant
light sources, and a
wholly interactive
environment that can
be programmed to
reflect the mood of
the room's occupant.

or be associated with). To do this accurately it may be necessary to have a number of the target audience present to ensure that the aspirational side of the board is correct.

__ZONE 5: PRODUCT UNIVERSE

Once the team has established the mood of the concept, and the nature of the consumer who will eventually buy it, it is now time to validate the legitimacy of the concept by placing it within the context of the product universe the consumer currently makes his or her purchases from. Again, a good workshop team may know this, but if they do not it may be better to work with the core consumer group in advance, and to ask them to bring examples to the workshop of the products they currently buy or aspire to. Some workshop facilitators will work with this group a week or two weeks in advance of the workshop, asking them to keep "product diaries" containing notes or photographs of the products they have bought, or would like to buy, over a particular period. These diaries can also be kept digitally – on a camera or cell phone – and then screened at the workshop or printed out and used to develop and understand the product universe within which the target consumer lives.

__ZONE 6: PRODUCT LANDSCAPE PORTRAIT

The words and phrases, and the visuals captured by the consumer or clipped from magazines by the workshop team, can now be used to visualize the product universe. Again, working from left to right and across pre-agreed categories, such as home products, wardrobe products, technology products, bathroom products, cars, etc., a mood board is created of how this universe looks. By doing so, the team can determine how the proposed concept or product will sit within this visual landscape (if indeed it does). Is there an obvious gap? Should the initial concept designs be toned down or should they be beefed up? Should they be made more functional, extravagant, minimal, or complex?

__ZONE 7: PRODUCT ESSENCE AND TAG LINE

Considering all of the above, the team should become marketers and advertising creatives for a moment. At this point, they need to "sell" the concept in twenty-five words or less, or to advertise it with one single coherent message or image. This will require debate and a reappraisal of the work that has gone before. It also requires the team to hone in on the essential characteristics of the concept, and how and why it should appeal to its consumer demographic. By reducing a brand, product, or service concept to its most essential components, the team is forced to consider its key elements, and to concentrate on the properties that make it unique, original, and relevant to the target market. The team is charged with asking what the one thing is that makes the product a compelling purchase. For the Dyson vacuum, for example, it is the fact that it cleans using centrifugal force (and its design); for Apple's iPod, it is its iconic white housing and a technological interface that is intuitive and easy to use. A product's key selling point does not have to be "tangible" or even practical, but it must be compelling, obvious, and unique.

The IDEO Aquaduct bike (which allows you to purify water as you peddle), the handheld magic window concept by Mac Funamizu (which lets you scan real buildings and products that contain virtual data tags), and the Hydro-Net city by IwamotoScott Architecture (which uses buildings to harvest energy from cross pattern wind currents) are all "what if" concepts that challenge conventional thinking.

At the end of the immersion stage you will have at least two concepts or products to grapple with: a short-term (defensive) one, and a long-term (offensive) one. The workshop visualizers will have synthesized all of the above into a carefully honed sketch or even a highly rendered visual of the product. But this is only the beginning of the mock-up process and we now move on to the "product development stage," where the idea is turned into an actual product.

> THE PRODUCT DEVELOPMENT STAGE

At this juncture, all concepts are presented to the participating teams by each of the team leaders. Because of the number of ideas being presented, the teams at this point may be asked to rank the top five short term ideas they most favor and the top five long-term ideas most likely to appeal to consumers. Once this has been done, the workshop leader will select a smaller working group – usually consisting of the design team, the brand manager, and the visualizers – who are tasked with developing more sophisticated mock-ups of the most rated products, and then taking them into the field or the design laboratory for testing, validating, and improving. These mock-ups can be made from balsa wood (a very pliable material) or created using an innovative piece of technology called "rapid prototyping," which uses a computer aided design (CAD) program to render the product in three dimensions on a computer screen, and then to "print" a copy of the product in solid form via a machine called a "fabricator."

__USABILITY TESTING
The process of field testing a product is known as "usability testing," and can take place in the confines of a design studio, where target consumers are asked to road test the product and offer their feedback. Designers record these comments, while visualizers make rapid changes to two-dimensional versions of the product until all changes suggested by potential users have been noted. If the concept is a store, for instance, miniature mock-ups are produced by model makers, or by theater designers if an actual three-dimensional model is required for a target group to comment on.

In each case, the comments of the targeted group are meticulously recorded and, when each round of testing is complete, a new model is developed and the group invited back for comment and feedback. This can be a slow, painful, but highly rewarding process for stakeholders as ideas that perhaps passed through the workshop unchallenged are now reappraised (perhaps unfavorably so) by the very people who were expected to like them. By this method of feedback from the target consumer, and the issues identified by the designers, the product is reshaped until a master product has been agreed on.

This process of consultation is sometimes referred to as "human factor design," because it is about developing products that have been created by collaborating directly with the end-user. This is a relatively new approach to design, which traditionally tended to be the work of a single person

Opportunity Cartogram

The concept and how it will look. Please answer the following questions using approximately 25 words for each.

01: Name of the product, idea, or brand extension you have identified.

....

02: What are the drivers for this product?

....

03: What trend or trends does this product stem from?

....

04: Who does this product appeal to and why? (Does it target more than one consumer group?)

05: How should this product be launched and why? (Consider viral campaigns, word of mouth, or direct marketing.)

....

06: When should this product be launched and why? (Consider timescale and time of year.)

....

07: What would this product look like? Use images below to visually define the look and feel of it.

Key images to describe the idea or product. Try to make them as specific as possible:

Images that capture the essence of this group:

Target market descriptors:

Products they like:

Your product / retail idea:

(or a design team) who worked the internal and external attributes of a product out for himself or herself before testing it (if indeed it was tested) on the target consumer.

The design consultancy IDEO is one of the most successful design consultancies in terms of embracing human factor design at all points of the design process, using every visual or model-making tool at their disposal to bring concepts to life as early in the development process as they can. As IDEO's Chief Creative Officer, Jane Fulton Suri, puts it: "In design research, ideas don't stay intangible and ambiguous for long: they are given form, whether as sketches, models, stories, video, or other kinds of prototypes. In this context, a prototype is simply a visible or tangible representation of an idea to be thought of as a probe or a thought-experiment; it is not a fully fledged pilot or a pre-production version of the real thing."[5] In itself, field testing products is a whole new sector for study and research. Here products may go through many versions before a "beta" (penultimate) one is tested on a larger swathe of consumers. Then, and only then, is the final one released to the market.

If your forecasting has been accurate, and your brailling of consumer needs focused and measured, you will find that the developed product will have a ready, waiting, and appreciative audience. But even here, however, the clever designer or manufacturer may not target his or her mainstream user straight away. Some prefer instead to "seed" the product among small groups of Innovators or Early Adopters so that it can be further refined by a group of people known for their inquisitive minds, innovative activities, and their ability to create buzz around a brand, product, or service they like. By this route then, new products can enter the culture and the whole cycle of fringe or niche products or activities becoming mainstream concerns begin once more.

> SUMMARY

In many ways, the activities described in this chapter – the trend funnel and opportunity cartogram – mimic the process of discovery, refinement, assessment, and re-evaluation all trends go through when they pass in and out of our culture. The zones within the trend funnel can be viewed as those zones within the culture occupied by Innovators, Early Adopters, and Early Majority. Within each zone, ideas are tested, discussed, challenged, and refined, and then with such changes made, passed on to the next zone or group where more refinements are carried out, so that the concept at each stage is made more acceptable, compelling, or appealing to the wider consumer.

In the opportunities cartogram, we see this work being done in a more visible, strategic, and assured way. Here the focus is on defining the by-product of the trend itself and articulating it in a way that captures all the design characteristics that resonate well with its target audience. Previously, this was a matter of designer trial and error but now designers use the strategy of human factor design – a process that involves small networks or groups of a product's target market in the design of that product – at the earliest possible stages. Thus a field that has been about a very singular vision is quickly becoming one

Innovation can be
about anything: here
VilaSofa furniture
store commissioned
Amsterdam-based
studio Tjep to
design a store
environment which
brings together
elements of the
warehouse and the
home, but can also
accommodate children
not keen to shop
with their parents.
Inspiration included
shipping containers,
storage containers,
children's
kindergartens,
and plastic and
kitsch toys.

that is about collaborations, about involving the few to define and assess the current and future tastes of the many.

In many ways this is what trend forecasting itself is about: a set of practical, intuitive, observational, and quantitative tools, skills, and strategies that allow you to assess the future needs and consumption patterns of the many by studying and empathizing with the activities of the few. As we have seen throughout this book, this has to be done by being alert and by being plugged into the new, the next, and the marginal. It is not a job for the incurious, the unimaginative, or those who are suspicious or sceptical of change: at its heart trend forecasting requires you to be aware of the now, to be welcoming of the future, and to be informed and fully cognizant of the past. It also requires openness, and a sense of adventure. Forecasters are always on the look out for new "stuff," for the seeds of change that drive our culture in new and ever more distinctive ways. They are always asking: "Where will this seed fall?" "How will this seed grow?" "Who will nurture it?" "What will it look like when it does grow?" "What will it become?" "How will it change as it matures?" "What seeds will it drop?" "Where will it drop them?" "Will I know where to stand when they do?" "How will they grow?" "What will they become this time around?" And so the cycle continues...

Notes

CHAPTER 1

1. "Losing My Edge," LCD Soundsystem, Capitol Records, February 2005.
2. Elaine Sciolino, "In the Lap of Luxury, Paris Squirms," *The International Herald Tribune,* January 15th, 2009.
3. Eve-olution, Lsnglobal.com, Inspire section, published 2009.
4. Richard Dawkins, *The Selfish Gene*, Oxford University Press, 1989.
5. Richard Dawkins, *The Selfish Gene*, Oxford University Press, 1989, page 190.
6. Everett M. Rogers, *Diffusion of Innovations,* fifth edition, Free Press, 2003.
7. Everett M. Rogers, *Diffusion of Innovations,* fifth edition, Free Press, 2003, page 31.
8. Everett M. Rogers, *Diffusion of Innovations,* fifth edition, Free Press, 2003, page 270.
9. Everett M. Rogers, *Diffusion of Innovations,* fifth edition, Free Press, 2003, page 220.
10. Everett M. Rogers, *Diffusion of Innovations,* fifth edition, Free Press, 2003, page 283.
11. Everett M. Rogers, *Diffusion of Innovations,* fifth edition, Free Press, 2003, page 41.
12. Everett M. Rogers, *Diffusion of Innovations,* fifth edition, Free Press, 2003, page 41.

....

CHAPTER 2

1. William Gibson speaking on NPR's radio program "Talk of the Nation," November 30th, 1999.
2. Online interview with Susan Choi, brailling the culture, 2004.
3. Malcolm Gladwell, "The Cool Hunt," *The New Yorker Magazine,* Annals of Style section, March 17th, 1999.
See also www.gladwell.com/1997/1997_03_17_a_cool.htm
4. The Future Laboratory, Spring/Summer dossier, 2008, page 13.

5. Mark Simpson, "Here Come the Mirror Men," *The Independent,* 15th November, 1994. See also his essay of the same name, "It's a queer world," published in the United Kingdom by Vintage in 1996 and in the United States by Harrington Park Press in 1999.
6. www.firstmatter.com
7. Interview with Liesbeth den Toom, August 2008.
8. Malcolm Gladwell, *Blink: The Power of Thinking Without Thinking,* Little Brown and Company, 2005.

....

CHAPTER 3

1. Igor Ushakov, *Histories of Scientific Insights*, Lulu.com, 2007, page 153.
2. In his Nobel prize-winning work, Roger Sperry tested ten patients who had previously had their brain severed in such a way as to prevent the left-hand side sending signals to the right. Experimentation on both halves proved that each half could still function and carry out certain key tasks independent of the other. Erroneously, it was assumed that only the right half could carry out creative and imaginative tasks, while the left could only carry out logic-based activities.
3. Eric Kandal explains in his autobiography, *In Search of Memory* (Norton and Company Inc., 2006) why memory, learning, insight, and even those seemingly inexplicable "eureka" moments we experience, have little to do with the psyche but all to do with distinctive and measurable molecular events which are determined by chemical changes taking place in the brain. His scientific work refutes the notion that the brain is divided into hemispheres that operate independently of each other (which they can do) and proposes that for humans to have the kind of thoughts, insights, and flashes they do, all parts of the brain – especially memories, real and imagined – are required.
4. Barry Gordon and Lisa Berger, *Intelligent Memory: Improve the Memory that Makes You Smarter*, Viking, 2003, pages 8–9.

5. Psychologist Gary Klein has written a number of books on how professionals with highly stressful jobs, such as firefighters and marines, use their instincts in a way that defies logic and expectation. While we expect such people to weigh up all the odds and then to act, Klein's researches indicated that they seemed to act first and rationalize their actions later. In actual fact, these people were tapping into their instincts to access previous experiences – their own and ones learned from colleagues – to determine a path forward. However, as soon as that pathway became problematic they abandoned it and tried out a new method. In other words, they were using a type of "historic awareness" (see pages 78 and 83), combined with presence of mind to predict a possible way forward. More detailed accounts of how intuition works can be found in *Source of Power: How People Make Decisions*, MIT Press, 1999 and *The Power of Intuition: How to Use Your Gut Feelings to Make Better Decisions at Work*, Currency, 2004.
6. William Duggan, *Strategic Intuition*, Columbia Business School, 2007, page 54.
7. William Duggan's book *Napoleon's Glance: The Secret of Strategy* (Avalon Travel Publishing, 2003) is an excellent account of Napoleon's campaigns and a must-read for forecast students who need more scientific and historically referenced proofs that the intuitive process has a long, honorable, and credible history associated with it.
8. Interview with William Duggan, July 2008.
9. Interview with William Duggan, July 2008.
10. Interview with Carsten Beck, May 2008.
11. Douglas Fox, "The Secret Life of the Brain," *The New Scientist* magazine, 5 November 2008.

....

CHAPTER 4

1. Chapter Two: Increasing Returns in Kevin Kelly, *New Rules for the New Economy*, Penguin Books, 1999.

2. James Surowiecki's book, *The Wisdom of Crowds* (Little Brown, 2004) is an excellent account of how we can harness the collective thinking of crowds in a way that is insightful and strategically useful for business. His book contains many valuable case studies on how trend forecasters can use this approach to their advantage.

3. Francis Galton, *Memories of My Life*, Methuen, 1908. Also quoted in James Surowiecki, *The Wisdom of Crowds*, Little Brown, 2004, page xiii.

4. Mark Granovetter, "The Strength of Weak Ties," *American Journal of Sociology*, Vol. 78, No. 6, May 1973, pages 1360–1380.

5. A full version of Mark Granovetter's original paper can be downloaded from http://www.stanford.edu/dept/soc/people/mgranovetter/documents/granstrengthweakties.pdf. This is comprehensive in its sweep and should be read by any student who doubts the power of weak ties, and the reason why networks need to be populated with un-like-minded members as opposed to contacts they are familiar with.

6. James Surowiecki, *The Wisdom of Crowds*, Little Brown, 2004, page 36.

7. James Surowiecki, *The Wisdom of Crowds*, Little Brown, 2004, page 37.

8. Interview with Liesbeth den Toom, July 2008.

9. Interview with Piers Fawkes, August 2008.

10. Interview with Piers Fawkes, August 2008.

11. Statistics provided by Internet World Stats: www.internetworldstats.com.

12. Metcalfe's Law. Bob Metcalfe, "A Network Becomes More Valuable As It Reaches More Users," *Inforworld*, October 2nd, 1995.

....

CHAPTER 5

1. thinkexist.com/quotes/Margaret_Mead.

2. Widely used by trend forecasters today, cultural triangulation as a method and term was first coined by trend forecaster Christopher Sanderson in 2001 to describe a three-pronged method for identifying trends and was further developed by The Future Laboratory.

3. Interview with Marco Marsan, August 2008.

4. Interview with Sean Pillot de Chenecey, August 2008.

5. Underhill's book, *The Call of the Mall* (Simon & Schuster, 2004), is perhaps one of the best books on ethnographic research and ethnographic forecasting in the commercial context. His previous book, *Why We Shop* (Simon & Schuster, 2000), should also be read in tandem with this book to provide you with more detailed insights into what makes people behave the way they do in a retail environment.

....

CHAPTER 6

1. Michel Godet et al, "Lipsor Working Paper, *Prospectives*, Strategic Foresight: Use and Misuse of Scenario Building," PDF downloadable from economie-gestion.cnam.fr/lipsor/UserFiles/SR10vEng.pdf.

2. *On Thermonuclear War* (Princeton University Press, 1960) by Herman Khan courted instant controversy on publication for a scenario dismissing the notion that there would be one outright winner in any thermonuclear conflict between the world's two superpowers at the time: the Soviet Union and the United States.

3. Art Kleiner, with forewords by Warren Bennis, Steven Wheeler, and Walt McFarland, *The Age of Heretics: A History of the Radical Thinkers Who Reinvented Corporate Management*, 2nd edition, Jossey Bass, 2008.

4. Peter Schwartz, *The Art of the Long View*, Currency Doubleday, 1996.

5. Transcript of interview with Michel Godet by Philippe Durance in September 2004, page 11. On page 9, Godet attributes the American change to an even more simplistic approach to the rise of the hippy movement in the mid- to late-1960s and to New Age thinking (a spiritual, intellectual, and visceral offshoot) that encouraged and embraced the belief in nature-based worship and in a more holistic, less rational, and hard-faced approach to problem solving. This transcript is downloadable as a PDF from http://www.cnam.fr/lipsor/eng/memoryofprospective.php. To further encourage and make easy the use of *la prospective*, all software programs and the methodology needed to use them are available to download free from the LIPSOR website (www.3ie.fr/lipsor/lipsor_uk), as are many of Godet's papers and teaching methodologies.

6. Interview with Carsten Beck, 2008.

....

CHAPTER 7

1. Kristin Thoennes Keller, *Malcolm X: Force for Change*, Capstone Press, 2005, page 26.

2. Interview with David Carlson, September 2008.

3. Interview with Marco Marsan, August 2008.

4. Interview with Marco Marsan, August 2008.

5. Jane Fulton Suri, "Informing our Intuition," *Rotman* magazine, Winter 2008, page 53.

Glossary

TREND FORECASTING IS A HYBRID, future-faced discipline that requires you to be inventive and imaginative when creating words that best suggest the trend you are attempting to describe or encapsulate. Following are some of the more interesting words developed by The Future Laboratory and its associates to name and capture the trends that are set to impact on tomorrow's consumer landscapes.

Alphaluxe – alpha + luxury: used to describe a style of luxury that is dominant, powerful, and singular in terms of its visual statement and aesthetic presence.

Brandtocracies – brand + democracy: as brands expand their activities on a range of social networks including Twitter, Facebook, and MySpace, they are also becoming more collaborative, open, and keen to listen to, and work with, consumers in order to develop more democratic relationships with them.

Bleisure – business + leisure: as technology blurs the distinction between work and play, the notion of the business and leisure traveler seems less and less relevant in an age when we are connected 24/7 and working in a world where we increasingly use social network tools like Facebook, MySpace, Twitter, and LinkedIn to conduct business as well as to converse with friends and family.

Blingimalism – bling + minimalism: used to describe an aesthetic that combines the less excessive aspects of "bling" (or bright shiny fashion and luxury) with characteristics that are more considered, refined, and less showy or visually aggressive.

Consumanism – conscience + consumerism: used to describe a consumer who proactively chooses brands, products, and services that have a social, ethical, civic, and environmental aspect to them.

Dreamtelligence – dream + intelligence: used to describe the creative possibilities inherent in splicing two or more seemingly contradictory skills, disciplines, or ideas together in a way that creates new possibilities or ways of problem solving.

Eve-olution – Eve + evolution: used to describe how brands, products, and services are increasingly designed to accommodate the emotional, aesthetic, and functional needs of a female target audience.

Freesumerism – free + consumerism: describes a growing trend or movement for offering consumers brands, products, and services that are free, or contain a free component within their economic make-up.

Freerange Living – used to describe the liberating impact wi-fi, GPS, and LBS technology has on how the new generation works, rests, and plays in spaces of an individual's own choosing.

Femtech – feminine + technology: used to describe a design aesthetic which embraces aesthetic, emotional, ergonomic, and technological "touch-points" that subconsciously appeal to female users.

Homedulgence – home + indulgence: used to describe the growing importance of the home as a proactive place to play, pamper, and entertain family and friends in a way that is more in keeping with how we normally entertain people in public spaces like bars, clubs, restaurants, and cafés.

Homesteading – used to describe how a generation of people in their thirties and forties are transforming their homes into proactive hubs or homesteads where vegetables are grown, energy harvested, and a focus placed on making the house as self-sufficient as possible.

Life-casting – life + broadcasting: used to describe how a growing number of consumers use their cell phones, laptops, and networks such as Twitter, Facebook, and MySpace, to broadcast all aspects of their day-to-day activities continuously and in a way that is live and "always on."

Localvores – local + carnivore: used to describe people who are keen to eat, drink, and buy products that originate from their town, city, or surrounding region.

Masstige – mass market + prestige: used to describe how brands have increased the overall "value" of a product by working with named designers and more prestigious materials, packaging, and marketing methods to raise their product's sense of prestige, or position in the market, without unduly increasingly its price.

Menaissance – men + renaissance: used to describe a generation of men who are determined to define masculinity and masculine roles in a way that is positive and affirmative without negating the role, influence, and status of women.

New Mass Affluents – used to describe a group of men and women who have a stated income of US$100k-plus and use it to support a lifestyle that is aspirational, global, and dominated by certain shared characteristics in taste, and in social and ethical values and mindsets.

New Sobriety – used to describe a mood whereby consumers are keen once more to embrace simple values, straightforward principles, and revert back to a more serious, sober, and socially-responsible mindset.

No Frills Affluence – used to describe a demographic with an US$100k income who are keen to live frugally, sensibly, and with a low carbon footprint despite their high annual incomes.

Nu-Luxury – used to describe a new sensibility in the world of luxury that eschews excess, brashness, and waste, and instead promotes an aesthetic and ideology that is more refined and low-key in its attitude and outlook.

The New Normal – used to describe how our lifestyles are set to change as the impact of climate change, the credit crunch, depleted global resources, technological convergence, the social media, and the rise of bioscience and GM forces us to reconsider what is and isn't normal, or acceptable, in the decade to come.

Previving – prevent + survive: used to describe how people are embracing health and wellness strategies that are designed to prevent them from becoming ill.

Prohibition culture – used to describe a shift in civic and social agendas that gently or overtly persuades people to follow more responsible, sober, stringent, and abstemious lifestyles with a view to curbing excessive, damaging, or unhealthy behaviors and appetites – whether these be nutritional, social, ethical, or moral.

Social niceworking – social networking + "nice": used to describe people, organizations, and NGOs (non-governmental organizations) that use social networks such as Facebook, etc. to promote "nice" activities such as volunteering, charitable giving, and social philanthropy.

Slash Slash – used to describe a group or "tribe" of teenagers and young adults who use the Internet and social network sites like MySpace and Facebook to carve out self-made careers or entrepreneurial endeavors that use the forward slash symbol on the keyboard to link the range of skills being promoted together as in DJ/artist/club promoter/fanzine editor – hence Slash Slash.

Vasstige – value + prestige: used to describe how some brands are embracing a strategy that promotes values such as being fair to their suppliers, caring for the environment, and having a strong ethical and social stance while maintaining prices that are reasonable and good value for money.

Womenomics – women + economics: used to describe the growing economic, social, and intellectual power of women in the world of business, science, technology, engineering, etc.

Index

Picture Credits

Numbers in **BOLD** refer to pages.

TIMELINE.
6: *From top left*—Le Labo Fragrance Lab at Liberty, London; Inexpensive mini Tata Nano Europa is an upgraded version of the $2,500 "people's car" going into production in India, Tata Motors Limited (as also shown on page 155); Triaphos is the sole owner of the Triaphos srl rights; Borbo Skin Balance Confections, © Borba Inc.; Green Depot flagship store by Mapos LLC, photo David Pinter; PictureMate printer, design Industrial Facility with Epson Design; TOMY xiao™ TIP-521 Digital Camera with Built-in ZINK©; The School of Life, photo Matt Stuart; Aivan slide radio by Mikael Silvanto. **7:** *From top left*—Clam-A-Leg table, design and photography Jorre Van Ast; X-halo for Delmedica by Philips Design; Worrell designed the look/feel of Gruve (www.worrell. com), Muve Design Team: Gary Stein, Marc Seaberg, Elise Brock, Joel Silverman; Gispen Globus by Michiel van der Kley – www.gispen.com; Kaleido R7 Wireless Digital Photo Frame by IPEVO Inc.; Semi Automatic at Mondrian in South Beach by Teknovation (as also shown on pages 87 and 163): Semi Automatic at Mondrian in South Beach is an innovative retail concept housed in an over-sized vending machine occupying an entire wall in the hotel lobby. The enabling-technology, robotics, and mechanical functionality powering Mondrian's Semi Automatic was created by Teknovation, the Automated retail specialists; Philips CX50 CompactXtreme Ultrasound System; Perricone MD Neutriceuticals, photo Colin Faulkner; "World Uniqlock" interactive campaign by Projector Inc. for Uniqlo; The "Immaculate" prosthetic arm by Hans Alexander Huseklepp draws on futuristic robotics aesthetics rather than trying to look lifelike. **8:** *From top left*—Flavors by Philips Design; 3D Printer by Desktop Factory; Tramspiral for Alstom by Rodolfo Ciudad Witzel, yopodesign; Living Colors by Philips Design; Aion kitchen designed by Antoine Lebrun, student work developed at L'École de Design Nantes Atlantique in partnership with the Fagor Brandt Group; *Viewpoint* #22, SynthCelebration, photograph by Metz and Racine, Art Direction by Caroline Till; Immersive Cocoon by Michael J Brown, Tino Schaedler, Oliver Zeller, Pia Habekost; Made in Transit by Agata Jaworska; Acqua Mineralis Concept, by Jenny Lundgren photo

Simon Fagéus; "Lilypad" A Floating Ecopolis for Climate Refugees concept by Vincent Callebaut Architects is a self-sufficient amphibious city designed for a future world defined by rising seawater levels – www.vincent. callebaut. org. Illustration by Pixelab – www.pixelab.be (see also page 149); Philips Panorama 0.6T MR system; Future Of Internet Search, Mobile Version, concept by Mac Funamizu (http://petitinvention.wordpress.com). **9:** *From top left*—Firo for a unique cooking experience on open fires by Andrea Nimtschke, www.nimtschke. de; Origen biodegradable urn by Christelle Boulé; Bees by Susana Soares, Royal College of Art; Philips Design; Podle™ Pocket Sprayer, innovation, design, naming, branding, and patent (closing system) – Cédric Francois, Laurent Fontaine, MWV Calmar: industrialization; Moixa Interface Sphere, Chris Wright and Simon Daniel, Moixa DesignProducts (www.moixadesign .com); Aquaduct concept vehicle, courtesy of IDEO; BMW GINA Light Visionary Model; Seed Archive by Brittany Bell; The Waterpod Project, courtesy of Mary Mattingly and the Waterpod team of collaborators, volunteers, and supporters; Yellow Tree House Restaurant Architects Peter Eising and Lucy Gauntlett; Colim modular camper by Christian Susana; Hydro-Net by IwamotoScott Architecture.

CHAPTER 1.
10: Double Octopus designed by Seyhan Özdemir & Sefer Çaglar for Autoban. **13:** *Clockwise from left*—Le Labo Fragrance Lab at Liberty, London; Gispen Globus by Michiel van der Kley – www.gispen.com; Christian Wijnants SS09, photograph by Shoji Fujii; V10 pocket projector by Mint Wireless and Aiptek; Mama Shelter, Paris, designed by Philippe Starck, © Photograph Francis Amiand; Font Clock by Sebastian Wrong for Established & Sons – www.establishedandsons.com; Antwerp's Narrowest House by sculp(IT) Architects – www.sculp.it, photo Luc Roynans – www.roynans.com; Hanger Chair by Philippe Malouin; The T-Mobile G1 with Google; Micro Compact Home (M-Ch) by Richard Horden, photo Dennis Gilbert. **15:** *From top*—Borba Skin Balance Water, © Borba Inc.; Sencha Shot Japanese Green Tea by Ito-En; Sip Drinks, packaging by Pearl Fisher; Y Water Trio © 2007–2008 Y Water Inc. **16:** Ettore Sottsass, "Carlton" room divider, 1981, www.metmuseum.org, © photo SCALA, Florence. **17:** *From top*—Bookcase by Grégory Parsy and Camille Debons; "Sculpt" cupboard by Studio Maarten Baas – www.maatenbaas.com, photograph by Maarten van Houten – www.maarten vanhouten.com; "Lathe" chair by Sebastian Brajkovic, courtesy of Carpenters Workshop

Gallery. **20:** *From top*—2140 Mini Notebook computer by Hewlett-Packard; Palm Pre, Palm Inc.; Westinghouse Digital LCD HDTV. **21:** Charles Anastase at Dover Street Market. **22–23:** Photo Mischa Haller – www.mischaphoto.com. **24:** *From top*—Facebook Head offices, Palo Alto by Studio O+A, photo César Rubio; Gem Kingdom, Amsterdam, Holland, interior design by X+L, designers Leon van Boxtel and Xander Vervoot; "Living kitchen," The FARM Project by Dornbracht ©; "The future on Your Plate" by Postlerferguson ©2007. **25:** Diamond-Shaped Trend Model by Henrik Vejlgaard. © Worldwide rights reserved. **27:** Photo Giles Price. **28:** *From top*—Aeolus Airship by Christopher Ottersbach; Manned Cloud by Studio Massaud with the scientific partnership of the ONERA; "Strato Cruiser" by Michael J. Brown, Tino Schaedler, and Pia Habekost for Nau; **30:** EAR ON ARM, STELARC, photo Nina Sellars.

CHAPTER 2.
32: "Gula" chair by Thomas von Staffeldt for Copenheroes, photo Mads Emil Hilmer; **35:** *Clockwise from left*—Land Rover LRX Concept car interior; Marian Cabeza Beauty Salon by Miguel Ángel Llácer photo Javier Ortega; Blossom light by Hella Jongerius for Beluxâ; Yauatcha packaging by Madethought; "Nothingness" inspired power tools by Johnny Jing Shi; Ultra Silencer by Pia Wallén for Electrolux. **37:** PSFK Snapshot Brooklyn, image design by Jenny Beorkrem. **38–39:** Photo Mischa Haller – www.mischaphoto.com. **40:** *From top*—Hoogvliet Heerlijkheid, Netherlands by FAT, photo Rob Parrish; Bricks and Mortar Chair by Sebastian Wrong and Richard Woods for Established & Sons – www.establishedandsons.com; Lego Brick Camera by Digital Blue Inc. and the Lego Group; "Step Stools" by Paul Loebach for Areaware, photo Jeremy Frechette. **41:** *From top*—Muli sideboard by ding3000, photo Philipp Nemenz; The Chankley Bore by Studio Maarten Baas for Established & Sons, photographer Maarten van Houten; **42:** Photo Giles Price; **43:** *From top*—"Touch Wood" treasure chest for Droog B.V. by Minale - Maeda; "Soft Wood" sofa by Front for Moroso. **45:** *Clockwise from left*—1 and 8 Marian Cabeza Beauty Salon by Miguel Ángel Llácer, photo Javier Ortega; 2 – Land Rover LRX concept car interior; 3 – Russel Wright paint by Angela Wijaya; 4 – Winds Hairdryer by Raffaella Mangiarotti and Matteo Bazzicalupo, deepdesign, photo Arturo Delle Donne; 5 – Givenchy Store, Paris by Riccardo Tisci and architect Jamie Fobert; 6 – Yauatcha packaging by Madethought; 7 – BMW GINA Light Visionary Model; 9 – Modular open source hardware by Bug Labs; 10 – "Two Timer" by

Sam Hecht and Industrial Facility for Established & Sons – www.establishedandsons.com. **47:** *From top*—Springfield Sofa Designed by Patricia Urquiola for Moroso with "Pixellated" fabric design by Cristian Zuzunaga, photo Mikolai Berg; "Stolen Jewels" by Mike and Maaike Inc. – www.mikeandmaaike.com; "Witness Flat"—Pixelated Chairs by Studio Makkink & Bey – www.jurgenbey.nl, photo Alain Speltdoorn. **48–49:** *Clockwise from left*—1 – Josh Goot, pre collection 2008; 2 – Beata light and Harper dining table by Pinch Design – www.pinchdesign.com, photo James Merrell; 3 – Magnolia, designed by Seyhan Özdemir and Sefer Çaglar at Autoban, built by De La Espada; 4 – Aesop, Mount Street, London by Studioilse, photo Lisa Cohen; 5 – "Box & Box" by Lissoni Associati for Artelano; 6 – Common Projects Training Boot in black nylon, designers Prathan Poopat and Flavio Girolami; 7 – "Lingor" phosphorescent light by Mark Braun, produced by Authentics photo Guido Mieth; 8 – Knives by Studio Giulio Iacchetti, photo Barbara Bonomelli; 9 – Cerruti menswear S/S10 – www.cerruti.com; 10 – "Bridge Chair" by Matthew Hilton for Case Furniture Ltd - www.casefurniture.co.uk; 11 – Acne men's footwear S/S 09; 12 – Hiroko Shiratori BuildStool by Okay Studio, London; 13 – Melon District, Barcelona designed by Gus Wüstemann with Animal, photo Bruno Helbling; 14 – Peg chair by Alex Hellum for Heals, manufactured by Ercol, photo Pelle Crépin; 15 – APC Olive Oil, photo Olivier Placet; 16 – "Mizu Spa" by Stanley Saitowitz | Natoma Architects, Inc.; 17 – Cerruti menswear S/S10 – www.cerruti.com; 18 – Slow and Steady Wins the Race, Spring 2009 collection – www.slowandsteadywinstherace.com; 19 – Albam A/W08, photo John Spinks; 20 – Aesop "A Rose By Any Other Name" hydrating body oil; 21 – Artek "Bambu" range – www.artek.fi, photo Matti Pyykkö; 22 – Gem Kingdom jewellery shop, Amsterdam by X+L, designers Leon van Boxtel and Xander Vervoot; 23 – Albam footwear A/W08, photo John Spinks; 24 – Cerruti menswear S/S09 – www.cerruti.com; 25 – Laminated stool by Jamie Ward; 26 – Givenchy Store, Paris by Riccardo Tisci and architect Jamie Fobert; 27 – Acne Men's Pre Collection S/S 09; 28 – "A Stacking Hommage" by Dirk Winkel; 29 – Task light by Ilse Crawford for Wästberg 2008; 30 – Yauatcha Packaging by Madethought; 31 – Stories Kaffe packaging by BVD for Turesgruppen; 32 – The Olde Bell Inn, Hurley, Berkshire, England by Studioilse, photo Lisa Cohen; 33 – ©LifeGoods design (LG Design SaRL), photo © Milo Keller; 34 – "Soft Parcel," upholstered furniture collection by TAF for Rossana Orlandi; 35 –

"Heutchy" shoe, fall 2008 collection, design by Wells Stellberger, photographyer Kris Locascio; 36 – The Olde Bell Inn, Hurley, Berkshire, England by Studioilse, photo Lisa Cohen; 37 – Organic Food from Marks and Spencer; 45 – "Steelwood" chair by Ronan and Erwan Bouroullec for Magis, photograph by Paul Tahon and R&E Bouroullec; 39 – The Olde Bell Inn, Hurley, Berkshire, England by Studioilse, photo Lucy Cohen; 40 – Common Projects Training Boot in white leather, designers Prathan Poopat and Flavio Girolami; 41 – Christian Wijnants womenswear, Spring/Summer 2009; 42 – Pendal sofa by Pinch Design, photo James Merrell; 43 – Irie Wash, Eau de Toilette; 44 – "Production" table by Frank for Established & Sons – www. establishedandsons.com; 45 – Plastic back chair by Raphael von Allmen, made at ECAL, photo Florian Joye; 46 – "Soft Parcel," upholstered furniture collection by TAF for Rossana Orlandi; 47 – Aldo, Hagui shoe, Spring/Summer 2009; 48 – Three champagne glasses and one water glass designed by Michael Anastassiades in collaboration with Ilse Crawford 2009. **50:** *From top*—"Exhausted Cutlery" by Kathryn Hinton; "Still Life Meltdown" by Marie Retpen, photo Ester Segarra. **51–53:** Photo Mischa Haller – www.mischaphoto.com. **54:** *From top*—1–2 Dining space, Grand Hotel Stockholm by Studioilse for Mathias Dahlgren. 3 – The Olde Bell Inn, Hurley, Berkshire, England by Studioilse, photo Lucy Cohen. **55:** *From top*—"Memory Chair" by Ole Jensen, produced by Normann Copenhagen; "Lazy Bastard" chair by Bertjan Pot for Montis. **57:** *From top*—"Lathe" table by Sebastian Brajkovic courtesy of Carpenters Workshop Gallery; "The Cloud" by Richard Hutten, produced by Ormond Editions Geneva, photo Tonatiuh Ambrosetti; "Bodyguard" by Ron Arad, © Ron Arad Associates, Courtesy of the Timothy Taylor Gallery, London. **58:** "Rotationalmoldedshoe" by Marloes ten Bhömer; **61:** Photo Mischa Haller – www.mischaphoto.com. **62:** *Clockwise from left*—Andrea Dall'Olios's beauty concept book; *Textile View*'s autumn/winter 2009/10 fabric directions for womenswear; *Pantone View Color Planner*, color palette for winter 2010/11; The Chiron textile inspiration book; Issue 24 of *Viewpoint* magazine, photo Mischa Haller – www.mischaphoto.com; Style board by The Future Laboratory for Australian denim brand Just Jeans, photo Mischa Haller – www.mischaphoto.com. **64:** OKES, Oak lifestyle bike by Reinier Korstanje, photo Niels Huneker.

CHAPTER 3.
66: Seed Archive by Brittany Bell. **69:** *Clockwise from left*—"Flow 2 Kitchen" by John Arndt and Wonhee Jeong of Studio

Gorm; Hamper by Fortnum and Mason; Givenchy Store, Paris by Riccardo Tisci and architect Jamie Fobert; Lunch Box by the Home Delicate Restaurant, packaging design by Pieke Bergmans; "Meet at the Apartment," photo Nathan Kraxberger; Baja BBQ by Mike and Maaike Inc. – www.mikeandmaaike.com; Eager Drinks Cocktail Box designed by David Hitner. **70:** Lifestyle publications by Promostyl, Paris. **71:** *From top*—1 and 2 – Andrea Dall'Olios's *Home Interior Trend* book, spring/summer 2010; 3 and 5 – Trend books by Carlin International. © All rights reserved; 6 – Style board by The Future Laboratory for Australian denim brand Just Jeans, photo Mischa Haller – www.mischaphoto.com. **72–23:** Photo Mischa Haller – www.mischaphoto.com. **75:** Trend books by Carlin International. © All rights reserved. **77:** *From top*—1 – Citroen C3 Picasso; 2 and 3 – Nissan Cube. **78:** *From top*—1 – Dust Pan Vacuum Cleaner by Il-Gu.Cha, Royal College of Art; 2 and 3 – UK Folding Plug System by Min-Kyu Choi; 4 – Radio Valerie by Valentin Vodev, Pixstudio. **79:** Photo Mischa Haller – www.mischaphoto.com. **80:** *Clockwise from left*—1 to 4 – Laurier restaurant, photo Sabine Pigalle; 5 – Laurier boutique, photo Michael Baumgarten, styling by Nelson Sepulveda. **81:** *Clockwise from left*—1 – Laurier boutique, photo Michael Baumgarten, styling by Nelson Sepulveda; 2 – Laurier restaurant, photo Sabine Pigalle; 3 – Li Edelkoort portrait, photo Marie Taillefer. **82 and 85:** Photo Mischa Haller – www.mischaphoto.com. **86:** *From top*—"Odd Cabinet" by Mathias Hahn for OKAY Studio; Gubble Bum by Jessie Kirsch; Robots by Rusti D for R 20th Century, photo Sherry Griffin; Tohato Caramel Corn. **87:** *Clockwise from left*—1 – 3D Printer by Desktop Factory; 2 – Acqua Mineralis Concept, by Jenny Lundgren photo Simon Fagéus; 3 – Flavors by Philips Design; 4 – Immersive Cocoon by Michael J Brown, Tino Schaedler, Oliver Zeller, Pia Habekost; 5 – Made in Transit by Agata Jaworska; 6 – Colim modular camper by Christian Susana; 7 – Hydro-Net by IwamotoScott Architecture; 8 – Transpiral for Alstom by Rodolfo Ciudad Witzel, yopodesign; 9 – Semi Automatic at Mondrian in South Beach by Teknovation; 10 – Bees by Susana Soares, Royal College of Art; 11 – Yellow Tree House Restaurant Architects Peter Eising and Lucy Gauntlett; 12 – X-halo for Delmedica by Philips Design; 13 – Living Colors by Philips Design. **88–89:** Skin Furniture desk by Nacho Carbonell Studio; **90:** *From top*—Anana Bench by Ayala Serfaty, photo by Alby Serfaty; Apaya Lamp by Ayala Serfaty, photo by Alby Serfaty; Ears Stool by Ayala Serfaty, photo by Alby Serfaty; Cow Dung Chair by

Karin Auran Frankenstein; Limited Fungi by mischer'traxler for Droog, photo Rene van der Hulst.

CHAPTER 4.
92: Computer generated image by Filip Dujardin ©. **95:** *Clockwise from left* – 1 – Brand Next: The Store for Tomorrow by Wolff Olins Limited; 2 – Pure Groove Records by Threefold Architects, photography by Charles Hosea; 3 – The Plug 'n' Drink bar at Studio SFR, Grande Epicerie de Paris; 4 – L Café, Tokyo; 5 – Nokia's "free" music subscription service. **96:** *From top*—Elements of Islay by Raj Chavda; Askul alkaline batteries by Stockholm Design Lab; Vienna Museum House Wine, © Bayer, designer Erwin K. Bayer; ELLG-Gourmet packaging by Joana Areal at thisislove studio – www.thisislove.pt. **99:** *From top*—1 – "Flare" façade system by Christopher Bauder & Christian Perstl, WHITEvoid interactive art & design, photo Uwe Eising, building by Staab Architects Berlin; 2 – "Pyrenees" sofa by Fredrikson Stallard, courtesy of David Gill Galleries; 3 – "Black Spacepot" by Bartek Mejor, 2007, porcelain, 52cm x 30cm; 4 – "Soft Intensions" by Daniera ter Haar – www.daniera.nl, photo Lisa Klappe – www.lisaklappe.com. **100:** Photo Mischa Haller – www.mischaphoto.com. **101:** *From top*—"You Fade to Light" by rAndom International and Sebastien Pons for Philips; "The Spy in the Shimmering Coat" by The Baupiloten, photo Jan Bitter; "Field of Light" by Bruce Munro, the Eden Project, photo Mark Pickthall; "Moodwall" installation by Urban Alliance and Cube-Architects, photo Roel van Lanen; Rotunda entrance by Glenn Howells Architects and Mindseye Lighting, photo Nic Gaunt. **102–103:** Photo Studio PSC. **104:** Photo Mischa Haller – www.mischaphoto.com. **107:** *From top*—"A Rose By Any Other Name" hydrating body oil by Aesop; Olive Oil by A.P.C., photo Olivier Placet; "Brand" packaging by Jesse Kirsch; Stories Kaffe packaging by BVD for Turesgruppen. **109–111:** Photo Mischa Haller – www.mischaphoto.com. **112:** Photo Sean Pillot de Chenecey. **113:** *From top*—Melt Chocolate packaging by Jesse Kirsch; Blind Mice socks, fall/winter 09 collection; Slap-dash table by Oscar Narud – www.oscarnarud.com, photo Luke Hayes; Interlocking tea service by Jenny Gibbs. **114:** Photo Mischa Haller – www.mischaphoto.com. **115:** *From top*—"Fracture," Acrylic chair by Israeli designer Itay Ohaly – www.ohaly.com; Josh Goot, wool twist mini dress, Autumn/Winter 2009; "Venus" natural crystal chair by Tokujin Yoshioka, "Second Nature" exhibition, 21_21 Design Sight gallery, Tokyo. **116:** Friend Wheel by Tom Fletcher, http://apps.facebook.com/friendwheel. Friend Wheel shows part of a social network.

Around the edge of the circle are the author's friends. If two of them are connected by a line, it means that they are friends with each other. Relationships between different groups of friends (eg. "Home friends" and "University/College friends") can often be seen in the circle. Friend Wheel gets its data from Facebook, and anyone with a Facebook account can generate a friend wheel showing the links between their friends.

CHAPTER 5.
118: Applause Machine by Martin Smith for Laikingland. Laikingland is a creative collaboration based in both the UK and The Netherlands. We design and manufacture beautifully crafted kinetic objects. Our first product the Applause Machine is designed by British artist Martin Smith. Just press the button and the Applause Machine enthusiastically claps its hands for you. Martin's design was created "for when your ideas are great but no one else agrees." **121:** *Clockwise from left*—1 – Aesop store, Flinders Lane, Melbourne by March Studio, photo Amanda de Simone; 2 – "Drawn from Clay" by Polder Ceramics and Atelier NL, photo Paul Scala, Libby Sellers Gallery; 3 – Flame Chair by Tom Dixon; 4 – Merci Boutique, Paris. © Merci; 5 – Rough Luxe Hotel designed by Rabih Hage Ltd., photo Marcus Peel; 6 – Hot Kettle bronze by Nacho Carbonell at Nacho Carbonell Studio; 7 – Damir Doma, Paris, photo Sybille Walter. **123:** *From top*—Superfruit Goji by Superfruit Scandinavia AB, Creative Director – Patrik Stenefjäll; Omega 3 Whole Food Nutrition Shake by Skin Nutrition; "Sip" water, packaging by Pearl Fisher. **125–128:** Photo Mischa Haller – www.mischaphoto.com. **133:** *Clockwise from left*—1 – Green Depot flagship store by Mapos LLC, photo David Pinter; 2 – LaboShop, Paris by Mathieu Lehanneur for Le Laboratoire, Paris. The LaboShop has a dual personality. By day it's a bookshop-sales outlet for the experiments, productions, and publications of Le Laboratoire. By night its shop furnishings levitate to become light-filled caissons, freeing the floor-space for guests invited to taste the molecular cuisine of chef Thierry Marx, prepared in the FoodLab at basement level. The arrangement recycles the system used in coal miners' dressing sheds, splicing it to the mobile lighting booms used in film studios. The floor-space of the LaboShop may be limited, but its ingenious remote-controlled pantographs make it a magic box that opens up inward; 3 – die kunstbar, Cologne, Germany by Studio Arne Qunize, photo Dave Bruel; 4 – Aesop, Mount Street, London by Studioilse, photo Lucy Cohen; 5 – Fabriken Furillen, Gotland, Sweden, photo © Johan Hellstyröm; 6 – The House at Cannes, by Jason Maclean, Maclean Interiors –

www.macleaninteriors.com. **134:** Projects for BMW by The Future Laboratory. **136:** Facebook Headquarters, Palo Alto by Studio O+A. **138:** *Clockwise from left*—1, 6, 10 – Rebekka Bay and family, and their home, photos Emma Hardy and Jasmine Labeau; 2 Daylesford Organic, Organic seasonal vegetable bag; 3 Ecover Cream Cleaner; 4 Innocent Superfruit Smoothie; 5 Les Editions de Parfums Frédéric Malle, Carnal Flower by Dominique Ropion; 7 Vaseline® Lip Therapy tins; 8 Melrose and Morgan, London; 9 Dorset Cereals; 11 Leica M9, © Leica Camera AG; 12 Kiehl's Facial Fuel. **139:** *Clockwise from left*—1 Moormann's Berge, Austria – www.moormann-berge.de, by Nils Holgens; 2 Diptyque Baies candle; 3 Aesop "A Rose By Any Other Name" hydrating body oil; 4, 6, 11 – Rebekka Bay family home, photos Emma Hardy and Jasmine Labeau; 5 Children's stools by Artek, photo Jouko Lehtola; 7 Barbour International Trials Jacket; 8 Rocking horse by Ulf Hanses for Playsam; 9 "Love Seats" by Ercol Furniture Ltd; 10 Josh Goot, pre collection 2008. **141:** Photo Giles Price; **143:** Jammer's visual portrait, photograph by Giles Price; **144:** *from top*—1 – Liz, Jeff and Jasmine Hancock; 2 – Tim Guthrie; 3 – Rachel Jones; all portraits by Emma Hardy.

CHAPTER 6.

146: Kristof Kintera, Bad innovation in the name of protection, 2007, painted metal, wheels, bulletproof glass. Courtesy Jiri Svestka Gallery, Prague. **149:** "Lilypad" A Floating Ecopolis for Climate Refugees concept by Vincent Callebaut Architects – www.vincent.callebaut.org. Illustration by Pixelab – www.pixelab.be. **150:** *From top*— 1 – Songjiang Quarry Hotel by Atkins. 2 and 4 – Bird Island, Kuala Lumpur by Graft ©; 3 – Concept illustration by dbox – www.dbox.com. **153:** *From top*—1 and 2 – Zira Island in the Caspian Sea by the Bjarke Ingels Group – BIG; 3 – Mandarin Oriental Tree-top Villas by Oppenheim, rendering by Vyonyx. **154:** *Clockwise from left*—1 and 2 –"The Continuous Enclave: Strategies in Bypass Urbanism" by Viktor Ramos at Rice University explores how new forms of habitable infrastructure might be used to connect fragmented Palestinian enclaves and Israeli settlements; 3 – "Landed," a mobile, free-standing unit by Eric Degenhardt and Richard Lampert, contains only the absolute minimum structure for living, offering flexibility and freedom from a fixed locale; 4 – Masterplan for a carbon-neutral resort and residential development on Zira Island in the Caspian Sea by the Bjarke Ingels Group – BIG; 5– The "Immaculate" prosthetic arm by Hans Alexander Huseklepp draws on futuristic robotics aesthetics rather than trying to

look lifelike; 6– "Seawater Vertical Farm" concept, Dubai, by Studiomobile uses seawater to cool, humidify, and irrigate crops in a series of stacked greenhouses. **155:** *Clockwise from left*—1 – Seed archive by Brittany Bell at Victoria University School of Design, New Zealand, mimics the architecture of a plant; 2 – A tree hotel in the far north of Sweden by architects Tham & Videgård Hansson Arkitekter – www.tvh.
se; 3– Tata Motors Limited; 4 – South African Paralympian athlete Oscar Pistorius, known as "the fastest man on no legs," won three gold medals at the 2008 Summer Paralympics in Beijing, www.ossur.co.uk; 5 – "Venus" natural crystal chair by Tokujin Yoshioka was "grown" in a self-built tank. **156:** *From top*—Abel & Cole, Family Organic Box – www.abelandcole.co.uk; Duskin, Bramley apple juice; Marks & Spencer, Organic Fairtrade Chocolate. **157:** Le Laboratoire, Paris, designed by Mathieu Lehanneur. **159:** Future Orientation, the Product Development Issue by the Copenhagen Institute for Future Studies. **160–161:** Photo Mischa Haller – www.mischaphoto.com. **162:** Books by the Copenhagen Institute for Future Studies. **163:** Semi Automatic at Mondrian in South Beach, by Teknovation. **164:** Futuristic holiday and leisure scenarios by dbox – www.dbox.com. **167:** *From top*—1 – No Mans Land by Phu Hoang Office; 2 – Port House Antwerp by Zaha Hadid Architects; 3 – Seed Archive by Brittany Bell 2009; 4 – Three Stone Performing Arts Centre by Fletcher Priest Architects. **168:** Ami-e-toi store, Arnhem designed by Maurice Mentjens.

CHAPTER 7.

170: The Toaster Project by Thomas Thwaites, photo Daniel Alexander. Under its rather unassuming name, The Toaster Project is a clever and humorous reflection on today's most burning issues such as sustainability, industrialization, mass consumption, child labor, DIY culture, etc. Its author, Thomas Thwaites is trying to make an electric toaster, from scratch. Beginning with mining the raw materials. And yes, that means extracting oil to make plastic and even processing his own copper (to make the pins of the electric plug, the cord, and internal wires), iron (for the steel grilling apparatus, and the spring to pop up the toast), mica (around which the heating element is wound), and nickel (for the heating elements! The end result (which will hopefully see the light of the day for the RCA Summer show in June) will be a fully functioning toaster. **173–175:** Photo Mischa Haller – www.mischaphoto.com. **176:** *From top*—1 – Design development of glasses for Absolut vodka, designed by Konstantin Grcic; 2 – LaChapelle table by Inga Sempe,

design developed and edited for David Design; 3 and 4 – Designboost "Sharing Design Knowledge," co-written by David Carlson; 5 – Carlson Ahnell, Skanör, Sweden. **177:** *From top*—1 and 2 – Adour Alain Ducasse at The St. Regis New York – Wine Library – © Eric Laignel/Rockwell Group; 3 and 4 – Inamo, London, photo Francesca Yorke – www.francescayorke.com; 5 – Minibar by Concrete, Amsterdam. **178–179:** Absolut workshop, photo Vicky Langdon; **180:** Carlin team, photo Carlin International, © all rights reserved. **181–184:** Marco Marsan in workshops, portrait by OMS Photography, Cincinnati, OH. **185:** *From top*—1 and 2 – Citizen M hotel, work living room, OSIB Operations Holding B.V.; 3 – Eight Moorgate, members club, London, www.eightclub.co.uk; 4 and 5 – One Alfred Place, London. **186:** *Clockwise from left*—1 and 2 – Life Medicine Resort, Design Hotels, Austria; 3 – Prayer and Meditation Pavilion, Khartoum, by Studio Tam Associati. **187:** *Clockwise from left*—1 – Ruta del Peregrino pilgrimage trail lookout, Mexico, by HHF Architects GmbH; 2 – Life Medicine Resort, Design Hotels; 3 – Uma Paro Como hotels, Design Hotels; 4 – Prayer and meditation pavilion, Khartoum, by Studio Tam Associati. **191:** Absolut workshop, photo Vicky Langdon. **192:** *Clockwise from left*—Style boards, photo Mischa Haller – www.mischaphoto.com; The Modern Pantry, London, Jump Studio, photo Rachel Smith, www.themodernpantry.co.uk; Project Kitchenette Bebek, Istanbul, Turkey by Autoban – www.autoban212.com. **193:** *From top*—Anna and Ray; Ban and Clair; Mark and Roberta; Rebekka Bay and family; all portraits by Emma Hardy. **194–195:** Photo Mischa Haller – www.mischaphoto.com. **198:** "Wow Suite," São Paulo by John Manku and W Hotels, photo Leonardo Finotti. **199:** *From top*—Aquaduct concept vehicle, courtesy of IDEO; Future Of Internet Search, Mobile Version, concept by Mac Funamizu (http://petitinvention. wordpress.com); Hydro-Net city by IwamotoScott Architecture. **202–203:** VilaSofa Store, Netherlands by Tjep – www.tjep.com.

Acknowledgments

WRITING IS NEVER A SOLITARY ACT – there are editors involved, interviewees, designers, picture editors, desk researchers, colleagues, partners, and an ever-demanding dog that reminds you to forget trends and throw him a ball! Jasper therefore must get the first credit, followed by Allison Weldon, my picture editor, and the trend forecasters, visual analysts, and creative directors like Kate Franklin, Jacob Strand, Ravi Khanna, Jasmine Lebeau, Caroline Till, Chris Sanderson, Vicki Langdon, Tom Savigar, Max Reyner, Anne Fay Townsend – all superlative forecasters in their own right – who identified or refined many of the trends identified throughout the book.

Thanks is also due to the many designers, forecasters, innovation experts, and scenario planners who are profiled – Ilse Crawford, Piers Fawkes, Henrik Vejlgaard, Li Edelkoort, Sean Pillot de Chenecey, Carsten Beck, David Carlson, Marco Marson, and again Chris Sanderson. And thanks also to the many names who were interviewed about the methodologies they used to make good forecasting even better and more credible: to Innosight's Scott Anthony, View Publication's David Shah, the author Malcolm Gladwell, Trendwatch.com's Liesbeth den Toom, *Viewpoint* editor Liz Hancock, and Maggie Norden at the London College of Fashion, who over the years has allowed many of the methodologies outlined in this book to be validated by her students.

Thanks finally to Emma Baines – for acting as a much put-upon editorial assistant, to Gerard Saint of BigActive, to Ed Vince – who worked with him on designing this book, to Donald Dinwiddie – my senior editor at Laurence King, who had to keep chasing me, and to Helen Evans at Laurence King, who commissioned the book. And particular thanks to Melanie Walker, my more-than-hands-on development editor, who shaped what was merely a set of ideas and not-very-well-explained concepts into a series of chapters – which, if followed carefully, will yield up the skills needed to make you a forecaster to be reckoned with.